INFORMATION TECHNOLOGY CHALLENGES AND OPPORTUNITIES

INFORMATION TECHNOLOGY CHALLENGES AND OPPORTUNITIES

By

B.B. Batra

PUBLICATIONS

KALPAZ PUBLICATIONS

DELHI - 110052

Information Technology Challenges and Opportunities
(*Information Technology*)

ISBN : 978-81-783-5064-6

Published in 2015 in India by
Kalpaz Publications
C-30, Satyawati Nagar
Ashok Vihar-III, Delhi-110052
e-mail: kalpaz@hotmail.com

Laser Typeset at: Alphabet, Delhi
Printed at : Chawla Offset Press

Preface

The twentieth century witnessed the rapidly accelerating advent of information technology (IT). The progress has been truly amazing. About 40 years, electronic communications and news media have become commonplace and indispensable; computers have proliferated, becoming increasingly fast, powerful, small and cheap, so that now there is scarcely a human activity in which they are not to be found, bearing an increasing share of the burden of repetitive information processing.

Now, information can not only be stored, retrieved, communicated, and broadcast in enormous quantities and at phenomenal speeds; but it can also be rearranged, selected, marshalled, and transformed. Until recently, these activities were the sole province of the human brain. While creative, judicious, moral, and aesthetic choices are still best left to people, all the tedious and mechanical mental processes can now be relegated to the accurate, fast, and tireless machines.

People thought of the future in terms of machines of ever-greater speed and capacity; centralised behemoths would hold all the world's information in gigantic data banks, whence major decisions would issue to be imposed upon the population at their mercy. With the emergence of powerful, cheap, mass-produced computers-on-a-chip, the picture has changed radically.

Today the information society is passing through various new challenges and opportunities such as information professional skills information management skills and up-to-date subject knowledge. The emerging technologies supporting computer and tele-communication provides new dimensions in business and industry in a productive way.

This book elaboratively discusses the challenges and opportunities of information technology in the new millennium. It will prove highly informative to all the media persons and students and teachers in the field of information technology.

Editor

Contents

1

Introduction

The origin of these far-reaching changes is to be found in the advances in new information and communication technology, progress speeded up by the digital revolution and the convergence of the computer, telecommuni-cations and audiovisual industries. Communication systems have unified, to such an extent that telephone transfers and television pictures no longer circulate on separate channels. Computers and television sets are one and the same thing, telephones are linked to the Internet and mobile phones are connected to laptop computers. These changes also have far-reaching sociological implications, not only in terms of the ways we use the new technologies but also in the ways we have recourse to their services, and for what purpose. At the same time, the fact that computers can now be interconnected has marked a new step in innovation with the emergence of worldwide communication networks. At the forefront of these is the Internet, a living encyclopedia which makes no distinction between telephone, satellite or television to route the information it contains. Optimum performance of the network will not be achieved, however, until very high performance circuits have become commonplace. That movement is now under way, through the growing integration and interconnection of new information technology with telecommunications resources. It can be seen in information highways, the synthesis of technological convergence resulting in widespread interactive multimedia offers. This break with the past, one of the major undertakings for the next century, symbolizes a society in which network distributed information and intelligence will be the major forms of wealth.

Most governments are persuaded that such is the case, and are already preparing vast schemes with information highways as their priority to enable their societies to take part in a new economy, to enhance the productivity of already existing industries and to create new ones. With this in mind, economic actors in all sectors of the information and leisure industries - including suppliers of telecommunications hardware and infrastructures - are already taking up their positions.

Groups are being set up for this purpose, launching intersectional alliances which have generally led to high market concentration and internationalization. These upheavals, both technological and economic are radically modifying the ways in which we use communication, both at work and in the home. New possibilities for training, education, employment and leisure activities hitherto reserved for an elite can now be afforded by all. People communicating now have powers of transmitting and receiving information undreamed of even ten years ago. That fundamental breakthrough, which backs up the concept dear to Bill Gate of 'introduction at your fingertips', both enhances individual action and at the same time questions the very nature of the state, national frontiers and cultural roots. Combined with geopolitical change, to raises a number of questions about legislation,, the gaps existing between nations and within them, the risk of rendering local cultures uniform, and the role of public services when forced to compete with domestic and supranational private programmes.

The accelerating progress in new information and communication technology is essentially based on three fundamental changes: the digitization of images, sounds and data; digital data compression; and the growing power of electronic components. These innovations have made possible the gradual replacement of analog equipment by digital systems that are clearing the way for greater interactivity between end-users and terminals.

Digital technology marks a true revolution which goes far beyond purely technical upheavals. On the one hand, it will lead to the integration of information transmission networks and reception hardware, and, on the other, it will simultaneously enhance a new relationship with the media and the way in which we consume the information they convey.

Basically, this revolution stems from the spectacular progress made in micro-electronics, leading to the digitization of images, sound and data. In conventional so-called analog systems, sounds and images were converted into electrical signals so that they could be transmitted on physical support systems such as wires and optic fibres, or in electromagnetic wave form via terrestrial broadcasting networks or by satellite.

With digitization, the same signals are coded into strings of numbers represented in binary form as packets of os and is, which then constitute a data processing file. The problem with these basic files, however, is that they are extremely demanding in terms of transmission capacity. Digital compression has solved the difficulty, by reducing the flow of information to decrease the time and therefore the cost of transmission, without modifying the quality and content of the information itself.

Moreover, digital compression makes more efficient use of the channels available and thus reduces or shares out the cost of transmission. After pervading telephones and computers, digital technology has now tackled the last link in the chain of image and sound broadcasting: use by the public at large. The consequences for television viewers and users of images will be greater than those affecting users of computer or telecommunications technology, since television is a consumer market with a much higher penetration rate than the other sectors of the communication industry.

The development of digitization and its applications is based on the extraordinary breakthroughs in electronic components. Ever since their invention in 1969 by Ted Hoff and other engineers at the American company Intel, their computing power has increased at an exponential rate. Gordon Moore, one of the three founders of Intel, as early as 1965 deduced a law which has dictated their evolution ever since: 'Microprocessor power doubles every eighteen to twenty-four months.' Thirty years later, the Moore law can still be seen to hold true.

The power of semiconductors doubles almost every two years, with a corresponding drop in their price/performance ratio. Each new processor launched on to the market contains approximately twice as many transistors as its predecessor, with market launches following on every eighteen months. Between the 2,300 transistors of the first microprocessor and the 5.5 million in a Pentium Pro, the number of transistors has already multiplied by more than 2,400. However, there is no let-up in the power-race between the industrial groups as a whole. With 8.8 million transistors, the new

K6 Advanced Micro Devices (AMD) computer broke all the records in 1997, including that of Intel, which had reached the figure of 7.5 million transistors with its Pentium 11.

Progress in this field has also been spectacular. In 1956, one of the very first hard disks, the RAMAC 305 (Random Access Method of Accounting and Control) could store 5 million characters (each character being represented in computer language by one byte, a group of eight bits), or some 2,500 pages of-text. It contained fifty disk platters, each 60 cm in diameter. In 1997, the latest hard disk from IBM, the Travelstar VP, has a storage capacity of 1.5 billion bytes (Gb) of data, weighs no more than 99 grams, is the size of an audio cassette and is only 9.5 rum thick. It can store 3.2 Gb, or 1.6 million pages of text. The miniaturization of components and memories and the enhancement of their technical prowess are ongoing processes, making them smaller, faster, more powerful and less expensive. Meteoric changes such as these provide the new information and transmission support media with new powers of communication.

The general process of digitization has resulted in the emergence of a new feature: the convergence of telecommunications, computer and audiovisual technologies, which were previously separated by techniques, legislation and modes of distribution. The new concept has given rise to different definitions and interpretations according to each operator, institution or researcher concerned. Harmonized, common development of convergence is difficult to find, because each state is strongly influenced by its own history and the different levels of development of its telecommunications and audiovisual sectors. However, the structural transformation of the public sector and new legislation look forward to the development of such convergence. Several angles of approach are possible.

Some authors see convergence as comprising three different features or levels: the technical convergence mentioned above, economic convergence and convergence in legislation. Others add the convergence of social customs and expectations. The Organisation for Economic Co-operation and Development (OECD) distinguishes three other types of convergence: technical, functional and corporate. Technical convergence refers to the use by the communication industry of signal digitization. It is evaluated according to the progress in the digitization process in the three communication sectors. Computer technology is by definition completely digitized.

Digitization in telecommunications is an ongoing process which is already highly advanced in terms of both transmission and packet-switching. Finally, the audiovisual industry is making giant leaps in the digital world. Technical convergence, then, refers to the adoption of the general process of digitization.

Functional convergence refers to the diversification and increasingly hybrid nature of the services offered by communication media which hitherto have been distinct. This means radio broadcasting services will be able to transmit signals other than information or entertainment programmes; in addition to the conventional services of dialogue and data transmission, the telephone industry will also be able to transmit entertainment; cable-based distributors on their side will be able to provide telephone services. Functional convergence may thus be summed up as free competition between the radio broadcasting, telecommunications and computer technology sectors, and the disappearance of the traditional boundaries between these three industries. Corporate convergence refers to the new capacities of the communication companies to diversify their sources of finance.

In this way, companies telecasting audiovisual program will be able to make viewers pay for them direct, and will no longer have to limit themselves to indirect revenue such as advertising or state subsidies. The same principle applies to telecommunications companies, which will now be able to seek other sources of finance than direct fee-paying alone. The distinction in technical terms, therefore, between the various sectors of the communication industry is less self-evident, owing to the fact that information is processed in digital form and that the transmission infrastructure itself is multi-purpose. Functional convergence and that of the companies involved is thus melting the barriers between the different sectors of activity. While opinions are unanimous with respect to the reality of convergence, particularly in terms of its technological nature, debate is still heated about the lead times that will be needed to provide each home with programmes that are interactive, easy and fast to use. Some believe it will happen tomorrow, others talk of its realization ten or twenty years hence. Convergence is, in fact, an ongoing process.

The speed of technical breakthroughs, and the political and economic uncertainty and even resistance they encounter and create, make any definitive analysis of the concept impossible. Convergence is basically a social construct, based on technological as well as economic, legal and political logic.

Most of the satellites in service before 1989 were low- or mid-power systems outputting signals whose reception required an expensive, large-scale dish antenna. They covered territories such as Australia, the United States or the (then) Soviet Union and provided telecommunications and radio broadcasting services for local relay stations.

The same process is still employed by a large number of cable TV systems in North America, Latin

America and Europe, and has been put into use in recent years in Asia. Concomitant with the upgrade to mid-power and recently to high-power satellites such as the direct broadcasting satellite, there has been a reduction in the size of dish antennae. With the emergence of the digital age, the new generation of satellites is likely radically to increase the supply of interactive services accessible to the general public. The digital satellite market is booming.

Market share is probably greatest in the countries of southern Europe and in developing countries where the penetration rate for cable TV is low, even non-existent. From South-East Asia to Latin America, most countries are once again targeting this market at a time when a new system of world coverage is being set up in parallel using constellations of satellites basically dedicated to the mobile telephone sector.

Cable TV uses a wireframe support in order to transmit several programmes simultaneously from the operator of a specialized TV station to subscriber households. With a few exceptions, the geographical coverage of cable TV channels in practical terms is confined to urban areas, owing to constraints in the field and criteria of economic efficiency. Cable TV operators today are fully aware of the new capabilities of satellite retransmission which, through data compression, have boosted the range of programmes on offer and brought new interactive services into being. To meet the competition from satellites, cable TV operators use various transmission resources and data compression to enhance their capacity on coaxial cable networks. They also rely on new optic fibre architectures and on progress in Asymmetrical Digital Subscriber Loop technology (ADSL). This is a digital transmission technique provided by telecommunications operators to broadcast pay-per-view video over their copper wire telephone network, hence the name

Video Dial-Tone (VDT). The process makes it possible to transmit up to four television signals at the same time as telephone conversation. In other words, the subscriber can talk on the telephone and watch a video programme transmitted at the same time over the same telephone line. The advantage of this type of technology is the ability to offer pay-per-view video type services over the telephone network without any major investment, as long as the home of the subscriber and the telephone switchboard are both equipped with transceivers.

The change which has had the greatest impact on the current radio broadcasting environment is without doubt the emergence of optic fibre (light modulation) cable as a potential means of transmitting communication signals. Thanks to optic fibre, telephone companies and cable TV operators can provide broadband video services which would be impossible with conventional metal wiring networks, or, at any rate, only at greater cost and with less efficiency.

Terrestrial broadcasting is still the main means of telecasting, enabling more than a billion television viewers worldwide to receive their programmes, despite the developments in other telecasting means such as cable or satellite, which offer greater capacity in terms of the number of channels available. Conventional technology has made a comeback through the new possibilities provided by a technology for digital data compression known as MMDS.

This process leads to improved picture and sound and above all makes it possible to broadcast four times the number of programmes received through the conventional analog technique, as well as enhancing spectrum management. In concrete terms, television programmes are picked up via a dish antenna which receives a multitude of programmes.

A specific MMDS technology transmitter with a range of 5 to 10 kilometres broadcasts the pictures. In surrounding villages or rural areas, a small receiver antenna can distribute the signals to between ten and fifteen households. Broadcasting each digital microwave stream, however, will require the installation of a special network of transmitters and relay links. The investment may be competitive compared with the cost of a satellite repeater, which is generally rented at around $600,000 per year. The technique is currently developing at high speed in regions such as Africa, the Middle East and the Russian Federation, as well as Central and Eastern Europe, where homes are too widely scattered for the installation of cable networks to be economically viable. There are a number of digital terrestrial broadcasting projects currently under way. The British Government was the first to propose the introduction of digital terrestrial broadcasting in the United Kingdom as early as 1998. Some thirty digital terrestrial channels will be launched prior to this date. Without having either their sets or their aerials altered, more than 70 per cent of British homes will receive these programmes with the aid of a special decoder.

The United States of America, however, was the first to develop a concept of a digital terrestrial broadcasting system, initially designed for high-definition television (HDTV). The Federal Communication Commission (FCC) sees the advent of digital terrestrial broadcasting as a means of enhancing the efficiency of spectrum management. To foster development of the system, the Commission recently decided to issue 10,000 licences. Finally, in Japan, terrestrial broadcasting of digital television will become possible between the years 2000 and 2005.

Mobile communications are booming today, thanks to their ability to 'free' the end-user completely of wire connection constraints. Mobile systems form the terminal link in a communication network, and provide the multi-purpose and integrational functionalities required by the recent trends in technological convergence.

A mobile telephone equipped with a modem and connected to a portable computer can thus be converted into a genuine mobile office, since it can receive and send faxes and files, and access e-mail services from anywhere around the world. It is in the cellular telephone market, however, that growth in mobile communications has been greatest. In the developed countries, which are well equipped with stationary communication systems, the cellular telephone matches the diversity of professional and personal uses and requirements. In the developing countries, it represents an advantageous solution, capable of making up for the shortcomings of the conventional telecommuni-cations infrastructure, particularly in underprivileged areas or those with a low population density.

In general, the mobile communications market has one of the highest expansion ratios in the telecommuni-cations sector, with an annual growth rate close to 20 per cent. In all, the number of subscribers worldwide should rise from 40 million in 1995 to 100 million by 1998. Mobile phones are thus switching from being upmarket to mass market. That development is likely to be to the detriment of wireframe networks, which may be abandoned by a vast group of end-users in favour of a telephone number that will follow them wherever they go.

In 1996, the installed base of cellular phone subscribers in the Asia-Pacific region (not including Japan) stood at 12.6 million, 7 million of whom were in China alone, where the network has expanded in spectacular fashion. The figure for the region should reach some 53 million by the end of the decade. In

Africa and the Middle East, the advent of cellular services has opened the door to the private sector, both foreign and local. The wave of liberalization since 1990 has resulted in the granting of licences to private operators. Since that date the number of subscribers to cellular services has grown by an average of 78 per cent per annum. From 2.3 million in 1995, the number should have soared to nearly' 13.7 million by the year 2000. In Eastern Europe and the newly independent states of the former Soviet Union, the number of cellular phone subscribers could reach 5.5 million by the year 2000.

The growth announced will be driven by heightened competition and further deregulation. All the above countries would therefore seem to have opted for the fastest and cheapest solution. The cellular phone is rapidly becoming something of a panacea above all as a result of the progress in worldwide telecommunications projects.

1997 has seen the emergence of a new type of radiotelephone service with the launch of the first generation of low-orbit satellites, which will ultimately render terrestrial relay links completely obsolete. These new satellite systems are fully-fledged telephone exchanges in orbit, designed to transmit communications by means of 'satellite-hopping' until they reach their destination. They ensure nothing short of complete and permanent coverage of the planet and a level of performance unequalled by any of the existing terrestrial infrastructures. By the year 2000, the satellite-based radiotelephone industry may well include five rival networks.

The first Iridium network, which was piloted by the American company Motorola, was launched on 5 May 1997. It is planned to have all sixty-six satellites that make up the system in place by September 1998. From that date the first subscribers will use a complex portable to receive and transmit by voice, fax or computer data, but at a price of around $2,000 in addition to the cost of the communications, i.e. $2 or 3 per minute. The cost will no doubt start to fall as other networks come onstream, for instance Globalstar, a competitor that is already in position to give infrastructure back-up for national operations. Competition will become even fiercer with the launching of the other constellations such as Bill Gates's network, Teledesic, which was given the goahead by the FCC in March 1997, and many others such as ICO, Odyssey, Skybridge or Orbcomm.

The Internet is a sort of worldwide co-operative society composed of a multitude of dispersed networks, in which individuals and social groups develop independently of any specific place, culture or country. The Internet has no owner. It is managed by a community of users, and finances its operating costs via its members, who pay connection fees to hubs (or network nodes) entrusted with routing the data exchange, or to local providers who connect up to the hubs. It is a tangible illustration of the way in which the general communication system has changed, and embodies current convergence by offering an ever-increasing number of services, with audio and video functions integrated with most applications. As a result, the Internet has become a tool for use by the general public and by private users, whereas it was initially designed to provide a communication medium for military and, subsequently, academic use.

The economic issues at stake are such that the battle has already started between two rival digital transmission standards. On the one side there is the American technology known as Multiple Access by Code Distribution (AMRC or CDMA), and on the other the European standard called the Global Standard for

Mobile Communications (GSM). Technically, the differences between the two are minute, but they are mutually incompatible. Mobile communications seem destined to a fate similar to that of video cassettes for VCRs: in the coming years, one of the competitors will have to go. That is why each type of technology, supported by its countries and companies, is redoubling its efforts to prove its superiority.

The battle is being fought not only in the European and North American theatres, but elsewhere around the world where the markets have yet to be exploited. The winner will gain equipment supply contracts worth several billion dollars, and thus reign single-handed over the mobile telephone market. It is also worth noting that discussions are open in international forums about Global Mobile Personal Communication by Satellite (GMPCS) systems to ensure the free circulation of terminals. The issue calls for worldwide co-ordination so that all telecommunications operators and public administrations can, among other things, ensure access to and free circulation of the GMPCS, define a utilization standard, and find a solution to distribution taxes.

Almost 200 countries were connected to the Internet in 1997. North America has taken a considerable lead in the use of the network, since it utilizes virtually three-quarters of all network access sites. The phenomenon is gradually gaining ground on the other continents, particularly in the developing countries. Despite the many difficulties due to the limited number of telephone lines, access by developing countries to the World Wide Web is growing fast.

The growth is particularly noticeable in Latin American countries, where almost every single university is connected to the Internet. In Africa, most countries are also connected to the Internet. In South

Africa, the number of host computers per 1,000 inhabitants grew by 147 per cent in the period 1994-95 alone, while the traffic in Burkina Faso is increasing at the same speed as in the industrialized countries (about 100 per cent per year).

The presence, albeit symbolic, of places such as Eritrea, the Faeroes, Fiji and Lesotho gives some indication of the globalization of the network. Furthermore, while the presence of a number of countries such as China, India and Indonesia is as yet quite modest, the size of their populations is bound to propel them into the front ranks fairly soon. In general, current growth in network use is exponential in the full sense of the term. Approximately 75 million people are equipped with an electronic mail-box, which they may or may not use, and almost 100,000 commercial service sites are currently listed. At the end of September 1996, at least 500,000 servers were in operation around the world, a figure which is estimated to double every three to four months. The result of this boom is that nearly 30 million pages of information are currently available.

According to Internet experts, if the trend continues, every facet of human knowledge will be on the network in less than ten years from now. In 1936, the Internet had some 40 million internauts (users). With a current growth rate of 12 per cent per month, it is estimated that by the year 2000 the figure will rise to 100 million people. With its worldwide expansion and the increase in throughput rates, the Internet is currently opening to other sectors such as the worlds of industry, electronic shopping, the various media, and scientific and academic information.

According to the various published estimates, data exchange on the Internet is distributed as follows: 60 per cent for trade, 27 per cent for research, 9 per cent for administration and less than 5 per cent for education. These percentages are likely to change in favour of the corporate sector, which is making increasing use of the Internet to penetrate markets around the world and for interchange with customers. Certain estimates indicate that trade activities could generate revenue of between $7 billion and $40 billion in the year 2000. More optimistic analysts mention figures of up to $150 billion. In 1996, however, network trading only generated sales worth between $600 million and $1.2 billion. A whole new industry is humming in, on and around the Internet: new software systems such as Java and Navigator have been developed to facilitate access to and navigation through the network, and new generations of machines such as network computers connected directly to the Web have been launched on to the market.

Companies enter the network and attempt to take advantage of it to engender savings in terms of management costs and/or to stimulate new markets. Banks and funding agencies are providing on-line services specializing in settlements, share trading and the transfer of financial securities. Finally, electronic trading is becoming increasingly widespread, with more and more intermediaries making purchases on the network.

According to some observers, the danger is that the massive influx of the industrial, financial and advertising worlds may make its use by scientists marginal and may even signal the end of the Internet as we know it today. Others estimate that the number of Web pages in circulation, unlike other media, is limitless and that the network can therefore absorb any such initiative. The risk is not so much the arrival in strength of the financial and advertising sectors, but the apathy that may spread through the Internet community when faced with the sheer wealth and quality of commercial service sites.

Today, each of the major media is setting up sites on the Web in an attempt to compete with the other 'conventional media in the fields of news, entertainment and leisure activities. Written press and television sites generally offer articles and photographs, and even audio or video recordings, while in recent months radio stations have started using the Web to broadcast programmes around the world, either live or recorded. Finally, the Internet is a serious threat for fax machines and even telephones. The use of e-mail is expanding at an infinitely faster rate than fax machines in their day.

The various telephone services available via the Internet at cut-price rates are worrying the conventional telephone companies, which have attempted in vain to parry the attack on legal grounds. According to the IDC consultancy firm, the number of telephone users on the Internet is set to rise from 500,000 in 1995 to 10 million in 1998 and 16 million in 1999. It should expand rapidly through the activities of the American software firms Microsoft and Netscape, which are integrating the telephone function into their navigation program on the Internet. In the United States, however, the Federal Communication Commission (FCC) has dashed their hopes by declaring telephony on the Internet legal.

The Internet offers infinite potential for training and education. It already forms one of the greatest sources of information and documentation accessible anywhere around the planet. Several thousand scientific and technical publications can be consulted, generally free of charge or for a modest sum.

Finally, it is one of the world's most extensive e-mail systems, with integrated newsgroup and discussion services (UseNet news) for joint projects linking universities. In the United States, an FCC objective since May 1997 has been to ensure 'universal' access to the Internet in the nation's schools and libraries. As of 1998, more than 100,000 schools will enjoy such access at a special low rate of between 20 and 90 per cent of the ordinary cost to the user.

In developing countries lacking libraries or documentation centres to overcome their scientific and cultural isolation and remain in close contact with the international scientific community. It will completely transform their conditions of work by enabling them to access the vast resources of the leading research centres and universities in the industrialized countries. With this aim in mind, several experiments have been set up in partnership with UNESCO or with scientific establishments such as ORSTOM (France) and non-governmental organisations such as Greennet.

The Internet can also be a valuable means of enhancing the image of national cultures. For the first time in Africa, Niger has set up a site to visit its archaeological riches, while Benin has launched a service dedicated to voodoo. The Internet, however, will prove its true value in the field of education only when the network can offer interactive functions with a much higher degree of efficiency, particularly in terms of sound and video images. Current research led by American academics sponsored by private partners is aiming to launch Internet 2 by 1998.

The new network should be faster and more powerful, and can be used for interactive training and distance learning, with real video-conferences between teachers and students, for instance. For their part, satellite operators such as Astra and Eutelsat are striving to develop a powerful broadband technology to download in particular games or entertainments of an educational nature which the public is using more and more. This is sure to provide the worlds of recreation and education with a real teaching aid, promoting and illustrating knowledge and know-how.

The Internet movement has therefore been launched. Various sectors within it are already taking shape (based on individual, collective, cultural, educational and commercial initiatives), implying a change in the ways in which we produce, exchange and learn everything.

The Internet will only reach maturity, however, by ensuring a harmonious balance between the various facilities and multiple interests present on the Web, and it is only by strengthening the networks reserved for education, training and culture, on the one hand, and, on the other, by reinforcing basic liberties and moral principles, that the Internet will form part of an ethical cyberspace.

Information highways can be defined as a high-speed global network capable of routing to subscribers at high speed a series of new interactive services, such as distance learning, data bank querying, teleshopping, telemedicine, pay-per-view television, picture phoning, etc. These would seem to be the basis for a true technological, economic and cultural revolution, destined to eliminate all geographical, temporal and cultural frontiers.

In industrial circles they are compared to the grand civil engineering projects of the nineteenth century, such as the construction of cross-continental railways, or the first motorways. They will enable users to upload or download information to and from any point on the network, and to obtain information tailored to their requirements. At the same time, information users can become information suppliers. Information highways are not a single physical network but a series of local, regional, national and international infrastructures linked to form a worldwide information highway. Like any other grand technological project, they have aroused heated debate which boils down to a confrontation between those who are for and those who are against their development. Some merely see them as yet another technique which will render the reality of social relationships even more *virtual', accentuating individualism within society and further widening the gaps in development not only between nations but also within them. Others, on the contrary, consider that if the information highways do indeed come about, they will lead to far-reaching changes, particularly in the sectors of creative art, education, adult training, health and culture - changes, they add, which are likely to create new demands for other services. Most states support the latter point of view, and have built the concept into their strategies to combat the increasing challenges created by international competition. As a result, information highways have become a focal point for political, industrial and cultural issues.

The project, since then baptized the National Information Infrastructure (NII), is led by an interministerial committee (the National Information Super Highway Task Force) in charge of the operation in its experimental design stage. The project, which has been allocated a budget of $1.5 billion, is the spearhead of the economic revival of the United States and will hopefully generate hundreds of thousands of jobs, either directly or indirectly. A number of pilot experiments are already under way which are precursors to information highways. The most ambitious of these include the Full Service Network set up by Time Warner in Orlando, Florida, which serves 4,000 homes and provides a complete Video on Demand (VOD) service, and the project launched by Bell Atlantic in northern Virginia which provides approximately the same services and aims to be in 8 million homes by the year 2000. The purpose of these experiments is to test the market and determine the consumer demand for such new services.

The European information highway project was set forth in 1993 in the White Paper entitled *Growth, Competitiveness, Employment.* It was a reaction and a response to the American challenge, and focused more on the concept of the information highway itself than on its infrastructures. During a meeting in Corfu, the Council of Europe discussed the community policy on the information society on the basis of the Bangemann Report (whose official title was *Europe and the Global Information Society. Recommendation to the Council of Europe*).

The recommendations, which gave special emphasis to telecommunications, favoured a liberal approach to the sector as well as harmonization of national legislation with respect to media ownership, the protection of private life and intellectual property rights. Three weeks after the meeting, the Brussels Commission adopted an action plan on the ways and means of setting up a 'global information society'.

With respect to applications, the United Kingdom launched the first experimental information highway, the British Telecom Interactive Television (BTITV). Italy has already initiated its first interactive television experiment in Rome and Milan, in partnership with the American company Bell-Atlantic.

Japan reacted in 1994 to the American information highway project mainly through two public institutions: the Ministry of International Trade and Industry (MITI) and the Ministry of Post and Telecommunications (MPT). The stated aim was to set up by the year 2010 a broad interactive communication network providing a range of high-definition multimedia services. The MPT started by setting up a pilot experiment in the region of Kansai. The innovative feature of the Japanese approach to entering the information society is the fact that it is focusing its efforts on the requirements of that society and on intellectual creativity. Since the advent of these projects, governments have become aware of these new challenges and have fostered debate or reports on the information society. In France in 1994, Gérard Théry, the promoter of the French Minitel videotex system, returned a report on information highways to the government and suggested that by 2015 every home and every company in the country should be connected to the new network. In Canada in 1994, the Ministry of Telecommunications published a report on the 'Canadian Information Highway. And in its report published in September 1995, the Information Highway Advisory Council presented the Canadian answers to the challenges of the highways.

In China, three projects baptized the 'Golden Bridge' (a high-speed digital network linking thirty capitals and 12,000 companies), the 'Golden Gate' (connecting corporate computer systems) and the 'Golden Card' (a network of electronic banking systems) aim at massive development of the communications and telecommunications sectors. To reach that target, China has budgeted expenditure of $61.7 billion between now and the year 2000. Two-thirds of that amount are dedicated to the construction of the 300,000 kilometres of optic fibre designed for the high-speed network.

Other countries, such as Australia, the Republic of Korea and Singapore, have also scheduled the development of high-speed networks and of the new technology they require to connect up homes, schools and companies to the information highways. South Africa, Indonesia and the governments of a number of developing countries have decided not to be left behind and are putting forward reports defining their strategies to be part of the information society. At the same time, and with the same aim in mind, regional and international organizations are developing initiatives around the information society. In 1994, the

International Telecommunications Union organized the first World Telecommunication Development Conference. On that occasion, the Vice-President of the United States, Al Gore, launched the concept of a worldwide information infrastructure-'GII, the global information infrastructure' - which he defined as a 'planetary information network that transmits messages and images at the speed of light from the largest city to the smallest village on every continent'.

One year later, at the invitation of the European Union, the group of the world's most industrialized countries (G7) held a Ministerial Conference on the Global Information Society. It outlined eleven pilot projects to guide the development of the information society, and undertook to associate the developing countries in discussions of wider scope. In pursuit of a common vision, in May 1996 at Midrand (South Africa), together with the European Community and South Africa, the G7 organized the Information Society and Development Conference (ISAD), with representatives from developing countries, the countries of the G7, those of the European Union, and United Nations agencies.

The giant task of constructing the information highways and the estimated cost of setting them up are a golden opportunity for computer manufacturers, software publishers, consumer electronics manufacturers, telecommunications network operators and other groups of information holders. The industrial task is that of making information highways and their applications available to a public about whose future behaviour nothing is known. No one can say with any certainty whether the public are going to want new interactive services. But for the manufacturers, the potential market is enormous, and justifies taking the risk. With this outlook in mind, numerous alliances between firms are being set up to control the global information industry.

Over and above the commercial and industrial mechanisms which for the time being seem to be the driving force behind the construction of the information highways. the cultural and scientific issues must not be neglected. The new infrastructures are not just technological vectors, mere solutions put forward by market forces. They also represent, according to certain official policy speeches, a new facility to which users around the world may have at least minimum access, on equal terms and enjoying equal quality, no matter what their geographical location.

There is a major risk, however, that access may become the privilege of high-yield markets, particularly where new value-added services are concerned, which therefore raises the problem of the predominance of private interests in the development and organization of the information highways. The issue, therefore, resides as much in the technological capacity to create an information society as in the ability to promote the conditions for harmonious social, economic and cultural development on an international scale and thereby ensure access for the greatest possible number.

Access to the networks presupposes a reliable universal service at an affordable price, meeting the fundamental needs of individuals for education, science and culture. This implies that users, whatever their origin, must be able to acquire the basic 'digital skills' and have sufficiently user-friendly interfaces to benefit from them. It is equally essential that the pluralism of opinions and ideas be guaranteed, and that software which is not necessarily of commercial value be developed. It is also necessary that the plurality of cultural goods on offer and participation by all linguistic and regional viewpoints be fostered, in order to avoid uniformity and standardization of network content. Finally, in a digital universe which is already deploying its networks and drawing its new frontiers, there is a strong risk that the differences in the levels of development not only between nations but within them may simply widen. This risk is particularly significant in developing countries, which will have to implement clear-cut, audacious strategies to enable users to take advantage of the information highways.

The temptation to seek to control access to them, on the grounds that some programmes do not correspond to either religious or political national standards or values, could result in highly prejudicial delays in developing the new communications infrastructures. The free flow of information is an essential prerequisite, not only for the exercise of democratic rights but also for social and economic progress. That being said, to reduce the current debate to questions of market forces or purely technological issues would be to miss the point.

The major challenge facing the countries promoting the information highways is a multiple one. On the one hand, the difficulty lies in ensuring that the greatest number of people have access to the highways, and for the same reason, in removing every obstacle or barrier of any kind that might impede or hinder the advance of the highways within nations and between them; the challenge, on the other hand, lies in promoting the diversity of programmes both in their content and in their origin, such that each and every community or sector of society is able to express itself and thereby ensure the survival of its culture, language and traditions, without being systematically tied down by economic considerations linked to market laws. In this connection, the concept of public service urgently needs to be redefined to adapt it to the realities of the information highways. In other words, thought should be given to the measures that must be taken at government level in order to ensure that access to the information highways is open to all, that the most elementary needs, notably in terms of culture and education, are guaranteed over and above purely economic considerations, and that the services meeting these elementary requirements are financially accessible to the greatest possible number.

2

Freedom of Information

The principle of freedom of information is enshrined in the major universal and regional declarations and conventions relating to human rights. Its first consecration occurred in 1789 with the French Declaration of the Rights of Man and of the Citizen, whose Article XI asserts that 'the free communication of ideas and opinions is one of the most precious rights of man', and that in consequence every citizen I can freely speak, write and print subject to responsibility for the abuse of this freedom in the cases determined by law' Two years later, in 1791, the American Bill of Rights proclaimed a number of amendments to the constitution of the United States, including that landmark legal provision, the First Amendment, which stipulated that 'Congress shall make no law . . . abridging the freedom of speech, or of the press'. This was a fundamental revolution, for it meant that truth had ceased to belong to any one constituted power, and pertained 'solely to the constituent parties, being immanent to individual reason' and no longer to the transcendent authority of the state.

During the Second World War, the international community became alive to the way in which people's attitudes and awareness were affected by total control of the, media. It was for this reason that, in 1941, President Roosevelt placed 'freedom of speech and expression everywhere in the world' in the front rank of the 'Four Freedoms' In the years immediately following the war, defending freedom of information naturally became one of the objectives of all efforts to rebuild the international system. In 1945, the Chapultepec Act, adopted by the Inter-American Conference on problems of war and peace' proclaimed for the first time 'the freedom of international information flows'.

The following year, the United Nations recognized the importance of freedoms relating to information. In 1946, the UN recalled in its resolution 59 that 'freedom of information is a fundamental human right and is the touchstone of all the freedoms to which the United Nations is consecrated' On 10 December 1948, freedom of information was enshrined in the Universal Declaration of Human Rights, whose Article 19 is the most categorical expression thereof. 'Everyone has the right to freedom of opinion and expression: this right includes freedom . . . to seek, receive and impart information and ideas through any media and regardless of frontiers.

The Munich Declaration adopted in 1971 by representatives of journalists unions, adopts an identical point of view: 'The right to information, to freedom of expression and criticism, is one of the fundamental rights of man.' UNESCO's own Constitution, adopted on 10 November 1945, assigns to the Organization in its Article 11, paragraph 2(a), the goal of 'advancing the mutual knowledge and under-standing of peoples', it particular by means of international agreements designed 'to promote the free flow of ideas by word and image' These principles were to be strengthened with the International Covenant on Civil and Political Rights, adopted by the United Nations

General Assembly on 16 December 1966, whose Article 19 provides that: 'Everyone shall have the right to freedom of expression; this right shall include freedom to seek, receive and impart information and ideas of all kinds, regardless of frontiers, either orally in writing or in print, in the form of art, or through any other media of his choice.' More than ninety states have already ratified this Covenant, thereby pledging to apply its principles.

Other victories for press freedom bound up with the development of the media have given rise to further international and regional declarations. All give pride of place to freedom of information as a precondition of democracy, truth as a basic duty, and respect for the human person as limit.

Among the many international legal instruments that establish freedom of information as a basic principle, mention may be made of Article 10 of the European Convention for the Protection of Human Rights and Fundamental Freedoms, adopted on 4 November 1950, Article 13 of the American Convention on Human Rights, adopted on 22 November 1969, and Article 9 of the African Charter on Human and Peoples' Rights, adopted on 12 July 1981. This principle was to be a driving force in the domestic legislation of the different countries.

The Declaration of Rights and Obligations of Journalists was adopted on 24 and 25 November 1971 in Munich by representatives of the journalists' unions of the Six countries of the then European Community. It has since been adopted by the International Federation of Journalists (IFJ) and by most journalists' unions in Europe. The declaration, which is quintessentially a code of professional ethics, states in its Preamble: 'The right to information, to freedom of expression and criticism is one of the fundamental rights of man. All rights and duties of a journalist originate from this right of the public to be informed on events and opinions. The journalists' responsibility towards the public exceeds any other responsibility particularly towards employers and public authorities.'

The Declaration of Chapultepec was adopted by some hundred professional journalists in Mexico City~ at a conference organized by the Inter-American Press Association (IAPA) in March 1994. It has been signed and endorsed by the President of the United States, by a dozen Latin American Heads of State, by the Secretary-General of the United Nations and by the Director-General of UNESCO. It is in line with the Santiago (Chile) Declaration on the development of the media and democracy in Latin American and the Caribbean. In addition to recognizing the fundamental role played by freedom of expression and press freedom in all democratic societies, the declaration condemns all forms of violence and coercion against journalists. It stipulates in particular that, in a truly free society~ public opinion alone has the right to reward or to condemn the work of journalists. All acts of violence directed against journalists must be 'investigated promptly' and 'punished harshly'.

The ten principles of the Charter for a Free Press were adopted in London in 1987 by journalists representing thirty-four countries and the main organizations working in the field of press freedom. The charter urges governments to:

— put an end to both direct and indirect censorship;

— prevent all discriminatory practices in regard to the independent media, particularly in regard to access to information, means of distribution and taxation;

- permit the free flow of news and the unimpeded movement of journalists and their equipment across borders;
- not restrict the practice of journalism through any licensing system;
- ensure that journalists enjoy the protection of the law and are recognized as civilians in war zones.

The charter was signed by the World Press Freedom Committee (WPFC), the International Federation of Newspaper Publishers (FIEJ), the International Press Institute (IPI), the Inter-American Press Association (IAPA), the North American National Broadcasters Association (NANBA) and the International Federation of the Periodical Press (FIPP).

However, in the period immediately following the Second World War, the free flow of information would very rapidly become a Cold War issue and constitute one of the major bones of contention between states. It was interpreted in terms of two fundamentally conflicting doctrines. That of the Western democracies was based on Article 19 of the Universal Declaration of Human Rights.

It advocated the dismantling of all barriers in the way of seeking, receiving and imparting information and ideas both within states and beyond their borders. For its part, the attitude of the Soviet Union and the peoples' democracies originated in Communist theory, which defined the media, as educational tools operating under state control for the purpose of expediting the construction of socialism. The media had a social function, and journalists, defined as intellectual agitators and propagandists, had a mission to -inform and to mould opinion. To the principle of a free and unimpeded flow of information, the Soviet Union and its allies opposed that of a controlled exchange of information, conducted on the basis of intergovernmental agreements, with due respect for sovereignty and the principle of noninterference in the domestic affairs of states. For their part, the developing countries declared themselves to be the victims of serious inequalities in the matter of information flows between North and South. and considered the manner in which the media of the North reflected the reality of their national situations to be exaggerated, distorted and even totally false.

In consequence, they called for a redressing of the balance of information flows, and hence implicitly for control over information emanating from the countries of the North. The Communist countries' demand for controlled information exchange between East and West and the developing countries' calls for a redressing of the information flow balance between North and South were both compatible and complementary.

These two groups of countries formed a united front within the international organizations concerned, first and foremost the United Nations and UNESCO, for the purpose of advocating, at the end of the 1970s, the establishment of a 'New World Information and Communication Order' (NWICO), regarded as being the counterpart of the 'New World Economic Order'. The discussions which took place on the subject within UNESCO were extremely stormy.

Tension reached a climax in the mid-1980s when the United States (1984) and the United Kingdom (1985) withdrew from the Organization. For their part, a number of international organizations representing professional media circles put all their weight into the balance in order to isolate UNESCO and to make the international community understand that the New World Information and Communication Order constituted an intolerable assault upon press freedom and the free flow of information. The political changes which occurred in the USSR at the end of the 1980s, and in particular the introduction by Mikhail Gorbachev of glasnost, had the result of radically transforming the overall situation in regard to NWICO. With the emergence of democracy, a number of Eastern and Central European countries began to adopt the liberal conception of information whereby freedom of expression and media independence and pluralism are an essential precondition of any properly functioning democratic society. The major upheavals which occurred in Eastern and Central Europe drove a number of developing countries as well to embark upon the path of democratic reform.

Freedom of expression, and with it press freedom and pluralism, thus gained a certain amount of ground. The new information and communication technologies, in particular satellite television - which ,enters via the roof, without having to go through the censor's office' - and the Internet, have shrunk the planet to a global village, and made information available to a growing number of people on every continent. True, information flows remain largely to the advantage of the North; but an increasing number of developing countries such as Brazil, Egypt, India and Mexico are becoming in turn producers, broadcasters and operators on a regional and even a worldwide scale. Moreover, it is worth pointing out that the smaller countries of the North are themselves becoming ever more dependent upon the output of the major international, and particularly North American, corporations, in regard both to information (large international news agencies supplying texts, pictures and data) and to entertainment and fiction films. The twofold dichotomy between North and South and East and West is gradually being superseded by a new subdivision between the large, populous countries, which have a sufficiently strong domestic market to cover the costs of their national productions, and the smaller countries of the North and South alike, which are far more numerous but which, because they do riot possess the necessary critical mass, are doomed to import foreign programmes in order to counterbalance the quantitative inadequacy of their domestic output. The public and private television companies of the industrialized and developing countries are indeed in danger of shortly finding themselves excluded from international deals in regard to the live broadcasting of the most popular sports events, such as the Olympic Games or the World Football Championship, since the charges for broadcasting rights are becoming, in relation to their domestic advertising market, quite prohibitive. What, then, can be said of the poorest countries of the South, in particular those of the African continent, which provide so many of today's world champions! These countries are already almost wholly dependent on the international market. In the case of some, the situation is so critical that the systematic pirating of satellite pictures and videotapes has become the sole means of survival.

Thus the disparities highlighted by the commission chaired by Sean MacBride, which served to justify the call for a new world order, the NWICO, still remain a burning issue. On the other hand, the map of these disparities has changed in relation to the situation prevailing in the 1970s and 1980s. Most Latin American and Asian countries are undoubtedly in a better position than they were twenty years ago, both in regard to media access and in terms of endogenous production. It must not be overlooked that large sectors of their populations, notably the poorest sections, have benefited but little from this favourable trend. In the industrialized countries, while access to the media poses no special problems aside from financial constraints, the growing dependence of the small countries on the major international suppliers of texts, images and data has become an extremely worrying factor. As regards the least developed countries, their situation has worsened still further in that many have become still more impoverished, and have been left on the fringe of technological progress.

Seizing the opportunity afforded by the ending of the Cold War to move beyond the sterile discussions on the NWICO, and concerned to support the process of democratization being pursued in several regions of the world, the General Conference of UNESCO adopted, at its twenty-fifth session in November 1989 - at the very moment when the Berlin Wall was crumbling - a 'new communication strategy' aimed at meeting the needs of the burgeoning democracies and the developing countries alike. Its goals were threefold:

— Encouraging the free flow of information, at international as well as national level.

— Promoting the wider and better balanced dissemination of information, without any obstacle to freedom of expression.

— Developing all the appropriate means of strengthening communication capacities in the developing countries in order to increase their participation in the communication process.

In respect of the first prong of this 'new communication strategy , UNESCO reasserted the fundamental principle of 'free flow of information' enshrined in its Constitution. In particular, it pledged to promote both freedom of expression, the cornerstone of the human rights edifice, and press freedom, itself a key component of all democratic societies. To this end, it provides assistance to intergovernmental and nongovernmental organizations whose mission it is to defend these fundamental freedoms, while at the same time preserving and developing its own means of action. In order to give concrete expression to its commitment to the democratic process in countries living through a period of transition, UNESCO, in conjunction with the United Nations Department of Public Information, has since 1991 organized a series of five Regional Seminars on Promoting Independent and Pluralistic Media. These workshops, which brought together in all several hundred media professionals, gave rise to the adoption of firmly worded and unambiguous 'declarations' which defined the preconditions for setting up and operating a free, independent and pluralist press. An unusual occurrence in the annals of the United Nations system, these various declarations, framed and drafted by the participants, themselves all media professionals, were later formally adopted in their entirety by the states represented at UNESCO's General Conference.

In addition, the United Nations General Assembly decided, in December 1993, on UNESCO's proposal to proclaim 3 May, the anniversary of the Declaration of Windhoek, 'World Press Freedom Day'. Finally, as its most recent initiative, UNESCO established, in 1996, the UNESCO/Guillermo Cano World Press Freedom Prize, which was awarded for the first time on 3 May 1997. In the light of the foregoing, one cannot fail to observe the developments that have occurred in the states since the end of the Cold War.

Unfortunately, in so far as respect for fundamental freedoms is concerned, there is frequently a major difference between official positions, adopted 'cold' in intergovernmental forums, and the reality of the situation at grass-roots level. The fact nevertheless remains that states taken as a whole have never committed themselves so far on such sensitive issues as press freedom and the independence and pluralism of the media. The second objective of UNESCO's 'new communication strategy' takes up one of the ultimate goals of NWICO, with this single - but major -difference: that it is no longer possible to curb or to prevent the free flow of information on the pretext that its dissemination is, unbalanced. Such an argument had in fact frequently been put forward by authoritarian and totalitarian regimes, in the 1970s and 1980s, in order to justify censorship of the international news agencies, to ban the distribution of foreign newspapers on national territory and to jam electronic media broadcasts transmitted from abroad. The new strategy does not seek to weaken the strong, but rather to strengthen the weak in order to redress the balance, in so far as is possible, in the exchange of information flows. Hence the third objective of UNESCO's 'new information strategy', namely, to develop communication capacities in the developing countries.

When the General Conference of UNESCO adopted its 'new communication strategy' in November 1989, the representatives of the developing countries, somewhat at a loss after finding themselves dropped by their traditional partners among the Communist states of Eastern and Central Europe, had greatly hoped that the industrialized countries of the North, having obtained satisfaction on the free flow of information issue, would do their utmost substantially to increase their financial support for the development of communication, and in particular for the International Programme for the Development of Communication (IPDC). This hope was strengthened in February 1992 when IPDC decided to change its rules of procedure in order to be in a position to help the media, in pursuance of a recommendation formulated some months earlier on the occasion of the Windhoek seminar. As a result, projects submitted by the private sector are henceforth admissible. In the light of the experience of recent years, it must be acknowledged that hope has been disappointed because contributions to the IPDC Special Account have failed to increase. It is true that, since the economic crisis which hit them in the first half of the 1990s, most of the industrialized countries have severely cut back their aid budgets to developing countries. It is also true that the needs born of the transition process in the new democracies of Eastern and Central Europe have siphoned off substantial sums, frequently to the detriment of the countries of the South. However, that does not explain everything, for assistance for communication development has lagged behind both in the East European democracies currently in transition and in the developing countries of the South. This situation is all the more surprising in that, throughout the Cold War, Western countries, and first and foremost the United States, had invested billions of dollars in order to ensure their supremacy in the strategic field of communication.

Those investments were far from fruitless, since it was the power of words and images that toppled the Berlin Wall. While it is understandable that, like the 'weapons of deterrence', the 'weapons of persuasion' should have suffered substantial budget cuts, it is difficult to imagine that only a few crumbs remain to consolidate the achievements of democracy in the communication field, since it is well known that the media were and are still in Europe, as in the other regions of the world, the driving force behind the transition to democracy.

The scant interest shown by the industrialized countries in the development of communication and information becomes even more surprising when one considers the fact that the communication sector represents up to 10 per cent of GNP in some countries of the North. It may therefore legitimately be wondered what reasons have led the national development agencies to devote less than I per cent of their financial resources to date to projects relating to communication development.

Satellite broadcasting, electronic printing, the explosion of the Internet and of e-mail, and the mobile telephone have resulted in a huge expansion of the potential for worldwide information flows and exchange. They have also facilitated the rapid and even instantaneous transmission of images from one region to another, transcending national borders even though some states still endeavour to raise all kinds of barriers by operating border controls, jamming radio broadcasts and banning the possession of satellite dish aerials.

All these defences are today increasingly eroded by the new progress being made by the media, the intensification of output and the higher levels of technical performance. The new communication technologies, or the new ways of optimizing the old, have become an essential dimension in all thinking about the issue. For they are capable of producing positive effects and helping to speed up the democratization process, just as they may constitute a curb upon, and a threat to, freedom of expression and democracy.

The media have played a key role in several countries in bringing about the democratic progress recorded throughout the world during the 1980s. Their ability to transmit, continuously and in real time, current national and international news has had the effect of both driving events along and speeding them up. Examples are legion. In the Philippines, the clandestine use of video (and also of photocopying) at the time of the assassination of the opposition leader Benigno Aquino, as well as the high-profile presence of foreign media during the 1986 elections, contributed in large measure to the fall of Ferdin and Marcos.

Radio Veritas was occupied by the citizenry during the 'people's power' movement in order to rally the Population against Marcos's army. In South Africa, in Haiti and in Palestine, the pictures of apartheid, repression and of the intifada prompted reactions solidarity and support throughout the world. They enabled the international community to condemn the abuses, to defend human rights and to encourage democracy. The impact of the media can also be of paramount importance when they describe and present to peoples deprived of freedom another way of life other political systems, other democratic values.

The example of the former communist regimes provides an excellent illustration. In the ex-German Democratic Republic, citizens could receive the radio stations and television channels of the Federal Republic of Germany. They were kept regularly informed about certain political and other events that their government preferred to cover up. That was how, in 1989, they learned of the great demonstration in Leipzig, the opening of the Hungarian borders and the first cracks that were appearing in the Berlin Wall.

After the fall of the Berlin Wall, the peoples of the neighbouring countries, who were following the events on foreign radio and television stations, decided in their turn to take to the streets. Here too, pictures invaded every sphere and played a crucial role in bearing witness to the process of liberation. They neutralized official pronouncements and undermined the authorities' position. During the same period, in Czechoslovakia, the students had installed television screens throughout the streets of Prague in order to show police brutality against the demonstrators, and to broadcast the speeches of the playwright and future President of the Republic, Vaclav Havel. In Poland, the majority of journalists found themselves on the front line with all other citizens calling for democracy.

Dailies such as Gazeta wyborcza exerted considerable pressure on behalf of the democratization process. In Romania, television played a key role in rallying the population and helping to spread support for the liberation movement, which was filmed, monitored and broadcast live throughout the world thanks to the famous Studio 4 of the Free Romanian Television company. In striking contrast to the macabre faking of the mass grave in Timisoara, this movement established itself as a formidable force in the fight for democracy.

Determined to bear witness on behalf of that revolution, citizens set up as amateur reporters to impose their video recordings by way of popular testimony in the first meetings organized by the revolution's leaders. Reaction to the events was extremely powerful, thanks to a press and television that, having thrown off their shackles, acted as catalysts in generating a genuine new awareness. In the Federal Republic of Yugoslavia, the popular demonstrations against the authorities' refusal to accept the results of the municipal elections won by the opposition were widely and favourably reported on the Internet. Several sites made it possible to monitor in real time the evolution of the protest movement. Sites such as 'Protest 96', named after the student movement, made their voices heard through-out the world by posting reports on demonstrations, and by publishing their 'Declaration of Decency', a manifesto on behalf of respect for constitutional rights. These sites also showed photographs of demonstrations, and of graffiti observed on the walls of Belgrade. The Internet was thus instrumental in enabling the popular movement to keep up a dialogue with the outside world by receiving thousands of e-mail messages of support from all over the world."

These non-stop demonstrations, monitored continuously by the international community, drove the public authorities to confirm the opposition's victory in the capital and in several provincial cities. In a similar context, the live broadcasting of the first trial in the history of the UN International War Crimes Tribunal has enabled international public opinion to discover the full extent of the atrocities committed in Bosnia and Herzegovina.

In other regions of the world, such as North Africa and the Near East, certain media have played and still play a key role in fostering the progress of democracy. In the Maghreb, satellite dish aerials, installed on a wide scale in the region, continue permanently to defy the public television channels operating under state control. Their unstoppable spread is breaking up monopolies and triggering off a veritable cultural and political revolution. In Algeria, the October 1988 uprising sparked a genuine democratic awakening that was immediately reflected in the emergence of a profusion of newspapers of every persuasion, and of go-getting journalists whose credo was and remains freedom of speech.

In Africa, use of the video recorder has greatly increased access to information sources and to a whole range of messages. This, technology has contributed to a relative democratization of African society, which neither radio nor television had managed to achieve, for it has provided access to a greater number and variety of programmes than are offered by the traditional networks, whose coverage is limited and which generally operate under state control., Such programmes have in most cases been used to supplement or even to replace the information made available by the official media. Thus the events of the century's closing decades have provided, ample proof of the close ties that exist between the media and democracy.

The two are intimately linked, and develop in tandem. They demonstrate that there is no more reliable criterion for judging the quality of a democracy than press freedom and the pluralism and independence of the media.

In most democracies, the press is perceived as both an outward sign and a guarantee of democracy. Regarded empirically as the fourth estate, it ensures that democracy functions properly, condemns abuses and clarifies the options available. Pursuing these aims journalists enjoy certain professional rights that are supposed to guarantee their editorial independence *vis-à-vis* both the public authorities and their employer. In practice, however, many media professional regularly denounce the restrictions which undermine their independence - clear proof that the struggle for press independence is never over in democratic countries, even if it has lost much of its intensity.

First and foremost, journalists are concerned by the curbs placed by many governments upon the free flow of information. Access to public information sources, which is a precondition for ensuring that citizens are kept properly informed, is often limited if not deliberately restricted. In most cases, states stir impose strict regulations. For example, press coverage of military conflicts is subject to rigorous control i certain countries. There is a growing trend to limb the war correspondent's autonomy, freedom of movement and access to the front. This development has been particularly striking since the Viet Nam War in the United States, where access to information has c several occasions been channelled by the Pentagon. In most cases, the culture of secrecy continues to hold sway, usually cloaked in a series of regulations, statutes and conventions that limit both the volume and the nature of the information which may be disclosed to the public.

In reality, as the international monitoring organization Article 19 contends, 'governments invoke a wide variety of reasons . . . for justifying secrecy... Many reasons lack justification in the sense that they are not recognized as permissible restrictions under international law, and in fact may have illegitimate aims, such as the suppression of criticism and unorthodox ideas'.

The French media historian and former Secretary of State for Communication, Jean-Noël Jeanneney, has pointed out that in a modern democracy 'we must beware of all secrets, and flush out everything that is hidden in the shadows: ultimately, all curiosity is legitimate'. Thus the obligation imposed in certain cases upon journalists to reveal confidential information which they alone possess, the common tendency to confuse secrets that could jeopardize the interests of states with those that would simply harm political administrations, and the repeated attempts to thwart journalists' investigative missions are all, generally speaking, detrimental to the citizen's right to information and, hence, to the public interest as a whole.

Furthermore, media professionals consider that they are not safe from threats and intimidation. Infringements of, and obstructions to, freedom of information increasingly take the form of a whole range of obstacles placed in the way of journalists: these include house searches, indictments, the forced suspension of publication, violence and even murder.

The use and the interpretation made of libel actions, of requests to exercise the right of reply, of public order disturbances, provisional or emergency measures, and actions for damages are usually governed by the circumstances of the moment. The enforcement of these restrictions, which are moreover considered to be outmoded by the profession, generates a climate of insecurity and suspicion that weighs heavily upon freedom of information. Certain court rulings are experienced by journalists as intolerable infringements of their professional rights and, consequently, of the public's right to be kept informed. In the field of electronic media, the threats exercised by the courts also remain extremely powerful.

In the print media field, trials relating to the disclosure of documents deemed to be secret or confidential are becoming increasingly common, and are usually aimed at smaller newspapers, whose limited financial resources reduce their ability to defend themselves or to pay the fines and damages awarded against them. Media professionals consider that these judgements represent a direct threat to freedom of information and investigative journalism, understood as the concern to go beyond official sources in the search for information. They face journalists with an unacceptable dilemma, since they are liable to be convicted of libel if they publish confidential information without providing proof of the facts revealed, and convicted for possession of stolen property if they hold and publish the evidence confirming their allegations.

However, the Munich Declaration emphasizes the right to information by affirming that journalists may claim free access to all information sources and the right freely to investigate all events that affect public life. It adds that the secrecy of public or private affairs cannot in such cases be adduced as justification for denying journalists these rights save in exceptional circumstances and on clearly stated grounds. This trend towards freeing access to information sources from legal impediments has been enshrined, in most states of the United States of America, in the so-called shield laws', which shield journalists against being forced to give testimony. It has also been regularly reaffirmed by regional and international courts of justice. Several recent cases have, for example, provided an opportunity to reassert the right of journalists to protect their sources. The one that attracted most attention was the ruling by the European Court of Human Rights on 27 March 1996 which condemned the United Kingdom for failure to respect journalists' rights in this respect. In countries in transition, acceptance of the principle of a press that is free, independent and openly critical of all the authorities is a relatively recent phenomenon. Theoretically, most of these countries support the principles set forth in Article 19 of the Universal Declaration of Human Rights and reiterate them in their new constitutions.

Nevertheless, such support, often solemnly proclaimed, has not solved all the problems affecting freedom of expression and the free flow of information. In many countries, particularly arbitrary forms of obstruction of and restrictions upon the freedom of information still remain. Such obstacles stem by and large from the prevailing system of media ownership and management. The majority of broadcasting networks are still state monopolies subject to strict controls. In countries with authoritarian or totalitarian regimes, the prevailing ideology leaves but little room for pluralism. The main dailies and weeklies are controlled, subsidized and administered by the state. Likewise, the co-existence of several newspapers or television channels does not necessarily constitute evidence of pluralism, in particular when their proprietors are close to the establishment. In such contexts, the public, the target audience of these media, is self-evidently not in a position to forge an enlightened and unbiased opinion of its own. Censorship may take a variety of forms, depending on whether it is practised officially or unofficially.

The ban upon satellite dishes in force in many countries, and the controls exercised on access to electronic media and the Internet, deprive citizens of alternative information sources. Moreover, various administrative measures may prove just as effective as overt censorship. These range from restrictions upon, for example, the use of newsprint and other professional materials and hardware, to more direct forms of interference: control over the printing at newspapers, monopoly on the importation of paper, right of scrutiny of newspaper circulation figures, control over the award of advertising contracts, exorbitant taxation of certain publications, etc. In order to explain the strengthening of their control over the print and broadcast media, and even to justify the censoring of news-reporting that does not serve their interests, the authorities generally put forward the same reasons: imperatives bound up with issues of national security and public order. Thus many countries grappling with terrorism and outbreaks of irrational violence have adopted public order measures that have inevitably eroded press freedom severely.

In Spain, the Bill on the secrecy of defence matters presented by the Spanish Government in June 1996, which was interpreted by media professionals as an attempt to restrict freedom of expression, was finally abandoned. The activities of the ETA continue to be publicized by Spanish news agencies and reported by the media. For its part, the United Kingdom adopted on 16 September 1994, as one of its measures to deal with the Irish question, a Bill known as the 'Ulster Rule Bill' which imposed very strict controls upon news coverage of IRA activities by the BBC. For example, the BBC was not allowed to grant air time to IRA representatives. In order to circumvent this ban, the Corporation hired Irish actors to deliver the terrorists' statements. The same restriction was imposed upon the independent British television stations, which were required to sign specific agreements regarding the coverage of terrorist activities. In Algeria, the Government published a decree in June 1994 relating to the reporting of security issues. That decree established a 'communication unit' to be responsible for issuing official communiqués exclusively through the Algerian news agency APS. Article 3 of the decree stipulates that in reporting on terrorist and subversive activities, all categories of media are required to disseminate only official communiqués'. Lastly, Article 4 provides that 'the dissemination of any information relating to security matters that is not covered in the framework of an official communiqué or a public press release shall be forbidden' In Egypt, the law on 'crimes of publishing' authorizes journalists to be held without trial for an indefinite period in accordance with the law instituting a state of emergency. The new law also makes provision for lengthy terms of imprisonment, should the court decide that a crime is involved, in the case of journalists found guilty of 'tendentious writings'.

Freedom of information may be limited by other entities than governments (terrorist and extremist groups, the Mafia, paramilitary groups, and drug cartels). In some countries, extremist groups resort to force in order to prevent families from picking up foreign television channels that spread values alien to their own. Others launch fat was against intellectuals, artists and journalists. Others still go to the extreme of murdering journalists and other media professionals. In this regard it should be pointed out that, in almost every case, inquiries into crimes committed against journalists have come to nothing, and neither those who carried them out nor those who ordered and paid for the killings have ever appeared before the courts. Concerned by this 'culture of impunity', professional organizations such as the Inter-American Press Association have set up their own committees of inquiry.

International Freedom of Expression Exchange Network was launched by several professional and non-govern mental organizations concerned to pool information more effectively and to enhance the impact of their interventions, which set up an electronic alert and co-ordination network to react whenever freedom of information is threatened.

Operational since September 1992, the network is run by the Canadian Committee to Protect Journalists, in Toronto, with the support of UNESCO and its International Programme for the Development of Communication (IPDC). The IFEX Network today has twenty-seven members, including the major organizations. The network, which is a vitally important point of contact for all journalists and professional media organizations, comprised in May 1997 more than 300 subscribers in eighty countries, 160 of them located in the developing countries. This was achieved thanks in particular to the International Programme for the Development of Communication, whose aid has enabled the professional organizations of those countries to form a majority within the network. In five years, the network has made it possible not only to improve the gathering, production and disorientation of news and information on topics relating to press freedom on an international scale but also to strengthen the development of South-South exchanges, and, finally, to set up a veritable system of alert and solidarity among all the protagonists: 1,600 alerts are issued each year, as well as a weekly press release in three languages. Joint campaigns are also conducted. A data bank has been created on the Internet which makes available the information gathered by IFEX on a World Wide Web server (http:Hwww.ifex.org).

In conflict-tom countries, gaining control of the media and their use for partisan purposes constitutes a major objective of the parties in conflict. This practice may lead to a downhill spiral with ever more dangerous consequences. In the former Yugoslavia and in Rwanda, for example, newspapers, radio stations and television channels, press-ganged into the service of the various factions, have begun to launch public calls to violence, ethnic cleansing and even to genocide. The self-styled journalists working for these media no longer see their mission as being to report on events in times of crisis but as a veritable combat on the side of one or other of the parties in conflict. By resorting to the procedures of totalitarian propaganda, based on techniques of crowd manipulation, conditioning and disinformation, such media, co-opted or hijacke, to serve as the tools of xenophobic and hate-filler, politicians, have become vehicles or carriers of way.

The authorities no longer confine themselves the, censoring publications that might damage their image, but seek to orchestrate the entire system of the media in order to turn it into a political tool. It is well-known strategy of totalitarian regimes. In the former Yugoslavia, the media have been turned into veritable war machines putting out ~ mixture of crude lies and war-mongering propaganda For nearly five years, they have sown the seeds of hatred between the Serb, Bosnian, Croat and Muslim communities.

The consequences have been tragic since they have fostered the emergence of various forms of chauvinistic and xenophobic nationalism Be it in Serbia, in Croatia or in Bosnia and Herze govina, most of the media have been used as instruments of war and intercommunity violence. Brought very early on under the control of the parties in power, they have embraced the most extremist causes. Their persistent rhetoric inciting to hatred and ostracism has been regularly condemned by the international community. In Rwanda, media such as the broadcasting stations Radio-Télévision Libre Mille Collines (RTLM) and Radio Rwanda, and the periodical Kangura, have contributed actively to campaigns inciting to racial hatred and genocide targeted against the Tutsis.

Although RTLM, which was set up in April 1993, claims for itself the status of a 'free', commercial station, it was in fact financed entirely by members of the family of President Juvénal Habyarimana, who was assassinated on 6 April 1994. Installed directly opposite the presidential palace, the station became the propaganda centre of the Habyarimana clan, well known for its hostility to the Arusha peace accords of August 1993 between the government and the opposition party, the Front Patriotique Rwandais (FPR). The station succeeded in winning a wide audience thanks to live shows and musical broadcasts distinguished by a degree of professional expertise. The station's presenters gloated daily over the massacres, and the non-stop flow of their commentaries, personal messages and jokes was tinged with racial hatred directed against the Tutsi minority. This process of 'ethnicization' clearly won support throughout the region of the Great Lakes. In Burundi Radio Rutomorangingo, a pirate radio station set up by Hutu extremists, as well as both Tutsi and Hutu extremist newspapers, have enlisted in the service of ethnic hatred.

Resistance and international support

Faced with this dangerous drift by the media towards hatred-inspired campaigns of disinformation, some journalists are nevertheless striving, frequently at the cost of their personal safety, to do their job conscientiously, reporting events in an honest and unbiased manner. In Rwanda, André Sibomana, editor of the country's oldest independent newspaper, Kinyamateka, founded in 1933, narrowly escaped the massacres on several occasions. Having been a victim of harassment, threats and censorship, this newspaper resumed publication in December 1994, thanks to aid provided by the international community.

In the former Yugoslavia, while many journalists have thrown in their lot with the nationalists by espousing their doctrines, others have opted for a professional approach and strive first and foremost - despite the threats and obvious risks - to report the facts and to tell the truth as impartially as possible. While the former have consciously consented to take part in campaigns aimed at manipulating public opinion, for example by stirring up feelings of hatred and vengefulness, the latter have by contrast done their utmost to give a balanced and unbiased picture of the situation. Today, the problem of the media's independence in these countries has still not been resolved, despite the efforts of the international community, and in particular of UNESCO, to create the conditions in which pluralist and independent media can develop and take an effective part in the process of reconstruction and democratization.

UNESCO in a period of conflict

During the war years, independent journalists in the former Yugoslavia came under heavy political pressure. At a time when the independent media were fighting for survival, access to unbiased information was also becoming increasingly difficult for the public. In December 1992, in accordance with its constitutional mandate 'to promote the free flow of ideas by word and image', UNESCO launched a pilot programme to assist independent media in conflict areas, special emphasis being given to the former Yugoslavia. After the signing of the Dayton Peace Accords in December 1995, UNESCO renewed its support to independent media so as to pave the way for democratization and the peace process, thanks in particular to the aid supplied by several donors, and in close collaboration with other United Nations agencies and professional media organizations.

In 1996, UNESCO was designated 'lead agency for assistance to independent media for the reconstruction period in former Yugoslavia' by the UN Inter-Agency Appeal. As such, the Organization has lent backing in Bosnia and Herzegovina, the Federal Republic of Yugoslavia and the Republic of Croatia to eleven TV stations, ten radios, seven newspapers, three press agencies and three production companies.

Aside from the extreme cases described above, there exist throughout the world dozens of conflict situations in which the media perform a more traditional but no less essential role as 'witnesses' Their supposed mission being to report everything that occurs in these regions and to reveal violations of the fundamental principles of humanity, the media are in a position to keep international public opinion informed and to alert it to the most horrendous situations. The journalist then becomes, as it were, a torch-bearer of democracy by reporting on what he or she has seen and learned in order to supply the citizen's basic need for information. A report on violations of the fundamental principles of humanity, whether enshrined in the Geneva Conventions or in the human right., conventions, can in itself serve to alert public opinior and thereby constitute a major exposure of the crime,, committed. In certain cases, such a report may serve to set in motion mechanisms or procedures for putting an end to those crimes.

However, in situations of armed conflict, the journalist's job is a difficult and dangerous one Opposition groups and civil and military authorities alike generally find it in their interest to conceal certain compromising realities. Some do not their hesitate to take appropriate steps in order to curb the activities of reporters. Harassment, threats and even murder are unfortunately becoming increasingly common in dealings with journalists who get in the way too much.

In this 'no-man's-land' of freedom, the reporter's sole means of protection is frequently his own experience and common sense.

At present, the status of journalists on professional missions in areas of armed conflict is defined in the first Protocol Additional to the Geneva Conventions of 12 August 1949, in Article 79 relating to 'Measures of protection for journalists' This article provides that 'journalists engaged in dangerous professional missions in areas of armed conflict shall be considered as civilians' As such, they enjoy general protection against dangers arising from military operations, and shall not be the object of attack, acts or threats of violence.

3

New Technologies

In many respects, managers are confronted with the same perceptual problems as our unknowledgeable observer. In a business organization, however, people are still primarily driven by their physical organization and would not be happy to respond to virtuality. This then brings us to the point of the chapter: to discover how the model of physical and virtual organization will help the manager. Unlike those in our submarine, most managers are not aware of their virtual organization. Like our observer, they will interpret what is going on through their physical organization.

In the same way that our unknowledgeable observer would not be able to act either effectively or appropriately in such a situation, so too are management teams not acting properly because they appreciate neither the existence nor characteristics of their virtual organizations. Therefore, merely to understand the virtual organization will probably make a manager more efficient. In some respects the two-organizations model is proposing that managements adopt a new culture within an organization. That may seem contradictory to this work's implied sociological approach rather than one of prescription. This has not altered. But there are inevitable consequences from all types of analysis which are bound to change our perception of the environment.

The impact of technology subsequent to introduction will drastically upset that balance which then requires positive management action which is not always forthcoming. We then have the seemingly paradoxical situation of increased efficiency accompanied by decreased effectiveness. The final point takes us to a certain extent onto a macro level of analysis. Because they do not understand virtual organization UK firms generally may not be as competitive as many of their competitors abroad.

A classic case is cited by Peter Drucker (management) who compared western business organizations with their Japanese counterparts, who are recognized as being more effective. It would be naive to put their success down to merely a more conscientious workforce. That may or may not be part of the equation. What is more important is that their societal culture is more conducive to the formation of a business organization. The often quoted Samurai and rice grower relationship allows for a successful management of these firms.

On the one hand, the worker is happy to work for a particular organization (all the individual's life, and from generation to generation is not uncommon) because to do so reflects their relationship with formal authority into which they have been socialized. On the other hand, the management, through this same social mechanism, feels a patriarchal sense of responsibility towards its workers. The net effect seems to be a well functioning and happy firm.

Without the benefit of an empirical study on this particular issue, NBS research nevertheless tends to support the view that there is a difference in attitude between UK-based Japanese firms and western-managed business organizations. The management culture within the Japanese firms seemed to be more sensitive to aspects other than resource manipulation. There is evidence of stronger links into the virtual elements of an organization through a management acceptance of having to deal with the employee as a whole person rather than as a physical resource. In other words, the Japanese organizational culture could allow for a more effective utilization of the virtual and physical organization. If this is so, then in any competitive situation the Japanese firms could have a head start. For this reason alone it is worth understanding virtual organization.

This chapter, therefore, issues a challenge to all managements which cannot be ignored. That is, to understand and use appropriately their virtual organizations or to go under. This understanding cannot come about overnight. It is socialized into all of us to conceive in the physical perspective. To change this needs training and education. If we are to survive the onslaught of computers and perhaps our foreign competitors this needs to be attended to sooner rather than later.

Virtual organization is an abstract thing, its relationship with physical organization can only be measured by consequential action and therefore we are effectively seeking to analyse a world constructed in the human mind. We cannot take a psychological or humanist approach, that is to set aside a group of individuals and study them either in or out of context. To do that would miss the whole point of the relationship between the two organizations. People have to be studied not only within context but also within their functional positions.

To take them out of that would be to create a different relationship and thus create a different virtual organization. But not to take them out means an impossible task for the analyst in gaining the necessary data. The problem is not easily surmountable. There is no quick and effective way of gathering the necessary data. In many respects the practitioner is best able to test the model through day to day experience and a feel for the organization. The specific objective of the NBS research project was to analyse the impact of information technology on the structural characteristics of organizations. In particular we were interested in the implications for human behaviour. This allowed us to gather data on a range of interactions before and after computer implementation.

The construction of such data into workable models led me to perceive the organizational context in terms of the physical and the perceptual. We found that the efficiency criteria of computer implementation generated physically-orientated relationships such as output management and structural change, whereas the effectiveness criteria of computer implementation generated the perceptual relationships such as political change and culture. It was obvious that the two were linked, particularly since managers seemed not to be attending to, the effectiveness criteria and yet that part of the organization was not static in terms of change. This suggested that linkage mechanisms between the perceptual and physical aspects were indeed working.

It was but a small step from this to create the model presented in this book which formally recognized the dynamics of the two domains and satisfied the NBS's objective to understand better the impact of information technology upon organizations. Information technology is important in the modelling of an organization because its poignant, perceptual characteristics have a greater impact upon virtuality than other phenomena. The two sides cannot be separated. The effects of computers cannot be understood without virtual organization, whilst the computer has increased the need to understand virtuality.

Where do we go from here? Empirical research alone is not practical for reasons already stated. The Silverman et al. action research approach has greater promise. This is where the individual analysts are involved within the organizational process and are insiders as opposed to outsiders. But then we shall get only their side of the story. This could be broadened further by having many analysts in one company, but then the numbers would encroach upon the characteristics of the firm and also possibly be an inconvenience.

An examination of an organization over a period of time could be carried out in a similar manner to the research conducted by Burns and Stalker. The results, however, would at best be only the consequence of the relationship we seek and not a reflection of its mechanisms. NBS research has already achieved this. It is, therefore, down to the practitioner, the employees of our business organizations. They are the physical and virtual organizations, it is through them that any organization has form and reality.

An easy thing to say, but it requires their considerable participation and understanding in any research that is conducted. But more than this, the virtual/physical dichotomy is an action. As such, it cannot be analysed like a piece of furniture. In many respects it has to be accepted as being there and action then taken In accordance with that perception. An act of faith it may be, more likely a 'suck it and see' approach. Unfortunately the nature of our social entities do not allow us the convenience of a comfortable and well defined research framework.

The computerization of editorial work has had a revolutionary impact on the techniques of journalism, creating new jobs and changing old ones. It has provided publishers with an opportunity to take part in the digital revolution which is now under way, notably by enabling them to provide on-line newspapers on the Internet. In the radio market, broadcasters have taken advantage of the new transmission systems to diversify the programme offer and improve listening comfort, the trend now being to provide high-fidelity digital satellite programmes, or even to create a site on the Internet.

In the television sector, data digitization and image compression techniques have led to a vast increase in the programme feed with a qualitative improvement both in pictures and sound. The same technology also provides new possibilities for interactivity that may, on the one hand, revolutionize the way we watch television and, on the other, enable viewers actually to affect what happens in the programmes.

New modes of information consumption

The increasing number of information media has encouraged non-stop growth in the range of programmes on offer, with theme channels, specialized magazines, and local radios of an associative or community type in particular, but has also resulted in fragmented listening and reading behaviour patterns.

The consequence of this enlarged, personalized form of consumption is likely to favour the transfer of the programming function from broadcaster to viewer. 'Zapping' and repeat broadcasts via digital programme streams or VCRs mean that users can consume video and audio services on demand, whenever and however they wish. Digital television will enable users to access a wide range of new services, such as pay-per-view TV, the downloading of video games or software, or channels specializing in sports or teleshopping. Based on the North American model, these services are currently developing with increasing speed by making viewers pay for programmes as they consume them, in the same way that they pay for their electricity or telephone services.

The requisite decoders are already on the market around the world and are the cause of industrial battles about rival standards. Their regulation is a vital issue in the audiovisual management of digital television, because they are the key to consumer households, the means of monitoring viewers' choices, and that of ultimate control over contact with the customer. The profusion of networks and audiovisual channels raises the question of what programmes are to be fed to them, since new support media will not sell if attractive, quality programmes are not developed to be shown on them. Content has become a precious, rare and costly commodity, resulting in bitter struggles for exclusive coverage rights and hence control over distribution.

New media environments

The technological advances used by the media, their internationalization, progress in democracy, and freedom of enterprise and expression have led to upheavals in the media landscape everywhere around the world. Clear-cut traditional geographical divisions have given way to a wider range of market diversity and subtler shades of distinction.

The conventional divides between a virtually uniform, poor Southern hemisphere and a wealthy, homogeneous Northern hemisphere have narrowed. New trends are emerging, with certain countries such as

Egypt, India and Turkey making inroads in the Dress sector, while others such as Brazil and Mexico are making their mark in the audiovisual field, having learnt how to compete on equal terms with the major industrialized countries. Yet it is still the case that the majority of the developing nations and small industrialized countries have neither the same financial resources nor the critical mass to feed their television channels with programmes.

The danger therefore exists that some nations may dominate the programme market, with the concomitant risk of a certain form of cultural standardization. And while the profusion of information systems provides users with greater freedom of choice, it also creates greater inequality - even within the same country - between those who can afford to pay for programmes and those who cannot.

In reaction to technological breakthroughs and competition from pictures, newspapers are seeking to maintain their market share by increased diversification, with a considerable degree of determination. They are players of increasing importance in the other communication sectors, including the audiovisual field, radio, telematics, publishing, bill-posting and direct marketing, and are gradually spreading their activities to include the multimedia market by offering their services on the Internet.

Technological developments and digitization have impacted a number of links in presswork, making newspapers more accessible and more convenient for readers who have now also become television viewers, as well as providing newspapers with new means of adapting more easily to competition from pictures. The same technical advances have also enabled the press to give greater emphasis to photographs in relation to text, to graphics over the written word, to colour over black and white. The prototype for this model is the American daily USA Today, which marked a milestone in the history of the press by opting for a new concept in the use of colour, in particular as a means of enhancing information and guiding the reader. These options have not been copied everywhere in the world press, however.

The computerization of editorial staff has caused a real upheaval in working habits but has also marked a genuine development in presswork. Computers fascinate some people and frighten others, and have fostered bitter resistance from print union representatives. The possibility for journalists everywhere to type their own articles, type copy and enter it directly into a computer system has completely transformed the profession. Keyboard operators previously responsible for inputting copy, and who themselves had replaced traditional typesetters, have already gone in some countries and will disappear in the medium-term elsewhere. Similarly, the manual mounting of pages previously prepared by the editing supervisor and carried out by typesetters and copy preparers is beginning to disappear in some publications, to give way to computer-assisted page make-up. On top of this, as a result of the automation of the printing sequence, the numbers of staff in newspaper printing shops, from reel hands to controller hands to typographers, graphic artists and photo-engravers, have been considerably reduced.

The advantage in microcomputing for journalists is that they do not have to be permanently present at the head office of the newspaper. For several years now, reporters with the major publications around the world have been using laptop computers to type their text (and their illustrations) on site at their assignment and front-end them into the production process via any telecommunications network. The widespread adoption of these techniques and their influence on the gathering, transmission and use of information have had an impact on journalism in general, which no longer entails working for only one of the media, as is still the case in some countries. Journalists now need to be versatile in order to be capable of switching from one branch to another. These new processes, enhanced by digital transmission, have penetrated the market because of the need common to every newspaper to go to press as late as possible in order to print the most up-to-date news and keep manufacturing costs down. Production has become more streamlined, but an entire breed of print workers is on the verge of extinction as a result.

As a result of progress in telecommunications and satellites, texts, photographs and graphics can now be transmitted by facsimile from one continent to another. Since the first transmission by the *Asahi shimbun* from Tokyo to Sapporo in 1959, which took half an hour per page, the process has considerably improved. From New York, the Wall Street Journal dispatches its pages to Hong Kong in less than three minutes. Today, facsimile is used at both ends of its capabilities. On the one hand it is used for short-haul transmission: in Algeria, for example, the daily newspaper *Le Soir d'Algérie* transmits its pages from its head office in Algiers, where they are made up, to regional printing shops in Oran and Constantine. In Switzerland, the pages of 24 Heures and the Geneva Tribune are transmitted to a common printing centre in Lausanne. At the other end of the spectrum, facsimile is used for long-distance international transmission. Dailies such as the International Herald Tribune, the Financial Times and the Guardian, and likewise the Egyptian paper El Ahram, the Japanese newspaper Mainichi shimbun, the Greek paper Avriani and the Italian Gazetta dello sport, are simultaneously printed in several sites around the world.

Photojournalism is a form of presswork has been impacted by major breakthroughs, notably in terms of digital storage and image transmission capacity. The current trend is towards complete digitization of the whole of the photographic image chain, from film-free cameras to the scanning and production of printing plates, via image processing on workstations where photographs can be displayed on-screen, to be cropped and retouched before being inserted into the final page make-up. Layout artists can thus make up the whole newspaper direct from computer to printing plate, without having to edit hard copy and film in order to copy the plate itself. Most of the leading news agencies such as Associated Press, Reuters and Agence France Presse provide their subscribers with equipment permitting the reception of digital photographs, and most dailies are equipped with a digital processing sequence to receive photographs transmitted either by their regional editorial staff or directly by news agencies.

Newspaper production is now fully controlled by computer. From web tension to ink feed, from the registration of four-colour prints to the inserting of quires, down to the counting of copies at the delivery unit - all these steps are programmed and executed by computer. Computer technology is equally present throughout the newspaper distribution system.

Every day, computers calculate the number of copies to be deposited at each point of sale, suggest optimized routes for carriers, control the printing of addresses and trigger requests for subscription renewals. Whereas almost all the editorial staff in industrialized countries have become 'computer literate', and many newspapers in Latin America and Asia have followed their example, newspapers in the Arab World and Africa have taken the leap to computerization only recently. Elsewhere, the move is taking place in small steps.

In democratic countries, the press is often considered as the 'fourth estate', responsible for keeping watch over the social pact between government and governed, thereby enabling citizens to make enlightened choices and to express their opinions. Its independence is given body and form in particular under Article 19 of the Universal Declaration of Human Rights, which, referring to the free flow of information, calls for the elimination of all barriers to seeking, receiving and spreading information and ideas, both within states and beyond their frontiers. In countries in democratic transition, the press is seen less and less as an instrument in the service of governments.

Freedom of enterprise and of speech together have disrupted the old monopolies and led to radical changes in the media environment, with competition between newspapers now even becoming heated. Readers today have a choice of several publications which are often critical of those in power, with the result that current threats are more economic in nature, such as limited or controlled advertising markets, prohibitive tax liabilities, hyperinflation, and so forth. In a minority of other countries today, the press is still a monopoly in the hands of the state and is used to serve political, economic or social aims defined by government authorities or the party in power. Elsewhere, in areas of unrest or war zones, certain sections of the press, controlled by either one of the parties in the conflict, are used to disseminate their propaganda and spread their ideologies.

Newspapers in these cases provide disinformation to manipulate the population, and in extreme cases may be transformed into hate-mongers, inciting to violence and crime. The examples of Rwanda and the former Yugoslavia are still fresh in our minds.

The daily press has developed to highly varying degrees, according to country, region and historical background. It is on the decline in the majority of the most developed countries and on the upswing in various developing countries. As far as dailies are concerned, in 1995 the highest circulation was the privilege of Japan, with the plethoric Yomiuri shimbun, which has a print run of approximately 10 million copies per day. One overriding feature of the high-run newspaper market is intense concentration, with a sector dominated by a limited number of large national private press groups. including Asahi in Japan, Bertelsmann in Germany and Indian Express in India, international corporations such as Pearson and the News Corporation in English-speaking countries, or publicly owned groups such as Dar Al Ahram in Egypt. Apart from The Wall Street Journal and USA Today, which are international in scope, neither Germany nor the United States has a press 'capital', the major dailies with nationwide circulation being located in several large cities such as Hamburg, Frankfurt, Munich, New York, Los Angeles or Chicago.

The United States remains the country where the local press is most highly developed, as was testified by the 1,532 titles in circulation in 1994. Market penetration by newspapers varies according to the size of the country, its journalistic history, its rate of literacy or even its technological development. A few facts and figures give an idea of their impact in various countries.

The 1995 figures for industrialized countries where readership is on the downturn indicate that Norway was in the lead with 610 newspapers sold per 1,000 inhabitants (the 1994 rate was also 610), followed by Japan with 576 (down from 580 in 1991), Sweden and Finland with 464 (472 in 1994) and Switzerland with 365 (372 in 1994). Still on the basis of 1995 circulation figures, readership has increased in other countries, such as Egypt with 67 newspapers per 1,000 inhabitants, India with 26 (up from 21 in 1991),

Malaysia with 123 (up from 117 in 1994) and Sri Lanka with 29 (28 in 1994). These figures illustrate the wide differences between countries and regions. In most African, Arab or Caribbean countries, there is a degree of convergence. Circulation and penetration are still weak even if certain titles that have emerged with democratization-such as the Vientiane Times with a print run of 350,000 copies in Laos, Liberté with 352,000 copies in Algeria, Evenimental Zilei with 120,000 copies in Romania, Motomoto with 40,000 copies in the United Republic of Tanzania-have revitalized the sector, generally as market leaders

Quality newspapers stand out for the wealth of their news and the depth of their investigation. Worth citing among many others in this respect are the Washington Post in the United States, the Independent and the Guardian in the United Kingdom, Frankfurter Allgemeine Zeitung in Germany, Le Monde in France, E Pais in Spain, El Mercurio in Chile, the Straits Time: in Singapore and El Watan in Algeria. Quality newspapers address a wide-ranging readership elite, generally decision-makers, with the result that their influence is considerable, even if their circulation figures *remain generally low (with print runs of a few hundred thousand).*

Newspapers in the Russian Federation from 1990 onwards were confronted with a radically new socio-economic situation, the repercussions of which were far-reaching. In 1992, more than 80 per cent of the newspapers published within Russian territory still belonged to the Communist Party. The decree by President Boris Yeltsin putting an end to the activities of the Party also deprived every title of most of its financial resources. Since that date, competition has hit the press sector, bringing in its wake the difficult process of reconversion to a market economy.

Since 1990, the situation of the Russian press has worsened as a result of economic difficulties linked to new market demands. Between 1991 and 1993, Pravda sales fell by 500,000 copies, while those of Izvestio plummeted from 4.7 to 1.1 million and those of Trud from 18 to 1.5 million.' In the small towns and rural communes the state of the press is even more critical, caused by the absence of advertisers, the low-level income of the population and the growing cost of distribution. In reaction to these setbacks, a law to support the local press was adopted by the Duma in 1995. It provides for the purchase of new printing equipment as well as coverage of the costs related to the production and purchasing of paper, while the public postal service is to defray the costs of distributing newspapers. This assistance for the local press does not include newspapers belonging to political parties or specialized titles. Despite these obstacles, in 1996, 59 per cent of the Russian population read a newspaper every day, 61 per cent listened to the radio and 86 per cent watched television. Very few of the newspapers or magazines they read, however, have acquired any real financial independence, whether from the state, political parties, industrial groups or banking syndicates.

With the liberalization of the economy, the Russian press environment has totally changed. Some newspapers have simply been renamed: the Leningrad Pravda has become the Saint Petersburg News, although the old editorial staff is still the same, and the Kornmunist review is now known as Free Thought. Although other newspapers, former mouthpieces for the Communist Party in particular, have changed owners, the majority of them are now controlled by a few large corporations in the banking and power production sectors. The leading Russian oil group Loukoil, for instance, has a 20 per cent stake in the well-known daily Izvestia and its print run of 550,000. Another, the giant Russian gas company, Gazprom, has acquired a 20 per cent stake in Komsomolskaya Pravda, which has one of the highest circulation figures in the whole of the Russian Federation. Russian banks also have interests in the press.

The Menatep bank, at the head of a veritable industrial empire, has a share in the Independent Media Group, which publishes an English-language daily and the Russian editions of Cosmopolitan and Playboy. Imperial, another bank connected to the Gazprom group, controls the economic daily Kommersant. Finally, the Most bank has created a modern-day empire with the daily newspaper Sevodnia, the radio station Echoes of Moscow, the television channel NTV and the news magazine Itogui. Concentration on this scale has aroused considerable debate in the Russian Federation. For some, the fact that large companies should have shareholdings in the media is a normal economic process common to every democracy. For others, the process is fraught with danger for pluralism and for democracy, all the more so in that the main groups that control the media are also close to the political power base.

The periodical press in various parts of the world has seen radical change and marked growth. One such market move is the specialization of the titles in this sector in order to address a specific readership 'target', addressing a common centre of interest for both men and women. Highlights in this sector include association magazines, such as the ADAC-Motonwelt review for motorists' associations in Germany, with a circulation of 9.2 million, and Modern Maturity for pensioners in the United States, with a circulation of 27 million. Other examples include specialized technical journals in the economic or professional sectors; general public magazines such as television reviews (TV

Guide in the United States, which sells 16 million copies, Sorrisi e Canzoni TV in Italy with a readership of 2.3 million); women's magazines such as Elle in France, Harper's Bazaar in the United States and Grand Hotel in Italy; news magazines, almost all of which are imitations of Time, which was launched in the United States in 1923, such as Der Spiegel in Germany, Espresso in Italy, Cambio in Spain or L'Express in France; intellectual, academic, quality reviews with low sales but high impact, such as Les Temps modernes in France or the New York Review of Books in the United States; the religious press, such as Le Pèlerin in France or La Croix du Benin in Benin; and finally the entertainment press for youngsters such as Mickey Mouse Magazine. Just as for dailies, the situation of periodicals around the world shows tremendous inequality. Most of the magazines are published in America, Asia and Europe. All the above publications differ in terms of the ways in which they are owned and distributed. Some of them are held by families, as is the tradition in Germany, Japan and provincial France. Others belong to large industrial companies, as in India (Tata) or Italy (Fiat), as well as to public authorities, as is the case in China, Cuba, Egypt and Tunisia. In most cases, however, they belong to press groups, this being often the case in Europe, Latin America or North America.

The development of these groups has resulted in widespread internationalization, notably in the periodical sector with the launch of magazines of international scope and status such as Fortune, Playboy, Elle, etc. Other differences in the press concern their methods of distribution: depending on the historical traditions of the country in question, newspapers are sold from kiosks or by newsagents, delivered to the doorstep or bought from vending machines.

In most countries, newspapers have gone through a serious recession characterized by a general downturn in sales, a loss of advertising market share, dwindling readership among the younger generations and a general decline in the influence of the press compared to radio, television and now to computers. On top of this should be noted the increase of distribution and production costs and the rocketing rise in the price of paper between 1994 and 1995.

The steep increase has come close to 40 per cent since 1995 and has weighed heavily on the financial position of newspapers. The rise is also held to be responsible for the difficulties that newspapers around the world are currently facing and even for the winding up of some papers. These restrictions illustrate the extent to which newspaper production is a capital-intensive industry, and the consequences of the crash it is currently facing for the other sectors of the press. In terms of circulation, in 1995 alone dailies in Europe were down 0.69 per cent and in the United States they lost 1.32 per cent.

Newspaper circulation figures in these two regions of the world have declined by 7 per cent over the last ten years, while periodicals have lost some 8 million readers. In Central and Eastern Europe there has been a major downturn in circulation, with a fall of 70.25 per cent in the Russian Federation and 20.07 per cent in Estonia. Only in Bulgaria, with a rise in readership of 74.19 per cent, and in Latvia with growth of 25.79 per cent, have the trends been upwards between 1993 and 1994.

On the other hand, newspaper circulation has increased in Asia and in Latin America, with growth in countries such as Brazil (22.68 per cent), Colombia (5.81 per cent), Malaysia (4.68 per cent), Singapore (5.87 per cent), Turkey (63.91 per cent) and India (28.51 per cent). In terms of sales, Japan tops the list with

72.7 million copies a day in 1996, i.e. an increase of 0.9 per cent over 1995. The United States comes in second place at almost 57 million copies per day. China is in third place with its 2,200 newspapers, of which the top ten total sales of 28.5 million copies each day. In terms of advertising revenue, the press is continuing to lose market share to television and radio. In many countries, notably in the European Community, there was a general recession in this area for the print media between 1991 and 1994. Since 1994, however, the situation has improved, and revenue from advertising is beginning to rally, indicating for a number of countries that the end of the slump is in sight. In the United States, revenue from advertising grew 5 per cent in 1995, with sales of $36 billion compared with $34 billion in 1994.

The greatest rates of growth since 1991, however, have occurred in countries such as Malaysia (with a rise of more than 120 per cent), Brazil (131 per cent), India (97 per cent) and South Africa (97 per cent). In China, the advertising market is positively booming, with revenues of $140 million in 1996, compared to a mere $12 million in 1991. Home China watchers say that this market is set to grow at an annual rate of 20 per cent in the years to come.

The reasons are twofold: on the one hand, there is the launching of new press groups, particularly private ones, the first of which has set up shop in the Guangzhou region; on the other hand, the state monopoly on distribution has come to an end. Already by 1997, 775 titles had their own distribution network using the postal system as well as door-to-door delivery.

The democratization process that began in the early 1990s in-Africa has resulted in the emergence of a privately owned, independent press in several countries. Although these newspapers are often produced on a small scale and have only limited readerships, they are all vying for position in the democratic debate. Many titles, such as *La Gozette du Golfe* in Benin, *Sud Hebdo* in Senegal or *Le Messager* in Cameroon, have met and continue to meet with widescale popular success. The role and the development of the private press have varied according to the traditions, region and type of political regime in each country. In 1997, there were approximately a hundred private newspapers published fairly regularly over the whole continent. Most of these are dailies, although some appear fortnightly or monthly, but almost all their business is concentrated in the cities. The independent press is confronted with a number of obstacles that are cultural, economic and political in nature including illiteracy, low purchasing power, the narrowness of national markets, etc. Mali, for instance, has four national dailies for its 10 million inhabitants, poor readership purchasing power, a high rate of illiteracy, distribution limited to large provincial towns and meagre advertising resources, not to mention the prohibitive cost of paper.

In addition, the role played by a number of titles in forming public opinion for some governments is a source of concern, and for others a source of inspiration in their attempts to silence the press, including making publication subject to prior authorization, the withholding of information, customs duties, exorbitant tax liabilities, intimidation and lawsuits brought against newspapers and their editors. Other, more direct obstacles stem from monopolies imposed by public authorities on raw materials and equipment, a form of control which is difficult to circumvent and which some simply see as another form of censorship in disguise.

On top of these problems lie other constraints linked to the general economic backdrop and to the devaluation of the CFA franc, which have led to increases in manufacturing and transport costs, rising numbers of bad debts and a fragile advertising market. In 1996, the latter represented little more than 20 per cent of newspaper revenue.

The companies that dominate the market are mainly foreign, and prefer radio and television or space advertising in the international magazines that have wide circulation in the region. Parallel to these constraints, the independent press in Africa has also made a number of slip-ups. The lack of qualified journalists due to the insufficient number of training programmes has led some newspapers to spotlight current events and seek the sensational stories, or to support partisan points of view and settle scores, and in many cases the development of ideas connected with political parties makes it difficult to distinguish between informative reporting and the press that specializes in commentary. Several initiatives have been taken to overcome the mishaps that are inherent in any young press sector.

A number of newspaper editors have created the Newspaper Publishers' Society (SEP), a pool of regional scope based in Benin that aims to unite local independent newspapers. Other publishers, such as the Sud Communication Group in Senegal, have organized press groups around several activities, including newspapers, radio, publishing and printing, and have set up their own training programmes. Finally, others again have tackled the issue of professional ethics with the creation in 1995 in Yamoussoukro, (Côte d'Ivoire) of an observatory on press freedom, ethics and a professional code of conduct (OLPED). In spite of these efforts, the independent press has yet to find its feet in the African media environment. It is still weakened by a restricted readership of literate people confined to cities and suburbs. In order for it really to take part in the democratic debate and win the fight for pluralism, it has to face a number of challenges, the most important of which are:

— Modernizing equipment (fax machines, word processors, desktop publishing).

— Maintaining and preferably increasing the frequency of publication.

— Finally, enhancing training facilities to improve professional skills and develop the spirit of enterprise.

Within this framework, from 1993 onwards UNESCO began setting up a project for the 'Development of an Independent and Pluralistic Press in Africa' in sub-Saharan Africa. The project includes the organization of in-service training activities, the supply of equipment, the installation of effective distribution networks and other operations connected with the exercise of the profession. In 1996 the project provided further training for 108 journalists, thirty-three of whom were women, in some twenty countries of Central and West Africa, as well as the creation of a pilot publishing centre in Cameroon.

More and more newspapers around the world are opening servers on the Internet in order to provide their readers with an electronic version of their content. In August 1996, there were more than 1,500 newspapers and international magazines available on-line, 1,400 of which were on the World Wide Web alone. The first attempt at electronic publishing dates from 1992 by the daily newspaper the San José Mercury News, which enabled computerized readers to access the electronic edition of their newspaper. By 1997, testing had widened to include the leading titles in the international press (the International Herald Tribune, Le Monde, Al Hayat, etc.), all of which are henceforth accessible on the Net.

The United States has the lion's share with 765 publications (almost 400 of which are periodicals), to which-should be added some 123 Canadian titles. With approximately 300 titles on-line, Europe is also present on the market, as are Africa, Asia and the Arab World, although to a lesser degree. Generally speaking, all the on-line newspapers provide a wealth of often personalized news items and at particularly high speeds. Some, such as the New York Times, complete their texts and photographs with spoken commentaries, while others have set up newsgroup debates with their readers. These technological innovations have enhanced the written press, enabling it to face up to competition from radio and television on better terms. In addition, via the network, local and national newspapers can address a diversified public, spread around the entire planet.

All these experiments are being closely monitored by the publishing world, which has been able to identify other potential audiences such as research assistants, students, journalists, financial analysts and teachers, forming a vast market that may in the medium-term provide sufficient return on development costs, estimated at several million dollars per year. Although they are fully aware that electronic publishing is not a miracle solution for the economic straits in which the profession currently finds itself, many experts feel that the written press may be able to overtake television again, thanks to the Internet. For the time being, few of the sites providing electronic publishing services are profitable.

Systems design

In large-scale embedded systems, the design process includes an element of systems design in which functions are partitioned into software and hardware functions. Until recently, these decisions were not particularly difficult to make because only standard hardware with known functionality could be used. Thus, the hardware structure of a system often resolved itself leaving the software to coordinate and control the hardware units. As the cost of special-purpose integrated circuits decreases and the speed of fabrication increases (for simple circuits, it is now possible to go from an idea to a delivered microchip in a few weeks), the borderline between hardware and software components is blurring. It is becoming increasingly cost-effective to delay decisions about which functions should be implemented in hardware and which functions should be software components.

The advantage of implementing functionality in hardware is that a hardware component delivers much better performance than the equivalent software unit. System bottlenecks can be identified and replaced by hardware components, thus freeing the software engineer from expensive software optimization. Providing performance in hardware means that the software design can be structured for adaptability and that performance considerations can take second place. It is outside the scope of this book to discuss hardware and VLSI design. What is important in the design process is to delay hardware/ software partitioning as late as possible in the design process, and this implies that the system architecture must be made up of stand-alone components which can be implemented in either hardware or software. Fortunately, building a design in this way is exactly the aim of the designer who is trying to design a maintainable system.

Effective software design is best accomplished by using a consistent approach to design decomposition. Until relatively recently, the usual mode of design decomposition involved considering the design as a number of functional components with the state information held in some shared data area. Although Parnas suggested an alternative view in the early 1970s and versions of Smalltalk were in existence in the 1970s, it is only within the past few years that an alternative mode of decomposition, object-oriented design, has been recognized as of value. These two modes of design decomposition may be summarized as follows:

(1) *Functional design* The system is designed from a functional viewpoint, starting with a high-level view and progressively refining this into a more detailed design. This methodology is exemplified by Structured Design and step-wise refinement. Methods such as Jackson Structured Programming and the Warnier-Orr method are actually techniques of functional decomposition where the structure of the data is used to determine the functional structure used to process that data.

(2) *Object-oriented design* The system is viewed as a collection of objects rather than as functions, with messages passed from object to object. Each object has its own set of associated operations. Object-oriented design is based on the idea of information hiding which was first put forward by Parnas and which has been described more recently by Robson, Abbott and Booch. JSD is a design method which falls somewhere between function-oriented and object-oriented design.

Top-down functional decomposition has been widely used for both small-scale and large-scale projects in diverse application areas. Object-oriented design is a relatively recent development which has not been widely tried but it is a technique which encourages the production of loosely coupled and highly cohesive systems. To illustrate the difference between functional and object-oriented approaches to software design, consider the structure of a compiler. It may be viewed as a set of functional transformations with information being passed from one function to another.

The objects manipulated by the compiler are central with transformation functions associated with object communications. Proponents of particular design techniques naturally become very enthusiastic about their particular technique and sometimes suggest that a technique is generally applicable and that other techniques need not be used. This is hyperbole. Large software systems are such complex entities that all of these approaches to design might be used at some stage in the design of different parts of the system, there is no 'best' design methodology for large projects and the pragmatic software engineer selects the most appropriate approach for each stage in the design process. In particular, functional and object-oriented approaches are complementary rather than opposing techniques and each may be applicable at different stages in the design process. To illustrate this, consider the software systems which might be part of a modern civil airliner. Some of these might be:

— The navigation system.

— The radar system.

— The external communications system.

— The instrument display system.

— The engine control system.

Our natural high-level view of the overall software system is as a set of objects (subsystems) rather than as a set of functions. Thus, at very abstract design levels, an object-oriented viewpoint seems to be appropriate. However, once the system is examined in more detail, its natural description is as a set of interacting functions rather than objects. For example, some of these functions might be:

(1) Display_Track (radar subsystem)

(2) Compensate_for_Wind_Speed (navigation subsystem)

(3) Reduce_Power (engine control subsystem)

(4) Indicate_Emergency (instrument subsystem)

(5) Lock_onto_Frequency (communications sub-system)

This functional view may be that taken by the requirements definition. Although it may be possible to convert this to an object-oriented view, validation against the requirements may be difficult because there is not a simple correspondence between design components and requirements definitions.

A single logical function in the requirements definition may be implemented as a complex sequence of object interactions. As the system design is further decomposed, an object-oriented view may again become the natural way to view the system. At the detailed design stage, the objects manipulated might be The_engine_status, The_aircraft_position, The_altimeter, The_radio_beacon, etc. Thus an object-oriented approach to the lower levels of the system design is likely to be effective.

Software design quality

Depending on the application and project requirements, a good design might be a design that allows very efficient code to be produced; it might be a minimal design where the implementation is as compact as possible; or it might be the most maintainable design. This latter criterion is the criterion of 'goodness' adopted here. A maintainable design implies that the cost of system changes is minimized and this means that the design should be understandable and that changes should be local in effect. Both of these are achieved if the software design is highly cohesive, loosely coupled and readily adapted. Some work has been carried out to establish design quality metrics to establish whether or not a design is a 'good' design. These have mostly been developed in conjunction with Structured Design and a description of possible metrics and their potential value is postponed until a later chapter on design validation.

Cohesion

— A software component is said to exhibit a high degree of cohesion if the elements in that unit exhibit a high degree of functional relatedness. This means that each element in the program unit should be essential for that unit to achieve its purpose; for example, sort a file, look up a dictionary, etc. Elements which are grouped together in a program unit for some other reason such as to perform actions which take place at the same time or which implement a number of distinct functions have a low degree of cohesion. Constantine and Yourdon identify seven levels of cohesion in order of increasing strength of cohesion from lowest to highest:

— *Coincidental cohesion* The parts of a unit are not related but simply bundled together into a single unit.

— *Logical association* Components which perform similar functions, such as input, error handling, etc. are put together in a single unit.

— *Temporal cohesion* All of the components which are activated at a single time, such as start up or shut down, are brought together.

— *Procedural cohesion* The elements in a unit make up a single control sequence.

— *Communicational cohesion* All of the elements of a unit operate on the same input data or produce the same output data.

— *Sequential cohesion* The output from one element in the unit serves as input for some other element.

— *Functional cohesion* Each part of the unit is necessary for the execution of a single function.

These cohesion classes are not strictly defined and Constantine and Yourdon illustrate each by example. It is not always easy to decide under what cohesion category a unit should be classed. Yourdon and Constantine's method is functional in nature and it is obvious that the most cohesive form of unit is the function.

A high degree of cohesion is also a feature of object-oriented systems. Indeed, one of the principal advantages of this approach to design is that the objects making up the system are naturally cohesive. A cohesive object is one where a single entity is represented and all of the operations on that entity are included with the object. For example, an object representing a compiler symbol table is cohesive if all of the functions such as Add a symbol', 'Search table', etc., are included with the symbol table object. Cohesion is a desirable characteristic because it means that a unit represents one aspect of the problem solution only. If it becomes necessary to change the system, that aspect can be discovered in a single place and everything to do with it is encapsulated in a single unit.

Coupling

Coupling is related to cohesion—it is an indication of the strength of interconnections between program units. Highly coupled systems have strong interconnections, with program units dependent on each other, whereas loosely coupled systems are made up of units which are independent or almost independent. As a general rule, modules are tightly coupled if they make use of shared, global variables or if they interchange control information.

Constantine and Yourdon call this common coupling and control coupling. Loose coupling is achieved by ensuring that, wherever possible, representation information is held within a component and that its data interface with other units is via its parameter list. If shared information is necessary, the sharing should be controlled as in an Ada package. Constantine and Yourdon call this data coupling and stamp coupling.

Other coupling problems arise when names are bound to values at an early stage in the development of the design. For example, if a program is concerned with tax computations and a tax rate of 30% is encoded as a number in the program, that program is coupled with the tax rate. Changes to the tax rate require changes to the program. On the other hand, if the program reads in the tax rate at run-time, it is very easy to accommodate rate changes. Perhaps the principal advantage of object-oriented design is that the very nature of objects is such that loosely coupled systems are produced. It is fundamental to object-oriented design that the representation of an object is concealed within that object and is not visible to external components. Conceptually, objects communicate by passing messages to each other, and any one object can be replaced with another object that responds to the same set of messages.

Changing a design component implies that the person responsible for making the change understands the operation of the component. This understandability is related to a number of component characteristics such as the use of meaningful names for design entities and the design documentation. However, perhaps the most crucial characteristic affecting the understandability of a component is its complexity. We use the term complexity here in an informal way. High complexity implies many relationships between different parts of the design component and a complex logical structure which may involve deeply nested if-then-else statements.

Complex components are hard to understand so the designer should strive for as simple as possible a component design. Most of the work carried out in the general area of design quality metrics has concentrated on trying to measure the complexity of a component and obtain some measure of the component's understandability. However, while complexity is one determinant of understandability, there are a number of others such as the component documentation and the style in which the design is described. Thus, as discussed later, complexity measures provide an indicator rather than a quantitative assessment of the understandability of a component.

If a design is to be maintained, it must be readily adaptable. Of course, this implies that its components should be highly cohesive and loosely coupled. As well as this, however, adaptability means that the design should be well documented, the component documentation should be readily understandable and consistent with the implementation, and the implementation should be expressed in a readable way. It is particularly important that the design exhibits a high level of visibility. This means that there should be a clear relationship between the different levels in the design and it should be straightforward to incorporate changes made to the design in all design documents. This is important because changes made to a design description but not included in all descriptions mean that design documentation becomes inconsistent.

Later changes are more difficult to make (the component is less adaptable) because the modifier cannot rely on the consistency of design documentation. As well as the relationship between levels in the design being visible, it is equally important that the relationship between the specification and the design be clear. It is in this respect that there is an advantage in using the same design decomposition technique as is used to express the specification. That is, if the specification is expressed in an object-oriented way, the design should also be object-oriented; if the specification is described as a set of functions, it may be best to design the software in the same way.

Although it is not impossible to maintain the relationship between a function-oriented specification and an object-oriented design, the differences in view can make this a difficult task as entities in the specification may be distributed over a number of design entities. For optimum adaptability, a component should be as self-contained as possible. This is related to but distinct from coupling.

A component may be loosely coupled in that it only cooperates with other components via message passing, say. This is not the same as being self-contained as the component may rely on other components, such as system functions or error handling functions. Adaptations to the component may involve changes to those parts of the component that rely on external functions, so these functions must also be considered by the modifier.

To be completely self-contained, a component should not use other components which are externally defined. However, this is contrary to good practice which suggests that existing components should be reused. Thus, some balance must be struck between the advantages of reusing components and the loss of component adaptability that this entails.

Design description languages

A design description language is a language with control constructs which allow the designer to write down the structure of a software solution to the design problem. It has been argued that the most appropriate notation for this is a high-level programming language such as Ada or Pascal. This has the obvious advantage that the design is executable if a suitable language compiler is available, but there are disadvantages to this approach:

(1) Programming languages must be compliable and so cannot be readily extended to encompass new concepts. For example, if a Pascal-based language is used and the designer wishes to describe an abstract data type, this is not possible.

(2) The data types, structures and operations available as primitives in programming languages are often relatively low level. This means that the representation of some intuitively simple high-level constructs such as an unbounded sequence of data items sometimes becomes detailed and confused.

(3) As thinking is constrained by language, the lower

the level of constructs available to designers, the more their thinking is liable to be influenced by language constructs.

(4) If an initial implementation of a design, specified in a programming language, must subsequently be reimplemented, it is difficult to carry out this reimplementation in a higher level language than the design specification language.

Rather than using an existing programming language as a vehicle for design expression, a better alternative is to use a design description language intended for documenting and communicating software designs. A number of such languages have been invented such as those described by Van Leer and Linger *et al.*.

Design description languages make use of the familiar control constructs of high-level programming languages to specify flow of control but allow the designer considerable flexibility in the description of operations. In this chapter, a variant of Ada (Ada/PDL) is used as a design description language. This notation has been chosen because Ada is likely to become the most common language for large system construction and because Ada has a rich set of constructs encompassing control constructs, data abstraction, exception handling and tasking. It is only rarely necessary to go outside the language for descriptive purposes.

The Ada design description language used here is not proper Ada but a notation where natural language text may be substituted for statements or expressions and where it is unnecessary to declare all items before their use. This is particularly important in a PDL as top-down design relies on identifying abstractions then designing their realizations. If a name cannot be used without being defined, a top-down approach is inhibited as the designer is forced to concentrate on the details of the named entity rather than the component being designed.

Generally, a design in Ada/PDL is refined through a number of levels of abstraction from a high-level statement of the operation to a detailed design whose representation is close to the programming language. For example, consider the design of a program intended to detect misspelled words in a document. Notice how named parameter association is used, where the formal parameter name is specified along with the actual parameter name, to help with readability. Thus, in the call of Lookup the, the formal parameter is called Dictionary and the actual parameter is English_dictionary. The conjunction of the function name and the formal parameter name gives the readable name Lookup_the (Dictionary => English_dictionary... It is sometimes useful to import a high-level design description into a refinement in the form of comments. Thus the comment symbol - -* means that the associated comment represents a higher level operational description.

One of the advantages of using a design description language is that new abstract data types may be introduced and used without previous definition. Naturally they must eventually be defined.

User interface design

Interface design should reflect this and should ensure that the computer is seen as a useful and powerful tool. The interface should not have human characteristics, otherwise the user may ascribe human abilities to the machine. Human abilities and computer power are complementary and it is the task of the interface designer to ensure that they work well together. It is now generally recognized that the user interface of a system is the yardstick by which that system is judged. An interface which is difficult to use will at best result in a high level of user errors. At worst, it will cause the software system to be discarded, irrespective of the functionality that it offers.

A badly designed interface can cause the user to make potentially catastrophic errors. If information is presented in a confusing or misleading way, the user may accidentally misunderstand the meaning of an item of information and, on that basis, initiate a sequence of dangerous actions. Although this chapter cannot cover user interface design in any depth, it is the intention to provide enough information for software engineers that dangerous design errors can be avoided. For a fuller discussion of user interface design, the reader is referred to texts such as that by Shneiderman or Monk. Since the first edition of this book was published in 1982, the possibilities open to the user interface designer have opened up enormously. It is now possible to assume that the user's terminal will include a significant amount of processing power and it is increasingly likely to have a bit-mapped high-resolution display supporting multiple text fonts and mixed text and graphics display. Many systems are now equipped with a 'mouse' which allows the user to point at items on the screen and this has opened up computer use to many people who are reluctant to type.

The most fundamental principle in user interface design is that the interface must be designed to suit the needs and abilities of the individual user. Users should not be forced to adapt to an interface because it is convenient to implement or because it is suited to the systems designer. Tailoring the interface to the user means that the interface must be couched in terms familiar to the user and that the objects manipulated by the system should have direct analogues in the environment with which the user is familiar.

For example, if a system is designed for use by secretarial staff, the objects manipulated should be letters, documents, diaries, folders, etc., at least as far as the secretary is concerned. In practice, these objects may be implemented using different files or database entities but the secretary should not be forced to cope with such computing concepts as workfiles, directories, file, identifiers and so on. The allowed operations might be 'file', 'retrieve', 'index', 'discard', etc. Examples of systems based on an office metaphor are now commercially available. In these systems, the user is presented with pictures (called icons) of familiar office objects such as calculators, trashcans, pencils, erasers, etc. To select an operation, the user points at the appropriate picture and that operation is initiated. For example, to perform calculations the user points at the calculator icon, to draw diagrams he or she points at the pencil icon, to discard items the trashcan icon is indicated and so on.

This type of interface is suitable for users with no previous experience of computers as they are not intimidated by the terminology associated with the machine. However, it has the disadvantage that completely new operations, which have no non-automated analogue, cannot be represented with a familiar icon. Indeed, it may be very difficult to devise any kind of icon for automated operations. For example, how might multi-file comparisons be pictorialized? The second principle of interface design is that the user interface must be consistent.

Consistency should be maintained within a system and across subsystems running on the same machine. Interface consistency means that system commands and menus should have the same format, parameters should be passed to all commands in the same way, and command punctuation should be similar. Subsystems which offer the same facilities as a menu should display these menus in the same way. A consistent interface means that when a user takes time to learn about one command of the interface that knowledge is applicable to all other commands in the system. For example, say system commands accept parameters which may be filenames or which may be flags controlling command operation. If it is necessary to distinguish flags from filenames by some means (such as preceding flags with a '-' character), this should be the convention for every system command.

If a particular flag name is used to signify a particular operation in one system command, exactly the same name should be used in all compatible commands. For example, if a command to print a file takes a flag '-d' specifying that the file is to be deleted after printing, the same flag name should be used in every other command which can delete a file, such as archive commands, copy commands, etc.

Interface consistency across subsystems is equally important. Many large systems are made up of subsystems which can be independently activated. These subsystems should be designed so that commands with similar meanings in different subsystems are expressed in the same way. It is dangerous for a command, say *', to mean 'keep this file' in a system editor and the same command 'k' to mean 'kill this transaction' in an information retrieval system. Users of both systems will inevitably confuse the commands at some stage, with possibly dire consequences.

The third principle of interface design is that the interface should have built-in 'help facilities. These should be accessible from the user's terminal and should provide different levels of help and advice. These should range from very basic information on how to get started with the system up to a full description of system facilities and how to use them. These help facilities should be structured so that the user is not overwhelmed with information when he or she asks for help. These principles set out the notion that the system design should be user-centred.

Computer users are trying to solve some problem using the computer and many existing systems concentrate on the fact that the computer is used rather than on the problem to be solved. The designer should always bear in mind that system users have a task to accomplish and the interface should be oriented towards that task.

4

Information Security

One hundred years ago, the few records that existed could tell us when a child was born, when a couple were married, when a man or woman died and what the boundaries of the land purchased by a family were. In those days, of course, only a handful of the American people went to college. Social security, income taxes, and life insurance did not exist. Three-quarters of the population was self-employed. Today, fewer than 5 percent of the American people work for themselves. And of the remaining 95 percent, almost half are employed by large corporations that collect detailed information about the education, health, family, and work habits of their employees.

Today, two out of three Americans have life insurance and nine out of ten are covered by health insurance plans. Insurance companies usually collect large amounts of information about their customers—revealing information such as whether they are seeing a psychiatrist, what drugs they use, and whether they have a drinking problem. Today, 60 million students are enrolled in schools and colleges that generally collect detailed personal and financial histories about both the student and his or her parents. The vast scale of information collected by government agencies, private corporations, and institutions such as hospitals and universities would not be possible without large centralized computers or, alternatively, linked series of smaller computers. It is also true, however, that some of these organizations did in fact collect some of this information before the computer. With armies of meticulous clerks, there were a few industries and a few countries like Germany and Chile that did compile massive handwritten records about the lives of an amazing number of people.

The computer, however, has powers well beyond that possessed by human scribes, no matter how numerous, and thus has fundamentally altered the nature of society's records. The first important change is that the computer mass-produces what has come to be called "transactional information," a new category of information that automatically documents the daily lives of almost every person in the US. Exactly when did you leave your home? Exactly when did she turn on the television? Exactly when did he deposit the check? Exactly when were the calls made from their telephone?

How many times have you driven your automobile? In the centuries before the computer, transactional information answering these kinds of questions was almost never collected. And in those very few instances where it was collected, it was not easily available for later inspection. With the computerized filing systems now available, the larger organizations of our society can easily collect and store this new kind of information. Equally important, they can combine it with automated dossiers containing the traditional kinds of information such as a person's age, place of birth, and the material contained in school and work records.

There is one more important development made possible by the computer: the incredible maze of electronic highways that can move the new and old information about the country in a matter of seconds at an astoundingly low cost. The automatic exchange of information between different data bases was not seriously considered in the first years of the computer age. But as the technology has become more subtle and sophisticated, it gradually is reducing the barriers between these giant repositories, increasing their ability to "talk" with each other. The contributions of these linked data bases to our daily lives are enormous.

The swift granting of lines of credit to a substantial number of American people would not be possible without the computerized data bases maintained by credit reporting companies like TRW and Equifax. The hundreds of millions of checks written each year by tens of millions of Americans could not be processed and cleared without the computerized data bases maintained by the separate banks and the Federal Reserve System. Easy movement about the US would be far harder without the computerized reservation systems of the airlines and car rental agencies.

The collection each year of nearly $500 billion in federal taxes from almost 100 million individuals and corporations would be extraordinarily difficult without the computerized data bases of the Internal Revenue Service and the large corporations who each year employ more and more Americans. There are a variety of reasons why understanding the true significance of all of these changes is very hard. First, there is the fundamental difficulty of putting anecdotal flesh on the bones of the abstract truth that information is power and that organizations increase their power by learning how to swiftly collect and comprehend bits and pieces of information.

This difficulty is greatly multiplied by the sheer force of the tools of the new information age: the machines that can locate a single item in a file of millions in the blink of an eye or that can swiftly develop statistical trends by massing these single items, and the communication links that can shuttle the collected information about the world at almost the speed of light. When thinking about the impact of these technical achievements, allow your mind to wander beyond the traditionally narrow boundaries of the computer debate.

Consider how the technology is altering the power of large organizations. Consider how the technology is affecting our social values such as the notion of checks and balances, the role of work, and the importance of spontaneity. Consider the far-reaching changes it is bringing to the nation's economy. What does it mean, for example, that the officials and clerks of the US government, each year armed with more and more computers, have collected 4 billion separate records about the people of the US, 17 items for each man, woman, and child in the country? What does it mean that an internal communications network serving just one multinational corporation now links more than 500 computers in over a 100 cities in 18 countries and has been growing at a rate of about one additional computer a week in recent years? What does it mean that 10,000 merchants all over the country are able to obtain a summary fact sheet about any one of 86 million individual Americans in a matter of three or four seconds from a single data base in southern California? What does it mean that a handful of federal agencies, not counting the Pentagon, have at least 3 separate telecommunication networks stretching all over the US?

Two of the world's largest and most complicated systems of linked data bases are controlled by the

American Telephone and Telegraph Company and the Federal Bureau of Investigation. AT&T's gigantic network was deliberately developed by the company's scientists, engineers, and businessmen. The FBI system, which seeks to link the computerized data bases operated by a majority of the 50 states, has developed in a more haphazard fashion. Because the information-collecting and distributing systems of both the telephone company and the FBI began to function long before the birth of the computer, they illustrate the important point that the new tools of information processing usually are extensions of old bureaucracies, not shiny stand-alone machines that can be considered on their independent merit.

A second trait shared by these two very different systems is that neither has been subject to much outside scrutiny during much of their development. AT&T is a private company regulated by 50 state utility bodies of widely varying quality and a federal commission that never had the staff adequately to monitor the company's interstate operations. And very few congressional committees or state legislatures have taken the time or possess the perspective to consider the impact of the gradually growing network linking the FBI to the states.

Computers generate transactional information for many purposes and many organizations. They allow the construction of huge, speedy, and low-cost communication networks to transmit many different kinds of information to thousands of different customers. But the very different information processing systems developed by AT&T and the FBI provide clear examples of how transactional information and mass networks have enhanced the impact of these two pre-computer bureaucracies on all of our lives. First, consider AT&T. Through its millions of miles of cables, microwave highways, and satellite hookups, the American people make 500 million calls a day—four calls, on the average, for each of the nation's 130 million telephones. Thanks to the computerized data bases that are tied into this massive electronic network at a steadily increasing number of junctures, AT&T has become the largest single holder of transactional information in the world. Buried in the computers of the system are records that can be helpful in drawing an amazingly detailed portrait of any single person, group, or corporation that uses the telephone. The astounding power of these records is not appreciated by the public, the courts, or Congress. But for government and industry investigators, they have become an important tool.

A few years ago, for example, the Senate created a special committee to investigate a very sensitive and delicate subject, the relationship between President Carter's brother Billy and the government of Libya. After many months of embarrassed manoeuvring, the Democratic Senate committee issued a report on the antics of the brother of the Democratic president. Almost every other page of the committee's 109-page final report contains a footnote to the precise time and day of calls made by Billy Carter and his associates from at least ten different telephones operating in three different states.

The report said that on November 26, 1979, Billy Carter and an associate began driving to Washington from Georgia. Shortly after beginning the trip, the report said, the two men stopped to telephone the Libyan embassy and request a meeting with a high-ranking official. The assertion was supported by a footnote to telephone company records showing that "a five-minute call at 3:43 was charged to Billy Carter's telephone from [a pay telephone in] Jonesboro, an Atlanta suburb." Another footnote said that calls were made from Carter's office telephone in Georgia to the Libyan embassy in Washington "on March 7, March 10, four times on March 11, twice on March 12, three times on March 13, three times on March 14, March 15 and March 17." The investigations of the special Senate committee were publicly announced and the telephone records that document the report were obtained by a formal legal process. But this sometimes is not the case. One of the top officials in the Nixon White House, for example, claims that, shortly after the automobile accident that claimed the life of Mary Jo Kopechne in Martha's Vineyard, the White House political operatives ordered the FBI to obtain the telephone credit card records of Senator Edward Kennedy.

These records, which almost certainly would have revealed who and when Senator Kennedy called immediately after the accident, obviously would have been considered useful to those Nixon advisers who thought Kennedy was a likely opponent in the coming elections. Though reporters for the *New York Times* determined that the records in question disappeared from the files of New England Bell shortly after the accident, they never found documentary evidence confirming the account of a top Nixon lieutenant that they were obtained by the White House. Both the Billy Carter and Teddy Kennedy cases illustrate why investigators are so interested in transactional information.

First, the information can be extraordinarily revealing. Only considering the data that can be collected from a telephone computer, investigators can learn what numbers an individual has called, what time of day and day of the week the calls were made, the length of each conversation, and the number of times an incorrect number was dialled. Considered as a whole, such information can pinpoint the location of an individual at a particular moment, indicate his daily patterns of work and sleep, and even suggest his state of mind. The information also can indicate the friends, associates, business connections, and political activities of the targeted individual. But there is an even more fundamental consideration at stake. Almost by definition, transactional information is automatically collected and stored in the data bases of the telephone company, the electronic equipment of banks and the computers of two-way interactive television systems. This means that transactional information can be obtained months after the instance when the particular event that is documented by the records actually occurred. This ability greatly enlarges the scope of any investigator. Before the computer age, it was extremely hard to develop concrete evidence about the activities and whereabouts of an individual unless someone had been assigned to follow him.

In most cases, investigators were limited to pursuing the handful of individuals they believed might undertake a forbidden act in the future. Now they can move back in time, easily gathering concrete evidence about any person of interest long after the forbidden act occurred. The broad broom of transactional information, however, can sweep up much more than the highly revealing computer tracks of an individual citizen. In at least two instances, for example, evidence has recently come to light where this same kind of computerized information was used by AT&T to track the activities of several large corporations and even the ethnic and economic groups living in a single state. A significant characteristic of the transactional information collected by AT&T and other major computer systems is that its reach is universal.

Transactional information is collected and stored about the telephone use and banking habits of everyone who lives in America, rich and poor, ethical and unethical, white and black, Republican and Democrat. Though the information ultimately may cast a revealing light on the activities of a single individual, it is collected about the activities of all. The system of data bases that gradually are being linked by the computerized network of the FBI does not share this universal quality. Instead, it collects and distributes information about one segment of the population, the millions of Americans who are arrested each year in the US.

The story of the FBI system begins almost a hundred years ago, long before the birth of either the modem computer or the FBI. The occasion was a meeting of reform-minded policemen who decided the time had come to ask Congress to finance an agency in the federal government to maintain a central record of all American criminals. The policemen, who called themselves the National Chiefs of Police Union, argued that the prompt exchange of information about "criminals and criminal classes" made possible by such an agency would improve the ability of their separate departments to control crime. Nearly nine decades later, in the summer of 1981, a task force appointed by President Reagan's attorney general, William French Smith, acted to bring the original proposal in line with current technology: the panel endorsed a plan to have the FBI make a significant change in its existing communication system to speed up the exchange of the records of millions of people who are arrested each year all over the US. As was suggested by the police chiefs in St Louis, the Reagan administration's task force said the adoption of the proposal would help the government curb serious crime.

There is a good deal of plausibility in the belief of both the police chiefs at the turn of the century and the Reagan administration today that the swift exchange of summary information about an individual's past contacts with the criminal justice system will significantly improve the ability of the police, prosecutors, and judges to catch and punish criminals. Careful examination of the sources of information that lead a policeman to make an arrest or a judge to decide an appropriate sentence, however, suggests that the nearly instantaneous retrieval of criminal history records may be considerably less useful than is generally thought to the business of crime-fighting.

Furthermore, the gradual computerization of criminal history records in most of the states and the development of a single computerized network to link all these state and local data bases raise questions that go to the heart of democratic institutions of the US. So profound are these questions, in fact, that they have provided a handful of critical congressmen, working with communication experts of the Nixon, Ford, and Carter administrations, with the necessary weapons to stall the construction of the federal network for the last decade.

But now, with the blessing of the attorney general's Task Force on Violent Crime, plans to have such a network constructed by the FBI appear to be nearing fruition. Should the FBI get its way, the single most powerful law enforcement agency in the US will control a computerized network linking a system of data bases of almost unimagined size and complexity.

The impact of the information that would be transmitted through the vast maze of telephone lines, data bases, and computer terminals is of even greater concern than the network itself. When FBI officials call for the development of a bureau-controlled network to speed the exchange of criminal history records—rap sheets—most Americans assume the proposal is designed to reduce the chance that they or members of their family will be the victim of a hardened criminal, an experienced mugger, or a drug-crazed rapist.

But the reality of trying to control crime in America is much more ambiguous and complex than is sometimes suggested by advocates of a greatly enlarged computer network for the FBI. For example, only a small portion of the millions of traumatic events logged yearly into the criminal history records involve what are now called career criminals-professional murderers, robbers, and burglars who repeatedly prey on their victims. The sad truth is that many of the murderers and rapists who terrorize the American people are not marauding strangers. Instead they are wives who have been driven to kill their husbands in the dark heat of the night. They are uncles who have been asked to babysit for their young nieces. They are old acquaintances who fell to fighting at the end of an all-night bout of drinking.

An astoundingly large number of Americans have at one time or another been arrested. Because some individuals have records in more than one jurisdiction, and because millions of those with arrest records have subsequently died, it is not easy to estimate how many people have actually been arrested during the course of their lives. A recent authoritative study done for the Labour Department by Neal Miller, however, concludes that about one out of five living Americans has an arrest record somewhere in the US.

In the past few years, local, state, and federal law enforcement officials throughout the country have successfully argued that society should provide them with statewide and national computerized communication systems that can instantly inform a policeman on the street whether the individual he has just stopped is currently wanted on suspicion of committing a crime. These systems make sense from the standpoint of protecting both the patrolman who is making the stop and society at large from the possibility of further hurtful activities by the person who is being temporarily detained. But the acknowledged value of a hot-line system to Inform a patrolman that the person he has stopped *currently is* a suspect for another crime does not necessarily justify a parallel system informing the patrolman that his target was arrested for a crime in a distant city at some possibly *distant period of time.* The computer panders to the natural human instinct to desire more information about everything. But there are some law enforcement officials who question whether more arrest records are actually going to help them do their work. They contend that the value of the arrest record has been greatly diluted, partly because so many Americans have been arrested for so many significant causes that it is hard to separate the wheat from the chaff. They further believe the records are of questionable value because they frequently do not disclose whether the case was immediately dismissed, whether the defendant was found guilty or innocent, and what sentence, if any, was imposed. Beyond the pragmatic judgment about the utility of providing the patrolman instant access to arrest records, they see a larger ethical and constitutional question: do the American people want their police making arrests for *current* activities partly on basis of *past* behaviour?

> The idea that a national rap sheet system would make an important contribution to our work here is just a bunch of baloney. Our problem is not to find out who the guy is Our biggest problem is, once we catch him coming out of a house with the goods, how do we keep

> him in jail and how do we make sure he stays in jail? If anything, we have over-information-oriented and over-computerized this department. These critical comments from the police are drawn from a 1981 report to the Office of Technology Assessment as part of a congressional effort to determine the impact—positive and negative—of the FBI's proposed system. This particular report was prepared by Dr Kenneth C. Laudon, a professor at New York's John Jay School of Criminal justice. During its preparation, Dr. Laudon interviewed over 140 experienced criminal justice officials working in four states and six cities. Dr Laudon found that the prosecutors and judges he talked with were even more doubtful about the utility of the FBI plan than the police.

The complaints of the policemen, prosecutors, and judges interviewed by Dr Laudon went well beyond simply questioning the utility of a summary record that has been lifted out of its original legal and social context. Over and over again, the users complained that the records being moved along the experimental criminal history segment of the FBI's communication network were incomplete and inaccurate.

The subjective judgments of the police officials, prosecutors, and judges about the poor quality of the information was supported by a second investigation undertaken by Congress's Office of Technology Assessment. For this second study, the OTA arranged for Dr Laudon to obtain access to a random sample of the criminal history records that recently had been dispatched to law enforcement and other agencies from five official repositories maintained and operated by three separate states and the FBI. The information in the records from the repositories was then compared with the information in the original records in files of the county courthouses. Procedures were followed that permitted the comparative analysis without disclosing individual names.

The findings are surprising. In North Carolina only 12.2 percent of the summaries were found to be complete, accurate, and unambiguous. In California 18.9 percent were complete, accurate, and unambiguous. In Minnesota the researchers found almost half the sample—49.5 percent—met the same standards. The quality of the FBI files, which of course rests on the information submitted by the 50 states, was not noticeably better. Based on a random sample of 400 records dispatched by the Identification Division during a single week in August of 1978, Dr Laudon found that 25.7 percent of the FBI rap sheets met the standards suggested by federal law. Assuming the one week sample was valid for the entire year, the OTA study suggests that 1.75 million of the 2.35 million records sent by the FBI to criminal justice and other institutions all over the country had various failings. The quality of the much smaller number of records disseminated by the Computerized Criminal History segment of the FBI's National Crime Information Center was somewhat better than that of the Identification Division rap sheets. In the computerized system, the comparison of the sample summary and the original records disclosed that 45.9 percent were complete, accurate, and unambiguous. At the request of OTA, Dr Laudon also checked a sample of 400 arrest warrants from the 127,000 contained in the FBI's "hot file" on a single day in August of 1979. Upon comparing the information on the FBI's warrant notices with the information in the local court records, he found that 10.9 percent of the sample already had been cleared or vacated. 4.1 percent showed no record of the warrant at the local agency, and a small additional number of warrants had other problems. Again, assuming the validity of the sample, it appears that on that single day in 1979, 17,340 Americans were subject to false arrest because the FBI computer incorrectly showed they were wanted when the warrants in question had been cleared or vacated.

Official records, of course, were subject to improper use long before the computer became an important part of every major public and private bureaucracy in the US. But an executive in a New York state agency explained how the computer has enlarged the opportunity to abuse. "Technology may not be the only villain, but it is one villain," the official said. "Before high technology, you could actually control information better; at least, it could not spread very far because it was impractical to transmit it. With the computer system, you can't control it any more, largely because of the automatic interfacing of the system, which makes it difficult for even us to know who's getting our information."

The Office of Technology Assessment asked a team at the Bureau of Governmental Research and Service at the University of South Carolina to try to determine exactly who was now receiving criminal history information and to assess the social impacts of computerizing these histories. According to the South Carolina researchers—Lynne Eickholt Cooper, Mark E. Tompkins, and Donald A. Marchand—the use of criminal records outside the traditional confines of the criminal justice system is enormous and growing.

All applicants for federal positions, all military recruits, many of the hundreds of thousands of citizens working for private contractors who are doing jobs for the federal government, and all new employees of federally chartered and insured banks are among the millions of persons who have long been subject to criminal history record checks for many years, the researcher reported. In addition, with the recent growth in the number of states and cities requiring licenses and permits for almost any kind of job, the population subject to criminal record checks has further exploded.

At the last count, more than 7 million Americans must obtain licenses to earn their living. In California, for example, 47 separate licensing boards, 50 state agencies, and 32 out-of-state agencies have access to the criminal history records stored in the state's computerized record system. In New York the use of criminal records by law enforcement agencies has declined in recent years, while its use by private employers has gone up. Through a variety of federal and state laws, society has made the collective decision that individuals *convicted* of certain crimes may be properly denied certain privileges. Sometimes such individuals lose the right to vote. Sometimes they may not run for public office. Sometimes they are prohibited from bidding on government contracts. The US also pays a good deal of lip service to the principle that an arrest or investigation, *without a conviction*, should not be sufficient grounds to deny an individual an honourable place in the job market. In late 1981, President Reagan provided an eloquent testimonial to this principle when asked why he had not asked three officials in his administration to remove themselves from office after they were accused of illegal activities.

The Labour Department study that concluded that 40 million Americans have an arrest record also estimated that just Under 26 million of them were in the job market. With so many people applying for so many different jobs, it is nearly impossible to generalize about the impact of criminal records on their lives. Certainly, the bank is on solid ground when it decides not to hire a convicted bank robber.

Certainly, no one would argue about a hospital personnel director who decides not to hire a convicted narcotics dealer.

But there is good evidence that some employers assume that any kind of record, no matter what the offence, no matter what the outcome, is a powerful mark against the individual. More than a decade ago, two sociologists named Richard Schwartz and Jerome Skolnick attempted to measure this kind of bias in an experiment in which a number of employers were shown the employment folders submitted by 100 men who were looking for a menial job in the Catskill area of New York. The applicants were broken down into four groups. The first group had no criminal records. The second group had been arrested for assault and acquitted of the charge with a letter from the judge explaining the presumption of innocence. The third had been arrested for assault and acquitted, but there was no letter from the judge. The fourth group had been convicted. The employers were asked whether they would be willing to offer the individuals in each group a job. Thirty-six percent said they would hire the men with no record, 24 percent said they would hire the men who had been acquitted and had a letter from the judge, 12 percent said they would hire the men who had been acquitted but had no letter, and 4 percent said they would hire the men who had been convicted. The findings of this simple study, replicated in a number of subsequent research projects, are a dramatic illustration of the powerful impact of a criminal record, even if the individual under consideration has been acquitted.

The implications of these findings—when considered in terms of the number of Americans with records and the accuracy and completeness of these records—are staggering. Computerized records being rocketed around the country would be a greater help to the police and less damaging to the public if they were accurate and complete. In the pursuit of this worthy goal, after failing to reach a compromise on comprehensive legislation to govern the NCIC, Congress adopted a brief amendment to the Crime Control Act of 1973. The 139-word amendment, which all parties regarded as an interim measure, contained three very simple principles. First, to the maximum extent feasible, criminal history information disseminated with the help of federal funds should contain disposition, as well as arrest data. Second, procedures would be adopted to require that the information is kept current. Third, the information would be used for law enforcement, criminal justice, and "other lawful purposes." As already noted, the exception for other lawful purpose has become something of a gusher.

The 1973 amendment also offered the citizen an apparent remedy. "An individual who believes that criminal information concerning him in an automated system is inaccurate, incomplete, or maintained in violation of this title, shall upon satisfactory verification of his identity, be entitled to review such information and to obtain a copy of it for the purpose of challenge or correction." Almost three years later, the government followed up on the 1973 amendment by issuing a vaguely worded regulation that nominally required the states to develop policies and procedures to ensure the privacy and security of criminal history records. Individual access and review was one of five specific areas the federal government said the states must cover in their regulations.

Ever since the computer became a major force in the administration of large government and business organizations in the mid-1960s, the individual's right to see and correct his own computerized record has been held up as a miracle cure for many of the potential abuses of the computer age. Alan F. Westin, in his pioneering 1967 book *Privacy and Freedom*, was among the first to find wonderful powers in the cure of public access. The principle was subsequently embraced by both the Privacy Act of 1973 and the 1977 report of the Privacy Protection Study Commission. But the OTA report indicating that more than half of the millions of criminal history records now circulating in the US are incomplete, inaccurate, or ambiguous is compelling evidence that the remedies prescribed by law and regulation are not every effective. And when the congressional researchers looked at the actual record-keeping practices of four states and six urban areas, they found strong evidence that the promises made in the 1973 Crime Control Act amendment are largely an illusion.

The California criminal justice system, for example, contains more than 3 million records, 1.1 million of which are in computers, the balance in manual files. In a recent year, authorized organizations made 5 million separate inquiries of the system. Despite the huge number of transactions, however, the researchers discovered that only 300-400 individuals each year ask to see their records, 80 find something they regard as incorrect, and 40 are actually successful in forcing California to make a correction.

A second approach to assuring accurate records is to require that the record-keepers periodically check their files and dump those that are inaccurate or incomplete. The government, at least in theory, adopted this alternative approach in 1976 when it required that all the states develop plans for regularly auditing and purging their criminal history files. In 1980 the Office of Technology Assessment sent a questionnaire to the 50 states about how they managed their criminal history records. One question was whether they checked the accuracy of the records in their files. Four out of five of the 49 states answering this question responded that they had never conducted record quality audits. So much for federal regulations. The astounding finding that only one out of five states has ever sought to audit and purge the information in its criminal history files may explain why so many of the records are inaccurate or incomplete. It also demonstrates how difficult it is for the federal government to force state and local agencies to meet a standard established by Congress.

Computer scientists and manufacturers purport to believe that their machines are neutral. This is true, of course, as long as the technology remains in the showroom. The neutrality evaporates, however, when powerful officials running powerful bureaucracies harness the computers to achieve their collective goals. Often both the goals and methods of achieving them are in the public interest. History tells us, however, that the organizations of fallible men sometimes lose their way. During the 1960s and 1970s the leadership of the FBI and a number of police departments throughout the country came to believe that their responsibilities went beyond arresting those who had committed criminal acts.

Their job, some policemen thought, extended to trying to channel the political thoughts and lifestyles of the American people along certain narrow paths. Police departments in such cities as Chicago and Los Angeles enormously expanded their surveillance of individuals who did not share conventional police values. The US Army ordered its intelligence agents to attend all sorts of political rallies. The FBI, with the explicit approval of J. Edgar Hoover, undertook a secret program in which it deliberately sought to have critics of the federal government fired from their jobs or otherwise discredited by mailing false and anonymous reports to their neighbours and colleagues.

The FBI's effort to expand its activities beyond the precise boundaries of criminal law did not stop with the anonymous smearing of thousands of Americans who did not happen to share Mr Hoover's view of the universe. From 1971 to 1974 the FBI harnessed the computerized data bases of the National Crime Information Center to pick up the movements of persons who were not criminal suspects. Under the public relations establishing the NCIC and how it would operate, the FBI declared that only the names of persons who had been formally charged with a crime would be listed in the NCIC computer. In July of 1975, however, John Tunney, then chairman of the Senate Subcommittee on Constitutional Rights, announced the discovery that the Bureau had violated its own regulations by using the NCIC "to keep track of individuals who might be of interest to the FBI for whatever purpose, including possible political reasons."

Three months later, the justice Department confirmed that from 1971 to 1974 the FBI had instructed its NCIC's computers to sound an alarm any time a local law enforcement agency sent a message to Washington indicating that any one of 4700 individuals was arrested. When it is remembered what a large part of the population have arrest records, and how many persons were being arrested during that particular period for taking part in civil rights and antiwar demonstrations, the automated flagging mechanism can be viewed as a potentially powerful surveillance device.

One indication of how embarrassed the justice Department was about the FBI's secret operation of a surveillance system outside the limits set down in its own regulation was the way the project was abruptly halted on the precise day that the Senate subcommittee staff made its first inquiry. But seven years later, there are indications that the FBI and other law enforcement agencies of the Reagan administration would like to resurrect the use of the NCIC computers to track persons who are not the subject of a formal arrest warrant. The first hint of this possible shift in NCIC policy came at a meeting of the NCIC advisory board in June of 1980 in a talk by Kier T. Boyd, an FBI inspector and the deputy assistant director of that part of the bureau that controls the FBI's very large computerized telecommunications system. According to the minutes of the advisory board meeting, Mr Boyd openly advocated the startup of the same kind of surveillance that had been so suddenly halted in 1974.

The official began by acknowledging that the tracking of the early 1970s had run into a wave of adverse reaction because "of the political climate of that time" and that the policy under consideration in the spring of 1981 "smacks of the tracking system which in the past has not been very well received by certain quarters of Congress." In an apparent reference to the growing power of conservatives in the Congress, however, Mr Boyd said he now felt "that the climate is very definitely changing and now we have an opportunity to raise the system to a new level."

In the summer of 1982, the justice Department approved the request of the Secret Service to use the FBI computer to keep track of persons it suspects may be a danger to officials. But Representative Edwards, the one-time FBI agent, asked the justice Department not to implement the plan until a thorough public examination of the issues had been completed and possible legislation considered.

Without a law, Mr Edwards said in a letter to Attorney General William French Smith,

> what assurances do we have that this system will not evolve into the sort of system maintained by the Secret Service in the 1970s when "dangerousness" and "threat" were interpreted to include political dissent? In 1972, the Secret Service had nearly 50,000 individuals on its lists, including such "threats" as Jane Fonda, Tom Hayden, Ralph Abernathy, Cesar Chavez, Benjamin Spock, and Walter Fauntroy. Among the organizations listed were the NAACP, the Southern Christian Leadership Conference, and the John Birch Society.

It is very hard to challenge a Secret Service request for a tool that it declares will provide improved protection for the President. But it is easy to understand that the principle of restricting the FBI's computerized telecommunications network to tracking criminal suspects is an important one. It also is easy to understand that changes in a powerful instrument of federal surveillance should not be made without public discussion, congressional hearings, and legislative authorization. The possible threats to a computing facility and the information contained therein determine the security measures that should be investigated. Internal threats come from within the organisation and are typified by fraud, embezzlement, and accidental programming and operator errors. Although external threats include the disruption of computer services, they usually come in the form of attempted access to confidential information. Threats can be grouped into three areas: natural disasters, accidental threats, and deliberate threats.

Natural disasters, which include not only fire, water and wind but also rioting and bombing, can be classified as either accidental or deliberate, they will be discussed separately because they have different characteristics. They tend to occur infrequently, can be very damaging, and are easily detectable. Accidental errors, on the other hand, tend to be much more frequent, much less harmful, and not necessarily detectable. Deliberate threats tend to be infrequent and can be devastating, but again are not always easily spotted.

Most of a computing center's security budget is geared to prevent or recover from natural disasters, because natural disasters have typically been very destructive and expensive.

Fire is a problem in any organisation but takes on slightly different dimensions with respect to computers for two reasons:

(1) the concentration of expensive equipment and valuable information, and

(2) that water, the most common cure for fire, is at least as great a threat as the fire itself.

One of the most spectacular fire disasters took place on July 3, 1959, in the Pentagon computer center. The fire was started in a vault when a 300-watt bulb was left burning on a "fireproof" ceiling. When the vault was opened, flames shot out. The entire computer area and all tapes were destroyed.

Water damage due to fire sprinklers and firemen can be more damaging than the fire itself, since computer circuits and magnetic storage media not even near the fire may be damaged. Other sources of water damage come from tropical storms such as Agnes, floods, activities of firemen on higher floors, leakage in the computer's water cooling system, broken pipes, sewers backing up, *etc.*

Other natural calamities that may occur to computing centers include explosions, earthquakes, tornadoes, aircraft crashes, war, lightning, industrial chemicals or gas, sandblasting near air conditioning intakes, *etc.* Accidental threats constitute the major problem computer installations. Some of the typical problem cussed next. The threat of small magnets causing havoc in tape libraries is somewhat of an overworked problem, discussed in detail by Beardsley. There is definitely a threat to information stored on magnetic tapes, since it is magnetic fields that are used to store, retrieve, and delete information. The magnet must be quite strong and held quite close to the tape to have any effect. What is more of a problem is sloppy storage. Temperature and humidity extremes or winding tapes too tightly can destroy information. Devices such as transformers, which produce alternating magnetic fields, can introduce errors in magnetic storage devices.

Most often, lost printout is the problem. and printout can usually be recreated. However, the loss of printed copies of files that have been deleted could be very costly. Lost cards could be either input data cards or source program decks. Stories such as the one about the touring garden-club matron who took a handful of punched cards from a tray as a souvenir of her visit to the data processing center emphasize the need for security. Destruction of cards could be caused by water, rodents, or card readers. Magnetic tape loss could be due to mislabeling in a large computing center or sending the wrong tape away from the center.

Most often, operator error comes in the form of mounting an important tape as a scratch tape, but rerunning jobs, restarting jobs at the wrong place, and canceling the wrong job are also errors that could be costly.

Hardware error could be caused by air conditioning failure, room temperature and humidity deviations, brief changes in line voltages, complete power failures, or transient or permanent hardware logic errors. The result could be a head crash on a disk, where much of the information will be permanently lost, the malfunctioning of a tape drive such that it does not write the data that it should, the disabling of memory bounds registers so that one user program can overwrite another or the operating system, and decoding failures or communication system switching errors, which can cause information to be transmitted to the wrong terminal or erroneous information to be stored on a file or processed.

When the transient error stops being transient, it is possible to track it down and fix it, but in the meantime the computer is down. This loss of computer time is a real threat, and some allowance must be made for it in operations' schedules. What is sometimes more threatening than computer downtime, from a security standpoint, is hardware logic errors, which do not cause the system to malfunction but rather just compromise the hardware security. In his article on the hardware aspects of secure computing, Molho states that in a study done on a 360/50 a total of 99 single-failure hazards were found in the storage protection hardware and three were found in the Problem /Supervisor state logic. Any of these hazards could compromise the system security without causing a system crash.

By using the telephone communication system, data signals are subject to the same threats of crosstalk as voice signals, and most people have heard other conversations on the phone from time to time. The threat of data crosstalk is not nearly as great as for voice, though, since the signals are unintelligible to those overhearing.

Program errors are by far the most common threat. Completely testing programs or systems of programs for all possible cases is not economical from both computer and programmer standpoints. Thus, when a situation occurs that was not tested, or possibly not even coded for, the program may act in a way that causes garbage to be written on a file or certain data to be ignored or processed incorrectly. Also, the program could abend, which may cause loss of information, if the running procedures are not set up correctly.

Programs in the testing stage represent a threat to concurrently running programs in a multiprogramming environment, since by mistake they may try to read or write data from or to segments of core that are not theirs. If proprietary information is read, this could be a security breach. If garbage is written, this could cause unpredictable results for the other program. The prevention of accidental errors is usually referred to as protection. The prevention of deliberate attacks on the system is referred to as security. Deliberate attacks are becoming more common for several reasons. First, more and more information is being concentrated at one computer site, and computer systems have become the lifeblood of many organisations. Also, psychologically, penetration of the data processing system is a more impersonal and challenging kind of attack than rifling someone's filing cabinet. It may even give the perpetrator the added satisfaction of demonstrating human superiority over a cybernetic adversary. This is not the whole picture, though.

The fact that penetration is relatively easy has a great effect. With the advent of time-sharing, some forms of attack could be considered analogous to trying to break into a safe when you have the safe in your own home without anyone knowing.

Deliberate threats have been subdivided into three areas:

(1) threats that do not require the subverter to be a user of the system, such as physical threats and data communication line threats;

(2) threats that may allow the subverter to become an illegal user in particular, threats to obtain user codes and passwords; and

(3) threats that require the infiltrator to be a user, whether he is legitimate or not.

Many of the threats to become illegal computer users are carried out for the purpose of taking over the system or accessing confidential files.

Divulgence of information via waste material is one of the most basic threats. Many jobs have to be rerun for one reason or another and the first output is discarded. Perhaps a new copy of a report is obtained, so the old one is thrown away. Carbon paper from multiple-copy forms can also be a threat. This waste is usually just set outside on the loading ramp for the garbage man or whoever else might be interested in the information. Akin to this problem is the tape residue problem.

Tapes that were used by one customer of a computer utility might not be needed and might subsequently be sent to another customer, who could easily read any information left on the tape. Even if the data had been erased from the tape first, the Watergate scandal reminds us that there are means of extracting the erased information.

Slightly more elementary is over-the-shoulder eavesdropping, or the scanning of someone else's card input or printed output. Important information, particularly user account codes and passwords, can be obtained this way unless safeguards are set up.

Procedural safeguards to avoid nonauthorised exposure to confidential materials are often not implemented. A case in point is the 'company in the highly competitive oil industry which housed its dp center in a $7 million fortress only to entrust highly proprietary printout to a commercial messenger service'. Theft is a threat that is, often for convenience sake, somewhat overlooked.

Program listings, cards, tapes, and confidential output are left on programmers' desks overnight so that they can get back to work quickly the next day. Since the security in programming or office areas is not nearly as tight as in the computer room itself, even petty thieves could duplicate or steal information without being noticed. Theft by company personnel is more common, however. One software thief worked on geophysical programs for an oil company. He took copies of the programs home to work on, and eventually tried to sell them to other oil companies.

The computer was programmed to show that the money was used to purchase stock, so when he sold the supposedly purchased stock he pocketed the cash. The embezzler need not be a manager or programmer, though. One adjustments clerk in the Department of Revenue transferred tax credits from one taxpayer's account to another until finally she put it in a relative's, all done via data she prepared.

Fraud and embezzlement through data tampering are usually detected only in retrospect, when the individual tries to actually lay his hands on the money. But the stealing of information has a lower risk of discovery.

There are several ways of stealing computerised information without being a computer user. The first scheme is physical access to the communication lines, a pickup device, a tape recorder, and a code book are all that is needed. If one wants to avoid decoding the information, a terminal or decoding device can be used to print out every message that goes to or from the terminal. With the use of just a tape recorder, the active wiretapper can record legitimate messages and retransmit them to the system at a later time. This could cause confusion and might even result in irremediable perturbation of the data files.

Electromagnetic emanation pickup is more common as a threat to non-time-sharing installations. These emanations are low-powered, shortwave radio transmissions resulting from changing magnetic fields. They have been known to have a range of 75 yards, so an interested party could pick up every message to or from the operator's console even though the installation was physically highly secure. Indeed, this has happened at a military computer center in the United States. Hardware tampering, by itself, is not as efficient as data tampering for embezzlement.

It is very efficient at disrupting computer service and in collusion with a user of the system, hardware tampering can be a serious threat. Any of the over 100 hazards discussed under accidental hardware threats could be effected by hardware tampering, and there are many more. For example,

> a clever subverter might seek to add some hardware logic to the CPU which would look for, say, a particular rather unusual sequence of two instructions in a program. Should the sequence appear, the added logic might disable storage protection for just a few dozen microseconds. Such a small hole in the hardware would be quite sufficient for the user to (1) access anyone's file; (2) cause a system crash; (3) modify anyone's file.

User-controllable changes like this are very hard to detect. To avoid detection, though, the subverter could disable the hardware countermeasures or add logic that uses the test signal to inactivate his own logic while the test is performed. This threat of user-controllable changes comes not only from those who have access to the computer hardware:

> A clever subverter could easily alter an engineering change wire list to include his modification, or could send spurious change documentation. A Customer Engineer would then unwittingly install the subverter's engineering change.

Utilisation of these hardware threats will be discussed in the section on deliberate threats by users. One can become an illegal time-sharing user in one of two ways. Either you determine the sign-on protocol of a legal user, or you simultaneously use the same communications line. There are many different ways to obtain the credentials of a legal user. Almost all the deliberate threats not involving terminal access can be used to get this information. Wiretapping, electromagnetic pickup, looking over the shoulder of a user, looking at waste or input-output, or breaking into a user's office and finding the procedure written down are all viable schemes.

Other schemes include briberzy, trial and error, and utilisation of operating system "trapdoors." Operations people are near the bottom of the economic ladder in the computing center; yet they typically have a lot of power with respect to information and general system security. Bribery of operators to divulge the security setup, divulge legal user sign-on procedures, or even to load a special version of the operating system with trapdoors in it is not inconceivable. Trapdoors are weak points in the computer system where access can be made while bypassing security controls. A penetrator could discover these by detailed study of the operating system, by collusion with a system programmer who put in the trapdoor, or by experimentation. Most current systems use a form of password scheme with a high number of possibilities so that manual trial and error is very time consuming. However, as Foster points out, minicomputers could be used to break the code. One could be hooked up to, say, 10 telephone lines and could syste-matically try all possible passwords.

It does not seem difficult to obtain the sign-on procedure of a legal user, owing to certain countermeasures it may not be desirable to use his credentials. Three threats that can be used without knowing his password are "piggybacking," 'between the lines," and extended sign on. These methods utilize wiretapping but also require at least a terminal compatible to that of the legal user. Piggyback entry is accomplished by "selective interception" of communications between a user and the processor, and then releasing these with modifications or substituting entirely new messages while returning an error message to the user. The subverter can then request confidential files to be printed or he can delete important information. However, by this scheme alone, he is restricted to accessing only the information that the legal user could.

"Between the lines" is very similar. In this scheme the subverter does not interrupt the legitimate user but enters his command between the commands of the user. Not wanting to interrupt the regular user limits the type of request the subverter may make, so to extend his access time he can cancel the user's sign-off signals so as to continue operating in his name. Although this is a threat, in this simple form it is not too dangerous, as most time-sharing systems give you a small report of computer usage and cost as you are signing off. These threats are ways of obtaining illegal computer access. In themselves, many are not really security problems. Knowing someone's password does no one any harm unless you use that information. The next section deals with some of the harm people with access to computing power, whether legitimate or not can do.

Assuming that a person has access to the system, either by his position as a legal user or systems programmer or through some of the means previously described, there are many ways he can disrupt or misuse the system, or extract or destroy confidential data. Many computer frauds and embezzlements are included in this section under the subsection on program tampering.

It is defined to occur when a user program is executing in the supervisor or master mode. Most computer instruction sets include privileged instructions that physically cannot be executed in user or nonsupervisor mode. To execute these instructions, which for the most part are basic input-output instructions, one must call the supervisor which runs in this privileged or supervisor mode. Once a user program attains the privileged state, it has access to all information that the operating system has access to, which is everything.

In privileged mode, the subverter can easily cause a system crash to disrupt other users. Allowing a user to get into privileged mode is definitely a threat, but how can a user do it? Palme has expounded some of the weak points found in operating systems, which include the following:

1. When a user program asks the operating system to do something, the legality of the request is not always checked.

2. The user program succeeds in changing its message to the operating system after it has been checked but before it has been performed. One

method of doing this is by spawning a subtask and having the subtask do the message changing.

3. The operating system stores information in the user memory area, and the user program succeeds in changing this information so that it will be misinterpreted later. A good example of this is the address of the access routine. If it is accessible by the user program, the user can simply change the address to be that of a subversive routine. Control will be passed to it in supervisor mode, so the user has taken over the system.

4. There is an intentional opening in the operating system, which was put in to help system programmers or to help advanced utility programs. But the opening can be misused by other programs. The opening might also be introduced intentionally by a system programmer for later subversive use.

A user writes a utility program for general use; this program does what it is supposed to do, but does not stop at that. It might, if given control in supervisor state, print out confidential files like the password file, or it might just take over the system. One example of this scheme involved a university campus time-sharing system. In this case hidden logic caused the operating system to read still another program into system resident memory and erase all trace of the Trojan horse code. The perpetrator could then gain complete control of the system at any time using a specified user code.

The hardware trapdoors can be very hard to detect and, as pointed out in the section on deliberate threats without remote terminal access, they can be used to go into privileged state just long enough to get valuable information or plant a software trapdoor. Once a system has been compromised, it is very difficult to determine if it will ever be safe from attack.

The reason for effecting many of the previous threats was to be able to look at, copy, or alter confidential information stored in computer files. Masquerading as a legitimate user is one of the more common means of doing this. The credentials of the user are obtained by theft, wiretapping, or other means. Then the subverter probably has access to the files of the user along with system files.

The difficulty of accessing other user files varies from system to system depending largely on the access control scheme implemented. These schemes and generalised models of them have recently been the topic of academic research. The threats depend on the scheme. In some cases there is no security and any user can access any file. He might or might not have to know the file name or tape serial number depending on whether or not he can dump the system catalogue or disk volume table of contents (VTOC).

In a more sophisticated system, maybe only the owner is allowed access to his files. Then, short of taking over the system, the intruder must masquerade as the owner. An ingenious method of obtaining the user id and/or password of other users was devised by a couple of enterprising high school students. For many applications, access permission allowed only to the owner is sufficient. However, data sharing is becoming more and more desirable, especially with the advent of large data banks. The threat of misuse of access privileges is being addressed by several researchers some of their results will be discussed later as countermeasures.

If the access controls are such that a user either has access or does not, then there is no means to control his access. You can tell him only to read or only update the file but he can do what he wants. On the other hand, if the access control has specification for read only, write only, read and write, *etc.*, you can control the above threat but still cannot control what is read, if read only is specified. Neither can you control copying the file or printing it for sale to a competitor. Even control down to the data-field level has problems.

Collusion between people with access to different fields of, say, a data bank of information on individuals could compromise an individual's privacy. Also, inference about data not accessible could compromise security. Access control specifications that are not specific enough are a threat in that information may be obtained without a "need to know,' the more serious threat is the misuse of information obtained with a need to know. He admits it is difficult to control what will be done with information released and also difficult to guarantee that the information will never be distributed to other, persons or agencies. Ways of reducing but not eliminating this threat will be discussed later. Although file access threats are by no means restricted to external persons, they are the major source of concern with respect to external subverters.

Program tampering occurs mostly within the organisation. The motivation is usually direct personal enrichment at the expense of the company, but disgruntled employees have been known to carry it out to disrupt business. Typically, a programmer doctors one of his programs or a program that he has access to. One programmer inserted a routine in the accounts receivable billing program of the company he worked for that transferred all charges from his own and friends' accounts to a suspense account.

The most publicised case was that of a programmer of a banking system who siphoned the truncated-off portions of customer interest into his own account.

Another bank programmer patched his program to ignore his own checking account when checking for overdrafts. He was not caught until the computer broke down and the bank had to go manual.

Many other schemes, such as deducting extra amounts from tax or other payroll deductions from all employees each week and transferring the money to your own account, or the use of breakage or tolerance allowance manipulation in conjunction with a large-scale theft, can go unnoticed by the victims. There are more subtle ways of effecting program changes than permanently altering the program. Because most programming languages and compilers are not secure, it is possible for a programmer to illegally access or modify any word in his program or in other modules of the program by simply exceeding the dimensions of an array or having inconsistent COMMON blocks between modules. Even a module that contains parameter validity checking can be compromised by transferring into the middle of the routine, thereby bypassing the security checks.

Tampering of programs can be used not only to steal money but also to steal information. To date, the combination of the facts that computer-stored information has not been sufficiently valuable and that other more simple means are available has discouraged the use of program altering for information access. However, as other security leaks are plugged and more and more information gets computerised, the economies might favour this threat.

When a user no longer requires a mass storage file, whether permanent or temporary, the VTOC pointer to the file is deleted, freeing the space. However, the information is still there. If another user requests space but does not write in it, he could dump the "residue" information left by the previous user. For tape files, often the tape is just reassigned to a new user, who may quite easily read the tape before writing on it. Core memory suffers from the same threat, although manufacturers are now starting to zero memory after use.

Manager's Policies

Managers of an organisation require policy statements regarding their activity and responsibility to the data assets of the business. Such statements are generally presented in very broad terms to encompass any assets of value to the organisation. Some typical policy statements are:

— The protection of assets such as employees, physical property, and information relating to the conduct of business is a basic management responsibility.

— Managers are responsible for identifying and protecting all assets within their assigned area of management control.

— They will assign asset ownership, responsibility, and accountability to proper personnel under their supervision.

— They are responsible for ensuring that all employees understand their obligation to protect company assets.

— They are responsible for implementing security practices and procedures that are consistent with generally accepted practice and with the value of the asset.

— Finally, managers are responsible for noting variance from established security practice and for initiating corrective action.

A corporate information policy represents only an official statement of position taken by corporate management. The policy statement must be supported with plans and programs for executing all actions necessary to safeguard the data assets. Several key management plans and programs' of particular interest are listed below:

The following are the plans

— Vital Records Plan

— Access Control Plan

— Emergency Response Plan

— Interim Processing Plan

— Restoration Plan

The following are the programmes

— Data Classification Program

— Risk Assessment Program

Collectively these constitute an asset protection program that is an integral part of, or directly related to, a disaster/recovery plan. *These plans and programs may have nothing or everything to do with data processing.* In some form they are generally already in place, to some degree! Most organisations may identify these plans and programs under different headings. In any event, they comprise the basic core of planned activity necessary to conduct the business on a continual "normal" basis. Unfortunately, in many organisations that profess to have them they prove upon examination to be any or all of the following:

— Incomplete

— Inaccurate

— Insufficient

— Infeasible

— Missing
— Misunderstood
— Out of date

Therefore, we shall now review each of these key plans and programs to gain insight as to their typical composition, nature, and requirements. This review may provide either a start for your data security program or a measure of comparison and assessment for your currently existing organisational plans and programs.

System security's prime purpose is to protect data and programs that are essential to ensure proper business operation and function. They may be totally unrelated to data processing, such as blueprints, drawings, and licenses, or they may be specifically a part of data processing, such as tapes, disks, printouts, manuals, and the like. Vital records are the business records that an organisation requires in order to:.

— Ensure capability to meet commitments to customers and creditors.
— Prevent the loss of large amounts of money.
— Maintain proof of stockholder interests.
— Safeguard employees' rights and equities.
— Carry out the effective and efficient reconstruction of its business following a disaster.

The vital records plan should present the most efficient and economical methods for protecting these records and for making them readily available for both emergency operations and disaster recovery.

Before vital records can be protected, they must be identified. Management must be involved in determining the organisations vital records. It is not a data processing responsibility; it is an organisational responsibility!

The steps and strategies in a vital records to the organisation's continued operation.

1. Identify those records which are vital to the organisation's continued operation.
2. Establish means to protect them.
   (a) Provide for conditioned, secure off-site storage.
   (b) Provide for adequately protected storage on-site.
3. Keep them current.
   (a) Develop-update cycles for on-site records.
   (b) Develop update cycles for off-site records.
4. Establish means to reconstruct records within a reasonable time if disaster should strike.
   (a) Access control plan.
   (b) Emergency response plan.
   (c) Interim processing plan.
   (d) Restoration plan.

All the basic management plans and programs for data security interleave one another. Each plan depends on and/or contributes to another. Obviously, there is no single best plan. Rather there are a series of preplanned processes for achieving the final objective: continuance of business operation on a near-normal basis. The access control plan pertains to general access to the business premises. Its purpose is to limit access to a location to only those people who work there. Evidence of such plans can be seen in guards, the installation of man-traps, and the coded badge, key, and card systems used in many organisations for security. A necessary provision in this plan is the controlled access of personnel during and immediately following a disaster.

Management cannot rely upon intermittent police surveillance for adequate control of the remains. Furthermore, should any of the remains be moved or even tampered with, the insurance on that particular resource may be voided. Several strategies may be used to strengthen general access control, as described below.

Delegate responsibility, authority, and control to as low a level as possible, so that each local area provides access control in addition to the customary grounds control of fences, guards, and patrols. Adequate training and drills are necessary to ensure proper responsiveness from all delegates.

Access within an area needs to be controlled. Therefore, using multiple control points in a concentric or ringlike arrangement enhances the security of the entire facility. The concept of protective rings of control is used for physical access as well as electronic access to organisational resources.

The size of an organisation definitely influences the control strategy employed. In small companies everyone knows everyone. This is hardly true in large organisations. Therefore, additional controls of varying nature must be used as the size or populace of the organisation increases. The most secure strategy allows no one entry! As entrances and exits are provided, security is compromised. Common sense points to having as few entries and egresses as possible. Sensitive areas within an organisation should have additional control barriers for admittance.

The use of keys, locks, badges, and cards may be all that is required for adequate protection in small populations. However, as the organisation grows, TV cameras, patrols, and computer-activated controls are to and from a defined location. This prevents inadvertent wandering or exploring by either employees or guests. Surveillance with responsive action to the effectiveness of an any abnormality increases access control program. Once again, security is everyone's responsibility. Employees should challenge any stranger entering or leaving their area. An awareness program can strengthen this facet of access control. It may be implemented by video-tapes, circulated in-house memos, meetings, or other effective methods for communications in your organisation. Many employees have no feeling as to just what is "normal."

For example, abnormal may be:

— Employees without badges
— Visitors without escorts
— Use of emergency-only doors
— Entry after hours
— Absence of guard
— Family visitation and tour
— Tailgating

All plans need to be tested in order to assess effectiveness. Authorized attempts should be made Periodically by selected strangers to gain access to restricted areas. The success and failure of all such planned attempts should be documented and later reviewed for possible corrective action.

A substitute guard may be assigned to:

— Allow an entry without ID

— Attempt entry into restricted areas.

— Be absent from his post

— Not file any due reports

Such tests should always be carefully controlled. Management notification and approval must be granted before toying with the current access system.

An emergency response plan permits immediate response to serious as well as noncatastrophic threats. Its purpose is to limit critical resource damage as well as preserve the business capability. It is not a recovery plan but rather an action plan to mitigate, if not avoid, loss of business essentials at the moment of occurrence. Threats from acts of God or acts of humans should be met with planned actions to preserve both the people and the business. Other related plans will assist in backup and restoration.

Several strategies may be used to initially limit damage to critical resources and protect business capability:

— Protect resources in order of human and business importance rather than their difficulty to be replaced or recovered.

— Communicate an alarm to all parties affected

— Evacuate and shelter people

— Protect essential equipment

— Test the emergency response plan

— Drills-regular though nonscheduled

Once the initial emergency has taken place, a plan needs to be available to handle the time period between loss of business capability and restoration. Such a plan, activated by the emergency response plan, is called the interim processing plan; it consists of a description of what both Data Processing and the business do to keep the business going after a disaster occurs until the normal DP capability is restored. This plan defines the expected and tested approaches selected for business continuity. These approaches are for user alternate procedures as well as DP contemporary processing alternatives. The interim processing plan provides for continuance of business capability via any means until restoration takes place. Its key strategies are:

- Definition of the user's responsibilities
- Organisational level-by-level alternate plans
- Individual action plans
- Identification of critical applications
- Identification of critical configurations
- Identification of DP temporary processing alternatives
- Assignment of interim processing duties and responsibilities
- Provision for adequate security in an interim Processing situation
- Testing of the interim processing plan

An effective interim processing plan is one that has previously completed all the key strategies before called upon for us.

That is, the plan must be in place before the accident occurs! This also prevents conflict in assignment of personnel to emergency, interim, and recovery plan activity. Employees may be assigned to more than one plan as long as there is no conflict and a secondary individual backup has been identified. The interim processing plan necessitates outside contact and support that is committed and bound by legal agreement. First, the more that is stated, the more restrictions are imposed on the capability for flexibility and alternative action. Second, a false sense of adequate security may be based on a committed document. Even a signed contract does not guarantee that such support will be granted at the time you need it. For example, if the owner of the support needs it also at that moment, he may simply tell you to "sue me." The only effective interim processing plan is a tested, workable, proven plan that is retested periodically with trained people.

The restoration plan is the third major link in the chain of disaster recovery and related asset-protection plans. Its purpose is to recover the primary data processing capability once lost. This plans is the responsibility of the provider of DP service. The scope of the restoration project is a function of the nature and extent of the damage experienced. The restoration plan complements the emergency and interim processing plans and, like them, must in all functions and at levels. The restoration plan anticipates the worst condition that might occur or be expected. Strategies must be in place to manage people, space, equipment, communications, data, and supplies in such an event.

Activities that may be an integral part of this plan are:

- Determining if the old site is usable
- Making definite personnel assignments
- Providing for personnel replacement and reassignment
- Establishing communications between management and all personnel
- Identifying alternate sites
- Identifying sources of replacement equipment, including communications facilities
- Providing for the availability of data and supplies
- Creating multiple copies of the restoration plan
- Distributing copies of the restoration plan to secure remote sites
- Walk through of the restoration plan

The data classification program differs from the vital records plan. Vital records were classified according to urgency and immediate need to maintain the business. Data classification is viewed in terms of sensitivity and cost. It focuses more on disclosing information that is constantly available. The classification names assigned are generally indications of the level of protection needed; for example, the familiar scheme used in the military assigns labels of Top Secret, Secret, Confidential, and Restricted.

The purpose of a data classification program is to label all media with a name best representing the level of protective measures appropriate to the data recorded on them. "Top Secret" as used by the military implies highly sensitive, highly controlled data. Rules, regulations, standards, and procedures are precisely defined for anyone coming in contact with a document thus marked. Many variables determine the who, what, where, when, why, how, and how long for use of the data.

A primary decision factor in classifying data is the consequences to the business of disclosure, modification, or destruction of the data. This determines not only sensitivity but also cost.

The most appropriate cost to associate with the data may be any of the following: Cost of replacement; Cost of correction; Cost of recovering property associated with the data; Cost of replacing property associated with the data; Cost of recovering property controlled by the data; Cost of replacing data controlled by the data; Cost of lost revenue associated with data service; Cost of lost competitive advantage; Cost of lost business opportunity; Cost of compensation for personal damage

Although it is management's responsibility to set forth the rules for data classification, the owners of the data perform the actual classification. They alone have the necessary knowledge for affixing the most appropriate label. The strategies to be employed in a data classification program are:

— Complete labeling

— Precise definitions of each label

— Discipline of violators

— Relating to awareness program

The danger in any data classification scheme is overclassification.

Does one word make the entire file "Top Secret"? It is generally best to keep the number of different classifications to a minimum. Furthermore, all classifications should have termination dates for reassessment. Rule of thumb: "Classify only what really needs classification, and then, limit the classified amount." Overcontrolled data is unavailable data to those who need it to meet their business objectives.

The security administrator is responsible for the physical and logical security of operational, procedural, and descriptive data and all other information systems resources using data. Obviously, no one person can perform such a task alone. Security must be treated as both a line and staff function across the organisation. It is institutionalized in that it permeates the entire organisation on a level-by-level basis. Each level of management is responsible for all owners, custodians, and users of data assigned to it. Managers have an umbrella-type responsibility to the organisation with respect to data security. That is, they have personal responsibility for the knowledge, awareness, authoritative assignment, education, control, plans and program for use or meet this obligation through judicious assignment and delegation of responsibility to others under their control. Much like a captain of a ship, each manager is responsible for activities under his or her command. The basic role of the security administrator is service to management to make proper security easy. Care should be taken not to assign to the administrator responsibilities that properly belong to line management.

The security administrator does just as the title implies. He or she administers the data security program. This necessitates direct contact and awareness of activity with:

— *Suppliers of service*: Network manager, operations manager, data center manager, data administration manager, systems programming manager, applications development manager, and change control manager

— *Users/owners*: User/owner managers and/or assigned representatives from all pertinent business functions, operations, systems programming, applications development, and change control

— *Management:* All levels, staff, and, in particular, disaster recovery and organisational security

— *Outsiders:* Consultants, legislative/regulatory agencies, security products vendors, insurance companies, and data security organisations

— *Audit:* Internal audit, EDP audit, audit committee, and external audit

— *Legal:* Internal council, external consultant

A more specific list of duties and responsibilities can be developed for the data security administrator as follows:

1. Provide direct administrative support for installed security systems to ensure the secure use of all on-line and information systems.
2. Negotiate with multiple levels of programming support management to assure integration of assigned security objectives with the long-range data processing strategy.

3 Continually review and evaluate security alternatives to determine course of action based upon technical implications, knowledge of business objectives, and corporate asset protection policy, procedures, and requirements.
4. Assure that assigned projects meet corporate security objectives and are completed according to schedule within committed costs; inform management as early as possible of problems that could materially affect objectives, schedules, and costs; recommend alternative solutions.
5. Monitor the use of all on-line and information systems to detect and act upon unauthorized access and use of proprietary business data.
6. Interface and coordinate with legal, insurance, and security staff handling internal security investigations on a highly confidential basis.
7. Conduct security audits, participate in security evaluations, and provide guidance and assistance, as requested, to facilitate the implementation of data processing asset protection programs.
8. Supervise documentation efforts associated with various internal security systems.

A data security administrator is a specially talented individual. This person must be capable of:

— Recognizing actual and potential security exposures.

— Developing solutions in a constantly changing environment of computer technology

— Correlating highly specialized confidential data to realtime as well as batch security systems.

— Setting security design standards for application programs.

— Negotiating and influencing middle and senior management on risk analysis issues concerning security versus utility of computer resources.

Such a position demands highly innovative action with little dependence on past experiences. Working with currently available, state-of-the-art tools affords the data security administrator minimal guidance in developing unique solutions to existing and future security exposures. The administrator must have the self-confidence and initiative necessary to perform his or her function using only broad management guidelines in determing both day-to-day and long-range goals.

There is no fully accepted (set) job description for a data security administrator. This job has multitudinous functions, depending on many organisational variables (its nature, interface with technology, location, size, industrial position, and so on). Nevertheless, it is possible for each organisation to determine who should be doing what, and what the specific responsibility of the data security administrator is, by using a functional matrix. The data security administrator may decide to work up a functional assignment matrix alone and then present it to management for review, discussion, and finalization.

A representative group of people affected by the assignments may develop the matrix collectively and then submit the completed document to management for approval. There is no one best way to do it. The key issue is getting it done! Such a procedure aids in affixing accountability. Although the data security administrator has general responsibility for all data security, the appropriate person or persons should be directly accountable for specific functional actions.

The functional matrix helps identify these people, resolve conflicts, build awareness, and establish the overall role of the data security administrator. It may be advantageous to repeat this exercise or one of a similar nature. The data security administrator's role definitely involve's a moving target.

Management has been slow to recognize data as a major resource. Viewed in its fragmented state, data appears to be meaningless and quite harmless. Viewed in total as an established database, however, it may constitute one of the most critical assets of the business. What gives such value to data? The answer lies in its worth to those who have it or want it.

They recognize that information is power-power to manage, power to manipulate, power to control. Often the value of data is directly proportional to how much it alters or influences action or behaviour.The computer and its associated storage media enable management to have the information it wants and needs.

Management does not always assign a high priority to its responsibility in managing and protecting the process through which it now obtains that information. Electronic data collection and dissemination systems are now pervasive in most organizations. Many of these systems were developed implemented with little or no management participation and direction.

Controls are not only poor but generally nonexistent. Some systems today are developed in the same manner. Perhaps control is lacking because the data processing, audit, or other management support function has not stressed or sold the need for it. Another reason may be that computer vendors and salesmen have emphasized simplicity more than involvement. Perhaps, too, management should share some blame for its lag in really stepping up its new responsibilities in dealing with computerized information.

Two major events have put information systems security in the fore ground of management's concern. First came Equity Funding. Although publicized as a computer crime, it involved the computer only remotely in the generation of bogus policies. Unfortunately, lack of reinforcement and continued support of this concern made the period of recognition very brief. Originally enacted by Congress to deter American companies from making improper payments to foreign officials, it was later enforced by rulings of the Securities and Exchange Commission (SEC) to require management to state in their financial reports that controls were adequate and functioning as intended. The Act, with provisions amending the Securities Exchange Act of 1934, made it mandatory that a company implement a system of internal accounting controls to meet four objectives:

1. Transactions are executed in accordance with management's general or specific authorization.
2. Transactions are recorded as necessary to
   (a) permit the preparation of financial statements in conformity with generally accepted accounting principles and
   (b) maintain accountability for assets.
3. Access to assets is permitted only in accordance with management's general or specific authorization.
4. The recorded accountability for assets is compared with the existing assets at reasonable intervals and appropriate action is taken with respect to any differences.

In addition, each corporation was mandated to demonstrate upon request that it has:

1. Assessed the current status of its control system.
2. Improved any deficiencies.

3. Continued to monitor the actual effectiveness of the system.

Violation could result in a five-year prison term, a $10.000 fine, or both for the responsible executives. Once again, this made the issue of computerized information system security and control one of management, major concerns. Direct benefits from this concern were the establishment of an EDP audit function, the appointment of asset protection administrators, and the preliminary formulation of specific information system security policies, plans, and programs.

The SEC withdrew a proposal to implement the accounting provisions of the Foreign Corrupt Practices Act by requiring managers of publicly held companies to report on the adequacy of their internal controls. In withdrawing the proposal, the SEC said it would rely on voluntary management reporting the fangs of the Act were pulled. Management has started to respond to its responsibility in managing and protecting the process through which it obtains computerized information, much still needs to be done. Computer crime is the latest development pushing the security of information systems into headlines for management's attention. However, what is misleading here is that computer crime appears to be the number one problem of data security.

The majority of problems arise from simple errors and omissions in the data life cycle. Granted, a so-called computer caper may result in a sizable dollar loss. Until the basic accesses to the system are controlled, however, it does not make sense to concentrate on the technical or exotic aspects of system control.

It is best to close the doors and windows before worrying about the cracks in the walls. Many systems today invite penetration owing to their lack of basic data security controls. The purchase of exotic and "pensive hardware and software security is foolish when many basic, Positive controls very little cost.

Some business organizations are doing an Outstanding job in securing their information systems. The need remains for the majority of organizations to follow their example. This group needs a constructive approach to identify what really needs to be done beyond a "knee-jerk" reaction to the sensationalism of computer crime.

— Recognize the need for setting basic data security standards and guidelines,
— Understand their role in the data security life cycle,
— Establish a formalized approach to data security, and
— Commit the resources necessary to properly administer the data security function, the doors and windows to their information systems will remain open.

One of management's priorities today must be the establishment of data security plans, Policies, and programs for the corporate environment. Also, management must be committed to participate in the design, installation, and operation of all sensitive data systems. New management personnel assist in this management function. Several key Positions are: Data Security Administrator, Data Base Administrator, Disaster Recovery Manager. In small organizations one person may wear many of these hats; even so, top management still has the responsibility for setting the overall guidelines for each function.

A cardinal principle of the accounting profession calls for "the adequate separation of duties and responsibilities." In data processing, any unreasonable opportunity for the inclusion of errors or the dishonest conduct of employees necessitates the application of this principle. Other principles, as discussed below, further support this basic one.

Segregation of duties means separating the activities of a process among several people. For example, in data processing, the data entry operator should not also have the responsibility for verifying that data. A programmer should not maintain his own code. A system designer should not be allowed to access application modules. When this principle is applied, transposition errors will be more readily caught before entering the system. And a user may discover an attempt by the designer to access control over his system. Collusion also may be required in order for a breach of security to occur; that is, more than one person is needed to break security, and the capability of detection is thereby enhanced. Quality assurance, systems review, or even maintenance may then have the opportunity of uncovering an authorized programmed routine planted in the program by the programmer.

Sensitive information is data that, if exposed, could influence the posture of a given business situation. Information by itself may lack significance, but combinations of such information may become sensitive. For example, a programmer may not be authorized to view employee salaries. However, the same programmer may have access to personnel location and statistical data. If so, by inquiring first, "What is the employee's address?" and second. Individuals who have access to both the primary asset and the control data governing it, such as inventory control data and inventory, present a definite security risk. The pilfering of funds at Union Dime Bank is an example. Union Dime Bank had a teller who not only controlled a primary asset but also controlled all data governing that asset. The teller took advantage of the situation and maneuvered money in and out of the accounts to cover his betting losses at the racetrack.

Employees should not be placed in a tempting position where they could convert and conceal assets for their own benefit. A common violation of this principle is the assignment of a single computer operator to the third shift. Long production runs with few operating procedures might appear to justify a single operator. After some time, however, the operator, out of boredom or need, might begin to make and sell copies of the production run output or might secretly develop a service bureau business paid for unknowingly by the employer. Even worse, the employee might print or copy available data files and sell them to competitors. The greatest opportunities for conversion and concealment of data, however, may not lie within the data processing production shop but rather occur outside it, where input/output communication with the data base is possible.

Information systems that have been designed with inadequate separation of duties and responsibilities and/or allow access to combinations of sensitive resources are ripe for a conversion-and-concealment violation. It is not the use of a computer or a computerized data base that creates this opportunity; it is the inadequate use of the control capabilities available. In fact, a computer and its data base can afford better control over a business than the manual system that they replace. Control is achieved through proper planning, design, testing, utilization, and management of the many control features available in today's computer systems.

To improve efficiency and speed of operations, it may be deemed reasonable to combine the process of origination and approval of transactions. However, even though this responsibility is entrusted to a long-term, highly respected, honest employee with an impeccable work record, such absolute control violates acceptable accounting practice. A system should do only what it is supposed to do and nothing else. It performs according to a planned set of specifications-even when it fails. It possesses the essentials of wholeness or completeness. Such a system has integrity. For example, a timer on a bank vault door will activate opening at only a preset time and no other; a read-only data set will refuse all attempts at change from any source; a check will be dispensed only to the proper individual at the right time for the right amount.

The test of integrity is predictability. If, for every stimulus to the system, the response can be predicted both when the system is performing properly and when it is failing, it has integrity. By way of illustration, indicates that a system with integrity, when met with an abnormal stimulus, is still predictable in its performance. The property of integrity provides the capability to respond with corrective action. Such a system greatly reduces the Potential for information exposure and thus raises the level of data security.

System that is auditable allows an independent reviewer to verify its activity with relative ease at any time. The system must demonstrate that it is performing to specifications, complying with control requests, being used as intended, and conforming with standards of good practice. In order to meet this criterion, the system should be constructed entirely of auditable components. It needs to be modular in design, each module capable of communicating with others only across a limited number of formally defined interfaces. Such a system therefore has the ability to record all the transactions at the interfaces. A test of auditability is accountability. A system should be able to fix responsibility for every significant event at the level of a single individual. It should be able to point to some time" or some "party" as accountable for any system action. Such a system would be capable of holding any person accessing that system completely accountable for his actions. Such a system must also have visibility. Variances from expected behaviour, use, or content must come to the attention of management in such a way as to permit timely and appropriate corrective action.

System that possesses controllability permits management to exercise a directing or restraining influence over its use, behaviour, or content. This property limits the capability of a system to pass other than intended or prescribed resources between domains. For example, we may be able to submit charges for legitimate business expenses but not be able to approve, issue, or redirect the payment of funds. Furthermore, we may be allowed to submit expenses only for particular types of charges associated with my department. To achieve such a control posture, each auditable module must be individually controllable. This implies that each module control its own domain, so that it passes to other modules only those actions intended. A test of controllability is granularity. Granularity requires that the size of the module to be controlled is small enough to constitute an acceptable level of risk. For example, if a payroll module includes the functions of requesting, authorizing, and making payments, it fails granularity. No one module should control a resource of such size that it can materially affect the continuance of the business. It is a management responsibility to set the level of risk acceptable at each interface.

A strategy for achieving the properties of integrity, auditability, and controllability is to place functional controls at each domain's interface. These controls protect the passage of information in the system from being compromised. They represent the system designer's greatest contribution in achieving maximum data security. The functions are best described in the sequence in which they are designed into a system.

The identification function allows us to establish identifier tor each system user and resource. Its purpose is to afford evidence of reality. In other words, this function identifies by some acceptable means the people, hardware, software and other resources available to a system. Identification implies only that a record exists in the system that associates an identifier with a defined user or resource. A claim to some identity has been established at this point.

The authentication function is the act of collecting evidence to an acceptable level of risk that the claim of identity is valid. Simply stated, it is acceptable validation of identity. It provides the capability to verify the identified user or resource. This may be accomplished by comparing something that this individual knows, has, is, or can do to a recorded reference. For example:

— *Something he knows*—password. A secret coded word known only to the user and the system.

— *Something he has*—Photo identification card. A picture of the individual that may be matched to the person presenting the card.

— *Something he is*—Physical appearance. A bodily comparison of appearance to memory on a face-to-face basis.

— *Something he can do*—Signature. A unique but reproducible behaviour such as the manner in which the name is written.

Authentication, therefore, normally relies on some "thing" that only one entity knows has, is or can do. For instance, when children are transported alone by airplane to their relatives, only the stewardess knows the name of their dog or teddybear. The children are not released into the custody of others until the so-called relative volunteers the name. The use of a password in a system acts in much the same way.

The authentication of the source of data in an information system is key to data security. It helps determine how much trust can be placed in the accuracy, reliability, and completeness of the information presented by that system.

The authorization function's sole purpose is to state who is allowed to do what to a given resource. This function generally relates a user with a resource through defined rules of authorization. That is, authorization establishes rules that restrict system users to exercising only predefined actions to the data resource. Each individual must first have explicit authorization by management for access to the data resource.

To maintain and apply the authorization function, delegation is necessary. Delegation provides for the origination, recording, and maintenance of the access rules. This function determines who, under what circumstances, may exercise or change the rules of authorization. In small systems this task may be accomplished by the security administrator. Large systems that have a complex structure of users, resources, locations, and activities may require a sophisticated delegation mechanism that allows management to update the rules in a realtime mode. Needless to say, such a mechanism needs to be controlled. As an example, IBM's software access control package "RACF" (Resource Allocation and Control Facility) provides extensive delegation functions. Group administrators and data set owners can be assigned and changed, and they can control other users' access to their groups and data sets. Like other controls in a formal organization, functional control is delegated downward. Several systems marketed today are designed so only the designated control operator can be delegated the authority to change operation IDs and passwords.

After identification, authentication, authorization, and delegation, the next step is the journaling of all meaningful activity that takes place. Journals provide written records of the use of the system's resources.

They offer three major benefits:

1. Providing for reconstruction, backup/recovery.
2. Fixing accountability-trace and identify.
3. Gaining visibility-see what is happening.

Systems should never be designed without a journaling capability. Journaling is the most effective way to monitor adherence to company policies, objectives, rules, and standards of performance. Generally, any point where a significant resource or accountability passes from one person's control to another's is a key area for audit-trail considerations. Audit trails, no matter how complete, are ineffective without the next function, surveillance.

Someone needs to review the journals. Someone needs to monitor the activity for variance from the expected behaviour, use, or content. This is the surveillance function. Not only must the system journals be reviewed, but appropriate action must follow. Management must be informed of irregular activity or any unexpected system behaviour. If warranted, management can take immediate, positive, corrective action.

Surveillance requires both internal and external system mechanisms. Once a variance is detected, the security system can immediately initiate a preplanned action such as a terminal lockup. Corporate management must still be informed of any irregularities to decide what additional corrective measures, if any, are most appropriate.

Control is the capability to exercise restraint or direct influence over a given situation or event. It is an action taken to make an event conform to plan. Some controls are passive in nature; others are active. That is, some controls require no feedback before a planned action is taken. For example, a key is turned in a lock and the door opens; or an order is entered and the control system automatically stamps it with date and time of entry. No other considerations or actions are necessary for initiating and maintaining this type of control. Others are quite active and require feedback for proper operation.

For example, a thermostat is a control device that takes action to heat or cool a room. The device may be set to any planned temperature. However, control can take place only when the thermostat is able to actively compare what was,planned with what is actual. Some controls in DP function much like the thermostat. They are designed to operate in a particular manner, depending on the conditions present at the moment. A password is an active control. It requires comparison to an established authorized code before a planned action is taken. This action may be to permit entry, prevent entry, detect entry or even take corrective action against such entry.

In DP systems, both active and passive types of controls must be used for effective reduction or elimination of data exposures. Controls are used wherever applicable. In DP systems, this includes input, process, output, security, environment, administration, ware, and so on. There are literally thousands of control uses.

One of the most common types of data security controls is the password. Passwords may be user-generated or system-generated. Each approach has definite pros and cons that must be examined by the practitioner. Generally, as the number of users and the necessity for frequent change increase, the use of system-generated passwords is favoured. However, many users today generate their own passwords. The key factor in a decision of this nature is the ease of password distribution, maintenance, and control. IBM has been using system-generated passwords in its administrative system. The latest security code has a five-character alphanumeric format. Previous code schemes worked much as follows: Users of this system must first key their employee number and their assigned security code password for complete user identification. The elimination of vowels prevents the generation of embarrassing password names.

The system checks employee number and security code as follows:

— If employee number is valid and the password is correct, a user is permitted access to the data base.

— If either the employee number or security code does not pass, the event is logged for later review and the user is requested to try again.

Three unsuccessful attempts to access the system will lock the terminal and alert the local security administrator. A new security code is mailed to each user through a computer generated self-mailer. The security code is on a detachable card stub with no other reference data. The receiver is instructed to immediately detach the code stub. Should the user now lose this stub, the finder would have great difficulty in associating the password number with the appropriate system and employee number. If the user suspects his code has been compromised, he can request a new code at any time. This technique is normally successful in protecting a system from any unauthorized terminal users.

A major mistake in approaching controls is to view them too generally, attempting to pick and choose from a massive potpourri in hopes of selecting something adequate for the system. Often the designer does not even understand the control selected. An "anticipation" control used by audit, for example, may be completely foreign to the design engineer. What is suggested, and can be put into practice immediately with very positive results, is the classification of controls by their basic purpose.

Controls serve three basic purpose:

1. To prevent the causes of data exposure.
2. To detect the causes of data exposure.
3. To correct the causes of data exposure activity.

All the various areas in a system where controls may be used fit into these basic purposes. Combinations of controls will dictate the adequacy achieved.

This approach is often referred to as the three-layer, ring, or barrier concept. Preventive measures form the outermost, or first, layer of protection to the system. These are followed by detective measures and then a layer of corrective actions. All data is susceptible to influence from threats existing in its environment. Preventive controls offer the first line of defense or barrier against the bad things that could happen to a data asset. They stop the majority of causal agents from accidentally or intentionally disclosing, modifying, or destroying the data asset. Preventive controls are a before-the-fact type of control. Recognition is given that particular causal agents exist, and certain preplanned preventive measures are employed to reduce, if not eliminate, their effect on the data asset. No control or set of controls are perfect in themselves. Some causal agents will still pose a threat to the data asset after the preventive barrier is established. The purpose of the first control layer, then, is to substantially reduce the number of existing undesirable things in the neighbourhood of the data asset. The few bad things that filter through the preventive barrier should be detected and corrected by the second and third layers of control.

Preventive controls generally have the following characteristics: they

1. Are passive, requiring no feedback
   - — Lock on a terminal
   - — Power-off switch
   - — Preset timer
   - — Fence
2. Guide, to align things to happen correctly
   - — Machine feed guides
   - — Forms design; formatted coding sheets
   - — Training program
3. Are inadequate alone, overlooking a certain percentage of violations
   - — No admittance sign
   - — Timelock

— Automatic door close

4. Reduce threat frequency

   — Computer facility inspection

   — Audit

   — Personnel background check

   — Segregation of duties

5. Are transparent; people are not conscious of their existence

   — Shatterproof glass

   — Encapsulated circuits

6. Are inexpensive

   — Door lock

   — Cover over an emergency button

   — Badge

Detective controls offer the second line of defense against causal agents that penetrate the preventive barrier. Since the bad thing has happened, these controls are an after-the-fact type. They are designed specifically to detect the presence of a causal agent.

Detective controls are seldom effective by themselves. They note an occurrence. However, unless some corrective action is taken, the potential for data exposure continues. Detective controls generally have the following characteristics: they

1. Trigger an alarm

   — Smoke detector

   — Voltmeter power-supply warning light

   — Beeper on an opened door

2. Register the threat occurrence

— Printout of happenings

— Automatic error counter

— Photographing of intruder

3. Terminate further system operation

— Shut down the computer

— Lock the terminal

— *Abend* a program

4. Monitor occurrence and range of acceptance

— Reasonableness checks

— Anticipation of an event

— Tolerance level

5. Alert personnel

— Siren, horn, buzzer

— Warning, flashing light

— Error reports

— Debug routines with diagnostics

6. Test preventive control operation

— Hash totals, check digits

— Balancing of control totals

— Reconciliation of accounts

Corrective controls are generally paired with detective controls. Once the penetration has occurred and is noted, a corrective action for that causal agent is executed. The purpose of the corrective control is to take action on righting a wrong or preventing more wrongs from occurring. Many corrective controls are of the management type: that is, they require stated policies, procedures, and programs for execution.

Corrective controls generally have the following characteristics: they

1. Take action to resolve a problem
   — Automatic error correction.
   — Graceful degradation.
   — Exception management.
2. Reset for reprocess
   — Corrected rejects resubmitted upstream
   — Approved exceptions returned to entry point
3. Are expensive
   — Parallel operation
   — Backup/recovery resources
   — Change control center
   — Quality control group
4. Provide investigative assist
   — Audit trail
   — Discrepancy report

The data asset may be vulnerable to an infinite number of possible causal agents in its environment. Trying to consider controls for each of these undesirable things would be very difficult if not impractical. Although that approach may be viewed as the classical method, it is as absurd as the listing of all possible exposures.

A technique was developed that limits the number of exposures and their causes that need to be considered for purposes of control. By describing the basic causes of the identified data exposures at CP1. For example, exposure Al is the accidental disclosure of a timesheet caused by an employee's leaving it unattended on his desk. The consideration of basic controls is limited to that specific cause.

Controls are considered not for the mass of possible causal agents but only for the specific causes described in the process of identifying exposures. This greatly simplifies the control problem and, as a result, reduces the time required to complete the control process. An effective approach to designing or assessing controls for causes of data exposure is now available for use.

A workpaper that may be used to facilitate he process of deriving and recording control data for each exposure at each control point.

The user of the form enters:

1. Proper date, system studied, control point examined, basic data exposure defined.

2. Description of the type and nature of controls to apply the specific threat causing the exposure.

3. An annualized cost of the recommended control or control set.

4. The probability that the defined control (set) will successfully eliminate this specific threat for this basic exposure.

The person or persons most familiar and/or involved with the particular exposure under examination should be called upon to:

1. Suggest their thoughts.

2. Estimate the probability of success associated with such controls.

3. Express an annualized "ballpark" cost of the control set.

Insurance may also be regarded by some people as a control. However, insurance is a means of recovering from a loss rather than preventing, detecting, or correcting a loss. Potential causes of loss are unaffected. Therefore, insurance will be considered only as a backup to the control measures that are adopted. One should focus on the key areas in a computer environment that have proved in the past to be critical to the system control, before concentrating on a methodology for designing or reviewing control in information systems. Identification of a weakness in any of these areas may warrant the direction of effort there instead of toward a methodological system study. It may be far more effective to assign resources in the management and protection of these areas than to application reviews, risk analyses, or design methodologies.

Adequate segregation of functions

Adequate separation of duties and responsibilities exists in present systems and is designed into new systems. In particular, it addresses the authority, responsibility, and involvement of DP personnel. For example, no programmer should be involved with the user's application program. If possible, each of the following functions should be performed by a separate person. Although in small organisations this is not feasible, one must recognize the possible danger as an individual assumes more than one of these functions:

— Application design

— Application programming

— Database administration

— Data entry

— Library management

— Maintenance programming

— Management
— Operation-job initiation
— Operation-data input activity
— Operation-data output activity
— Output distribution
— Program testing
— Scheduling
— System library maintenance
— Systems programming
— Other management and control areas

An organisational chart or grid that plots personnel vs. function is an excellent tool to determine the extent of such separation.

Centralisation of change control is critical to all systems. Although a system may be designed with the highest degree of data integrity and control, this 'Protection will be defeated by a failure to control any or all changes to that system. Each DP organisation should have an established change control group. In a small organisation with few applications this group may be only one person. The group's primary function is to provide independent checks and balances on all suggested and approved changes to the system. They review all requests for stated purpose, need, cost, impact, and authorisation. This group may also control the use of all system penetration tools and utilities such as SUPERZAP, SUPERZAP is an IBM software program that permits change to an operating system program at machine-code or object-code level. Such changes are quick and generally unrecorded. Although SUPERZAP is an effective tool for maintaining higher production levels, it does present a security control problem. IBM today recommends the use of its

System Modification Program (SMP), where possible, since it offers control over whatever changes are made. Control of such tools as SUPERZAP by a change control group strengthens the total system's accountability and auditability properties.

Most problems reported today in change control are the result of "quick fixes." Many quick fixes use computer software tools to break into a system, bypass the problem, and patch a continuation linkage between the two segments. Temporary unauthorized code inserted at this time may go unnoticed and remain a permanent part of the program. A quick fix often occurs because a problem arises at an inopportune time. Although the operator's motives and intentions are admirable, the security of the system has been broken and its integrity is now questionable. All tools and procedures for quick fixes need to be controlled!

The need exists for handling and controlling data that is rejected and/or reentered. In past systems this area has been a favourite spot for theft to occur. For "ample, an employee who works in data entry for a large department store can simply spindle, mutilate, and miscode his or her personal purchase input documents, causing rejections. The employee then discards the rejected documents. A separate control function is needed in all systems to provide for the proper handling and disposition of all rejects and reentries

Every point in a system where man interiaces with machine, is a critical point for control. This includes not only DP operations but external points such as terminal entry as well. First, a control check should be made of the physical environment. Is the machine in a secure area? What precautions exist to protect the machine from acts of God and humans? Needed next is a study of the personal interfaces.

Who are the users? Are they trained, qualified, responsible people? A review of user procedures with direct observation of user performance often points out weaknesses. For example, the password entry is not masked; messages are retained on the video display unit (CRT) unless erased by the user; passwords are taped or printed on the console; the system is open to be played with by anyone during user's absence; and user input repeatedly "locks" the system owing to entry mistakes. The external controls at any data entry point are just as critical as the system's internal safeguards.

It is the combination of controls both internally and externally that determines the actual degree of system protection. The designer and auditor should review both types of control not only for security purposes but also for sources of error and inefficiency. An area of great concern for security today is the interface of word processing to the main computer system. Although the main system may have excellent controls, the tieing in of word processing presents the opportunity for system penetration. For example, many such tie-ins are done on a test basis 'that allows circumvention of existing controls in order to facilitate integration. Investigations have indicated that this occurrence is generally a case of management oversight.

Tapes and disks in most organisations today represent the information resource upon which the business functions. If the information resource were lost or modified, the business might not survive. Just as banks must account for every dollar in their inventory, an organisation must have controls to account for every item in its information library. Inspections and examinations of library documentation, procedures, operations, and even personnel are mandatory. Every library item and its activity needs to be logged and checked for availability, accuracy, usage, and maintenance- Far too many organisations today have library files openly available to users, programmers, and operators. In fact, many organisations have multiple libraries whose existence is unknown. Division, branch, and plant site locations may have minicomputers that fostered the development of independent libraries not reported to the main site location.

Many organisations, however, emphasize or give training in security only during new-hire orientation. As the employee continues to work, there is no reinforcement of that initial assignment of responsibility. Each organisation should have a security awareness program that reviews and emphasizes the continued security responsibility of each employee. Effective techniques include film sessions, staff meetings, and customized forms such as IBM's Security Assessment Questionnaire The importance of security may be emphasized by policy statements such as IBM's original 2-109A and current corporate instruction CI-104, which state that "fulfillment of DP asset protection responsibilities must be mandatory, and should be considered a condition of continued employment." Furthermore, an annual, signed certification by the employee that he or she has read and understood the company's published "Asset Protection Guidelines" and "Data Security Guidelines" reinforces the organisation's level of security awareness.

The purpose of disaster/recovery planning is to take steps in advance to ensure continuity of business information if the DP capability is lost. A disaster is defined as the loss of DP capability. Recovery plans are measures to be taken to restore the business on a near-normal-as-possible basis. Disaster encompasses far more than major catastrophes such as earthquakes, tornadoes, or floods.

The focus in disaster/recovery planning should be on recognition of emergency conditions and implementation of planned processes for returning the business to a normal operating mode as soon as possible. An event that causes a loss of DP capability qualifies as a disaster. Therefore, the extent and severity of possible disaster vary widely. Planning effort and responsibility is an organisation undertaking that is, not only DP but also management, users, and other affected parties participate in the program. In the event of loss of DP capability users are responsible for the continuity of their business function unit DP meets its responsibility to restore processing capability. This is a key element of disaster recovery planning.

A plan by itself is incomplete. Each plan needs to be tested and action taken to correct the discovered inadequacies. In other words, this is a continual planning process, where the process is even more important than the plan itself. It is the process that affords understanding and readiness. All organisations should have an up-to-date, tested, organisation disaster recovery plan. The end product, first and foremost, is not a paper document but a tested, proven capability to recover. Testing is the vehicle that changes disaster recovery planning from a concept into a reality.

In order to protect the most valuable data assets in an organisation, the data resources must be classified, and each must be assigned to a level of business need. The following four basic classifications may be used:

The loss of vital records could terminate the business. Their information often is irreplaceable and is needed immediately for the business to function. Examples might include key programs, master records and files, operational documentation, disaster recovery plans, and certain input/output data.

Essential records: The loss of this information would certainly disrupt the operation of the business. Although the business might survive, the level of operation and productivity would be seriously affected. These records can be reproduced, but generally extra expense, time, and effort are called for. Examples might include secondary programs, operational logs, and business histories.

Important records: The loss of these records causes inconvenience but rarely disruption of operation. Usually they are readily replaceable. Examples might include general systems documentation, special programs, and procedures for testing old applications and future system prototype data.

Useful records: The loss of these records creates nary a ripple in the operation of the business. They are often viewed as nonessential and may be found to be no longer necessary. They are nice to have, but their absence creates no problems. Examples include various management, user, and data processing reports.

Vital records may be further subclassified. Such breakdowns may or may not provide additional benefit. The key to a vital records Program is the recognition of the data that is necessary to the survival of the business-the vital records. Controls, safeguards, and tested plans are mandatory. This program includes a tested disaster recovery plan and all related backup plans.

The control of test libraries and test programs from production libraries and production programs is key to a system's integrity and security. Production is defined as those applications and systems that have been tested, approved, and made part of the actual operation of the business.

Many DP organisations have no actual physical record of a data, assets residing in their shop. Worse yet, many have no record as to where they are located. Each program, utility, routine, software package, and the like that belongs to the organisation should be accounted for. The tape/disk library is the repository. Copies of unique routines developed by programmers must be declared company property and properly controlled. Many such routines reside with the programmer who developed them, locked in personal drawers and viewed as his or her personal property.

Development of policies is the factor keys in on the management aspect of data processing systems. Although a System may be designed technically perfect, its administration may render useless the benefits derived from implementation. Management must state its policy with respect to the protection of DP assets.

Contracts that bind the organisation's personnel to selected services should all be reviewed by legal and audit. Often what is not said is what the organisation inferred was offered. Data processing will be involved in contracts for hardware, software, service centers, consulting, programming, time sharing, and insurance, to name a few. All of these need to have their stated provisions monitored and reviewed.

5

Globalisation of Communication

The development in cross-border TV stations accelerated powerfully at the end of the 1980s. Some are privately owned general-interest channels (Super Channel, Star TV) or public service systems (TV5, BBC World Service), while others are specialized in newscasting (CNN, Euronews, etc.), sport (Eurosport, Screensport, etc.), leisure (Disney Channel) or music programmes (MTV, MCM). They reach millions of homes around the world via cable networks or via collective or individual reception of satellite signals. In order to overcome language obstacles and increase their audience, cross-border stations are investing increasingly in national-language programmes (CNN, NBC, Star TV) or multiplex sound channels enabling televiewers to choose among several languages (Eurosport, Euronews).

As a rule, TV stations are basically financed by revenue from commercials on the domestic market but are increasingly likely to target the international scene. In addition to commercials, some channels (CNN, Star TV) obtain a growing share of their revenue from pay-per-view systems via cable TV networks, as well as from hotel and individual subscribers. The success of cross-border television is due to a series of factors that are basically technological in nature: the boom in satellites, the proliferation of installed bases of dish antennae over vast regions of the world, progress in the miniaturization of TV control rooms, cameras and small-scale transmission stations which together have done away with distance and time.

CNN is the channel which best embodies the instant, global, worldwide status of television. The channel today can reach every region around the world via a network of satellites covering the whole planet. In 1995, the channel was distributed in more than 120 countries, beaming its programmes into more than a thousand hotels around the world and reaching more than 70 million homes. But it was the coverage of major events such as the abortive coup d'état in the former Soviet Union or the Gulf War that pushed the channel to the forefront of the planetary news system.

The aim to serve an international audience means that it repeats part of its newscasts every twenty-four hours to provide televiewers worldwide with a panorama of the main news at any time, hence the importance of CNN International, the version of the channel's news bulletin tailored for international audiences. It combines the international programme of CNN and televised newscasts from Headline News, the other non-stop news channel of the Turner empire that telecasts a summary of the day's events every halfhour.

CNN and Headline News are the most profitable products of the Turner Broadcasting System (TBS), the mother company that also comprises Turner Network Television M and TBS Superstation. In recent years, the group has been putting into practice a diversification strategy by exporting its various models worldwide.

In June 1997, CNN regionalized its news programmes aimed at North and South America, Asia and Europe. The revised formula consists of adapting the editorial content to the targeted regions. Broadcasting is in Spanish for the South American market and English for the rest of the world. The channel operators have announced plans for alternative cultural and language versions, aimed in particular at the Arab, Indian, Japanese and Russian markets. This new policy does not rule out the extension of the TBS network round the world. In Europe it has become the majority shareholder in the German non-stop news channel NTV and in the Russian station TV6 Moscow. Targeting the European, Caribbean and Central American regions, it has also recently launched two channels which are already highly prosperous in the United States, one specializing in animated cartoons.

The Cartoon Network, and the other in films, Turner Network Television (TNT). The TBS group, with earnings in 1995 of $3,437 billion, has just merged with the Time Warner company to give birth to the largest global communication group in the world, ahead of Walt Disney-ABC. Observers expect the synergy generated by the two groups to buttress CNN's news potential, particularly in view of the journalistic input from the Time Warner group. Notwithstanding this important influx, however, CNN has to contend with other competitors surfing in on the wave of satellites, players who have also become aware of the strategic power and potential of information.

The BBC World Service ranks as a serious alternative to CNN. A subsidiary of the BBC, it covers practically all five continents. It broadcasts a non-stop news programme twenty-four hours a day. To cover its operating costs it receives neither licence fees nor state subsidies and strives to balance its accounts through sales. In addition to its newscasts every hour, the BBC

World Service adds news magazines and the best documentaries produced by the BBC. In recent years, it has improved its coverage through partnership agreements with regional or local channels such as the South African pay-TV network M-Net, and American and Japanese channels. While the BBC World Service seems to be the main rival for CNN, other news channels with specific linguistic or regional viewpoints are joining the throng.

Euronews is the leading satellite-based multilingual European news channel, jointly set up by eleven European public service channels. Via the Eutelsat 11-Fl satellite, it covers all of Europe, including the central and eastern regions, as far as the Near and Middle East. Televiewers have access to programmes broadcast non-stop twenty-four hours a day on a separate frequency for each of the six languages available: Arabic, English, French, German, Italian and Spanish. The originality of the channel is that the news bulletins are image-only telecasts, with voice-over journalists simply commentating on the pictures, reports and magazines provided by members of the European Radio-Television Union (UER). According to its proponents, by presenting a coverage of regional and world current events from a European point of view and in six different languages, Euronews can claim to be the European equivalent of the American channel CNN.

Other networks have spread over all five continents. The largest of these today is that of the Rupert Murdoch News Corp. group. It is the fourth largest communication empire in the world, with a 1995 sales figure of $9 billion (profits of $626 million from the press and $400 million from television). The Murdoch Group has a worldwide television network connected by satellite, notably comprising the fourth-ranking national American network FOX TV, the British encrypted BSkyB and the Star TV channel. After starting out as a small programming stream in Hong Kong, Star TV has grown to seven channels and is now the largest network in the Asia-Pacific region. It covers practically all of Asia, with a perimeter that includes Australia, China, Japan, Pakistan and even the Near and Middle East. The network includes news, sport and music channels, and has seen spectacular growth, particularly in South-East Asia and in India. Finally, Rupert Murdoch has announced his arrival in the near future in Japan with JSkyB, the United States with AS-KyB, and the United Kingdom with the launching in 1998 of a digital stream of 200 theme channels and services. The American operator Direct TV also has the same target, and is developing joint ventures with partners from different regions around the world.

In Latin America, the company intends to launch a stream of 142 channels, telecast in Spanish and Portuguese. After consolidating its presence in Asia, the operator intends to target the Japanese market in 1997 by going on-air with Superbird C, a stream of a hundred specialized theme channels. The company also intends to penetrate the African and Indian markets with the forthcoming launches of Direct TV India and Direct TV Africa. The French-language channel TV5 is also battling to gain planetary coverage by using four satellites: Eutelsat II-FI to cover the whole of the region from Helsinki to Casablanca, Statsionar 12 for the whole of the African continent, Anik El for North America and finally PanAmSati to reach Latin America and the Caribbean.

Since its start-up in January 1984, TV5 has operated continually in an associative French-language framework including the French-language Belgian Radio and Television Authority (RTBF), the Swiss Radio Broadcasting authority (SSR), France 2, France 3, the French National Audio-Visual Institute (INA), the Financial Broadcasting Authority (SOFIRAD) and the

Canada Quebec Television Consortium (CTQC) comprising the main broadcasters and producers in Quebec and Canada. The programmes on the channel basically comprise televised newscasts and magazines presented as the counterpoint to CNN, together with fiction, entertainment and theatrical and musical productions by the various French-language television channels. Another network with planetary status is the MTV music channel, which was launched in 1981 in the United States and has not ceased to expand since then It has consolidated its position in every region of the world with MTV Europe, MTV Asia, MTV Brazil. Mandarin MTV and MTV India. This regional fragmentation is part of the new strategy of the channel, which consists in adapting to the cultural conditions of each region. Also worth noting is the arrival of new channels specializing in financial news such as CNBC, Dow Jones, Bloomberg and Reuters, which are vying for position on the world money market.

Although the international circulation of televised programmes has always been dominated by the developed countries, notably in North America and in Europe, major changes are taking shape. The trend is towards enhanced co-operation and a somewhat timid balancing of the flow of communication. The international circulation of programmes is becoming less of a mismatch as a growing number of Latin American, Arab and Asian broadcasters launch their own satellite TV channels. In this field, the conventional North-South cleavage appears somewhat narrower in relation to the other gaps between regions or major language communities.

Asia, Latin America and the Middle East are asserting their presence and expressing a greater demand for news with a regional focus, while channels with international or regional status are developing and often competing with those of the Northern hemisphere. In Latin America, the Mexican broadcaster Televisa has invested more than $250 million in the Panamsat company to set up its own satellite TV channels. The Mexican operator provides a pay-per-view service in the United States and in Spain. In Argentina, the Canal Sur channel telecasts a selection of news and entertainment programmes representative of South America over both American continents. For the Arab world, the Middle East Broadcasting Centre (MBC) channel telecasts from London via Arabsat to the whole of the region. Funded essentially by Saudi Arabian capital, it is picked up every day from Morocco to Iran with a programme featuring news, entertainment, cinema and religious broadcasts.

News nevertheless remains the priority focus of the channel, with the recent acquisition of the UPI news agency networks and the modernization of the studios and the editorial department. MBC today is fully equipped for digital broadcasting, but that eventuality will be possible only with the launch of Arabsat 2.

Now that it has gone global, television displays whatever is happening around the planet, from the fall of the Berlin Wall to the massacre of Srebrenica or the genocide in Rwanda. It has become a bona fide worldwide counterculture that undermines totalitarian regimes and renders state control of content ever more difficult and illusory.

However, even if international television has enabled peoples that were previously deprived of images to open their windows onto the world, many feel concern about the power, the spirit of conquest and the scale of the networks, which have become nothing short of empires.

Regulation is a means of reconciling the economic interventionism of public authorities and the market forces in the audiovisual field. Domestic regulatory systems for the audiovisual sector feature a number of factors linked to the political, economic and cultural specifics of each country but also to economic and technological change around the world. The radical technological upheavals of the 1980s, combined with the expansion in television stations broadcasting by satellite and their increasingly international nature and structure, have caused major changes in the audiovisual field in every country. First of all they attacked the monopolies held by national broadcasting authorities which traditionally have always controlled the various functions of programme production, programming and broadcasting. Marketing and globalization have also brought the development of new markets with the emergence of private operators and that growth in their numbers, thereby undermining the conventional balance that existed between public and private sectors.

These changes have been further amplified by the new possibilities of transmission opened up by digital broadcasting, as well as by the emergence of multimedia groups against a backdrop of internationalized markets, and finally by the growing importance of private interests in the audiovisual field.

Faced with these new upheavals - which are likely to amplify during the course of the next few years - certain states have drafted a number of laws or taken decisions of a statutory nature. National contexts call for different strategies according to political traditions or patterns of media ownership. In countries where radio and television are a state monopoly, their management is generally controlled by the executive body, which governs the administration and guides decisions concerning the production and broadcasting of programmes. This structural concept tends to disappear as the democratic process evolves.

A public broadcasting authority is distinct from a state-controlled television service in that it enjoys editorial independence guaranteed by law and operates in a highly competitive environment. The state manages frequencies in order to prevent them from being used in an uncoordinated manner, and often supervises the financial management of the enterprise. On the other hand, regulation, wherever it exists, is controlled by independent authorities entrusted, according to the country in question, with regulating or supervising the programming activities of the private and public television operators. The authorities are generally placed outside the administrative hierarchy and are theoretically free from any judicial or political influence. Some are endowed with decision-making powers enabling them to organize the domestic audiovisual market-place and to control the legality of the conditions in which programmes are broadcast by private and public operators, and are even authorized to sanction occasional breaches of the law.

It would be difficult in a single chapter to quote all the texts issued by regulatory authorities or legislative bodies. It is possible, however, to highlight a number of systems and illustrate concerns common to them all.

Generally speaking, different countries have different approaches to the authority in charge of regulating the audiovisual and telecommunications industry. In some countries, there is a single statutory body. This is the case in the United States, where the 1934 Communication Act entrusted the regulation of the vast area of the telecommunications and audiovisual sectors to a single agency, the Federal Communication Commission (FCC). The FCC is responsible for frequency management, supervision of the telecommunication networks operators (prices, service quality, network interconnection, etc.) and regulation of international communications on behalf of the United States. The organization of statutory authorities in Canada is quite similar to that in the United States.

The regulatory body is the Canadian Radio-Television and Telecommunications Commission (CRTC), set up in 1961; its main assignment is to allocate radio and television frequencies and to define the operating conditions of each licence-holder, particularly with regard to the quotas of Canadian works broadcast and to the enhancement of domestic production. Since 1976, the CRTC has also monitored the telecommunications market, in which it strives to maintain a balance among the different operators. In Japan, the Ministry of Post and Telecommunications (MPT) is responsible for communications in the broad sense of the term, including postal services, telecommunications and broadcasting.

In Italy, the Bill presented by the Italian Government in July 1996 provided for the creation of a higher authority to supervise the audiovisual and telecommunications sectors. In other countries, the two branches of communication are governed separately, for example by the Office of Telecommunications (Oftel) and the Independent Television Commission (ITC) in the United Kingdom, or the Autorité de Regulation des Télécommunications (ART) and the Conseil Supérieur de l'Audiovisuel (CSA) in France. In practice, no country has a completely unified statutory structure, and it is only as a result of convergence pressures that attention is being brought to bear on the information and communication industry.

With the digital revolution and the convergence between the older industries such as the telephone and cable sectors, many conventional communication services, such as audiovisual services, can be routed through telecommunication networks. In some countries, cable operators can provide audiovisual and telephone services via the same physical medium. With the liberalization of telecommunications, new markets are developing and new operators are claiming the right to use competitor services on the same transmission system. The United States was the first country to take this change into account with the new telecommunications act adopted in February 1996, which completely opened up the communication industry to competition. The act enables the three major operators - long-distance telephone companies, local telephone companies (the seven Baby Bells) and cable operators - to compete in a general free market system.

Anti-trust laws have been introduced into national legislation. They usually place ceilings on shareholding in the capital of television channels. If a closer look is taken, however, and the legislation mentioned above is kept in mind, regulation in this area particularly in the United States 'and in Europe is more akin to deregulation than regulation of the audiovisual sector, a finding in keeping with the principle of liberalization which is characteristic of most countries nowadays. In the United States, the provisions of the 1984 Act on the concentration of operators on the American market have been slackened. The Act stipulated that no audiovisual consortium was allowed to reach more than 25 per cent of the American population, and it was out of the question to leave two stations on the same local market in the hands of a single owner. In the latest version of the law, the admissible percentage of the nationwide audience for all the stations controlled by a single owner was raised to 3 5 per cent (it is currently 25 per cent). The networks today are also authorized to have their own cable companies. In the United Kingdom, the Bill to amend the 1990 law which was submitted to Parliament in July 1996 came into force on 1 November the same year.

The new terms of the broadcasting Act relate to plurimedia ownership. They are intended to boost synergy between progress groups and local radio and television operations. Planned acquisitions have to be submitted for approval to the Radio Authority and the Independent Television Commission, whose task it is to see that the public interest rule is applied on the basis of diversity of opinions and programme content.

Many countries around the world have adopted rules that are both economic and cultural in their objective, forcing broadcasters to comply with quotas for programming and production of national works. By legislating on the quota question, states have sought to react to the consequences of the process of internationalization of the media on national television and film production and on the circulation of goods and services. In Canada, the regulations stipulate that 60 per cent of all programmes broadcast annually must be Canadian in origin, and 50 per cent of those broadcasts must be during prime time. On Radio Canada stations, a 60 per cent minimum of Canadian programmes must also be broadcast during prime time.

Canadian pay-TV stations have to allocate at least 20 per cent of their revenue to the production of Canadian programmes. In Lebanon, the audiovisual law adopted by the Lebanese Parliament in November 1994 stipulates that 40 per cent of all the programmes broadcast on national channels must be Lebanese in origin. In France, statutory requirements include quotas for broadcasting films and audiovisual production, conditions for telecasting films, advertising rules and regulations, the protection of children and adolescents, and due regard for the French language.

The effectiveness of these measures seems somewhat debatable, given the fact that viewers are free to watch other international channels if the domestic programmes do not suit their tastes, with the result that the ultimate effect of the measures may be diametrically opposed to their initial purpose. On the to allocate part of their resources to production may be a viable alternative to broadcasting quotas.

European regulations for the audiovisual field are based on the celebrated 'Television without Frontiers' directive of 1989. The purpose of the document was to co-ordinate certain provisions laid down by law, regulation or administrative action in member states of the Union concerning the pursuit of television broadcasting activities.

The most controversial aspect of the directive was the obligation for all European television channels to devote a majority of certain time-slots to broadcasting programmes of European origin. The requirement resulted in considerable disagreement during the drafting of the directive and in the somewhat thorny dealings with the United States during there trade talks of the Uruguay cycle at year-end 1993.

Compliance by TV channels with the above-mentioned obligation has yet to become the subject of any systematic monitoring, and this feature of the directive remains one of the main concerns for the industry professionals and legislators alike. The revision of the directive and its effects on the improvement of the circulation of European audiovisual works within member states of the European Union will be items on the agenda for the European Commission and Parliament in 1997.

While the 'Television without Frontiers' directive remains the key document in the audiovisual policy of the European Union, another White Paper on *Strategic Options to Strengthen the European Broadcasting Industry* was published in April 1994 and constitutes the basis for the current agenda, which aims to outline a community policy on these questions for the future.

5

Economic Change

This new technological paradigm affects every other branch of the economy, in terms of both its present and future employment and skill requirements, and its future market prospects. It has resulted in a drastic fall in costs, as well as vastly improved technical performance both within the electronic industry and outside it. This combination is relatively rare in the history of technology, but it means that microelectronics satisfies all the requirements for a Schumpeterian revolution in the economic system.

By contrast; the newer biotechnologies, although they certainly also have enormous future potential, have not yet reached the point where their macroeconomic impact could be great enough to carry the entire economy forward in the next decade or two. This illustrates the importance of the Mensch debate. It is the diffusion of the innovations of the 1950s, 1960s, and 1970s, rather than the first innovations of the 1980s, that must provide the main impetus for a new economic upswing. The new biotechnologies will provide very important auxiliary growth areas and will ultimately revolutionize agriculture, the food industry, and the chemical industry; but the main elements of the new technological paradigm for the fifth Kondratiev cannot come from this source.

Still less can nuclear technology play this role. Its applications are extremely limited. Its capital cost is astronomical, so that a large program would severely aggravate any capital shortage problems. Its cost advantages are even now dubious, and there are strong environmental, social, and political arguments for limiting its diffusion, especially in the case of the fast breeder reactor.

There are of course innumerable other types of technical change that affect particular processes and products, many of them important for individual industries. But our research, like that of similar work elsewhere, points unambiguously to the conclusion that the dominant new technological paradigm is associated with the combination of microelectronics, computers, telecommunications, and information technologies. This new paradigm may be loosely described as the "information revolution."

What are the implications of this revolution for investment and employment? We must emphasize at the outset that we have attached great importance in our research to the changing relationship between capital investment, output and employment. In most sectors of the economy we see the relationship between physical capital and employment as "clay" rather than "putty." In the course of the program we have attempted to develop a "vintage model" of the changing capital stock in each of the 40 main sectors distinguished in the Cambridge model of the British economy. This vintage model enables us to get some feeling for the potential future growth of employment in each sector on various alternative assumptions about the pattern of demand, future investment, technical change, and international technological competition.

From the evidence of past long waves of development, we assumed that there will be some tendency for the employment-generating effects of new technologies to be strongest in the early period of growth. At this stage there is little standardization of components or subsystems, and a specialized industry supplying capital goods has not yet developed. However, as growth accelerates, economies of scale, specialization, and standardization lead to a more capital-intensive pattern, and in the downswing of a Kondratiev cycle the pressure to reduce costs and combat the erosion of profit margins generates an increasingly job-displacing pattern of technical change.

Therefore we did *not* postulate (as many growth models do) an unchanging capital—output ratio. On the contrary, we expected that, as an industry grew and matured, there would be a tendency for capital productivity to decline. This tendency we expected to be associated with a diminishing increment of employment associated with each new vintage of investment. If these tendencies were general, then they could induce stagnation in the economy generally, via two mechanisms:

— diminishing marginal efficiency of capital leading to a slowdown of investment: this was the problem that Keynes described in the *General Theory*, but whereas he saw it as a secular trend, we see it as a cyclical problem, and not a permanent one;

— capital shortage problems in the sense that the rate of investment needed to generate a return to full employment could be so vast as to strain the resources of the capital market, even if the prospects of profit were good.

Both of these problems could be exacerbated by weaknesses in international technological competition, such as those experienced by the UK in the past 30 years. If they were not overcome or counteracted by social policies, such tendencies might generate conditions leading to a weak recovery and a prolonged period of mass unemployment as in the 1930s. In our empirical work, in relation to each of the major sectors of manufacturing and services, we have found confirmation of these tendencies.

Marginal capital productivity *has* been falling in most sectors of manufacturing for a fairly long time, and international comparisons indicate that this is by no means simply a UK problem, but a feature of the world economy. In the past experience of long waves, such tendencies in mature industries and sectors have been overcome on the one hand by structural change—i.e. a shift in the pattern of demand toward more labour- intensive sectors, with lower-than-average investment needs per unit of output—and on the other hand by major technical changes in various sectors of the economy, which brought about a rise in capital productivity, reversing the previous trend of the downswing of the long wave.

We certainly would not underestimate the importance of the remaining labour-intensive areas of employment in advanced economies. On the contrary, we would stress that there are certain types of services that are in principle rather labour-intensive, in the sense that direct human contact is the very essence of the service or activity. These include many types of caring and personal service, such as child care, psychiatric care, counselling services, many types of health care, and much education and training. They also include many types of creative work, including artistic, scientific, and craft activities.

The provision of these services has depended historically on a combination of growing public provision (usually on a non-profit basis) and voluntary part-time provision. The growth of such services is, we would maintain, one of the hallmarks of a civilized society; but for that growth to be sustained, and employment growth to continue in this area, it is essential to sustain high rates of productivity increase in the rest of the economy. The impetus to a major upswing of the economy could come in principle, as it has come in the past, from a major new technological paradigm.

Carlota Perez has pointed out that each of the major new technological paradigms has involved a drastic reduction in *costs*, so that it became managerial and engineering "common sense" to take advantage of the new technology in product and process design and in relation to all types of business decision-making. This occurred with respect to the fall in transport costs and in steel costs during the nineteenth century, and the fall in energy costs (especially oil) in the twentieth century. It is happening now with information technology and microelectronics.

It is essential, however, not to underestimate the vast scope of institutional change that is needed. It will involve enormous changes in the pattern of skills of the workforce and therefore in the education and training systems; in management and labour attitudes, in the pattern of industrial relations and worker participation; in working arrangements; in the pattern of consumer demand; in the conceptual framework of economists, accountants, and governments, and in social, political and legislative priorities. Perhaps the most important point is that "intangible" capital investment must now be recognized in its own right as more important than the transitory physical capital investment, which is today the main focus of attention for most managements, accountants, and economists. For a long time firms in the computer industry have devoted more resources to R&D, education and training, information services, design, and software development, than to physical capital investment. This balance will now be tilted even more toward intangible investment as the information systems available to firms, government departments, and other institutions are becoming their most critical resource.

This applies both to formal information systems and data banks and to the costs of developing, educating, and training the people involved. The scale of the change in skills and in occupations is still underestimated. Even in a period of high unemployment, there arc still persistent skill shortages for certain types of labour, particularly in relation to electronic engineering, software design, and systems analysis. In addition, there are many types of skilled people whose level of training and qualification is inadequate for the new types of work that they are being called upon to perform, or ought to be able to perform.

The information revolution also affects the whole climate and conduct of industrial relations. It makes possible the most sophisticated centralized type of "Big Brother" time and motion study, whether of sales workers in a supermarket or of miners operating an underground shearer-loader. But it also make possible a very high degree of decentralization, local responsibility, and initiative. Rosenbrock's work has shown the importance of designing production and management systems that leave a high degree of autonomy, responsibility, and skill with the workforce; otherwise the alienation effect of centralization and deskilling could generate social tensions even greater than those on the Tayloristic assembly line. Computerization will also facilitate the introduction of much greater flexibility in working hours. In many occupations flexi-time has already been introduced, and the scope for this will be increased.

Part-time work and work-sharing are likely to become more widespread. But here again, this social change can take a variety of different forms. It *could* be introduced as a means of depressing wage levels and of reducing social insurance benefits, if part-time workers are treated as a lower-grade type of labour. Or it could be introduced mainly as a response to the desire of many workers—male as well as female—at various stages in their working lives to work part-time, so that they can spend more time with young children, on pursuing education and training, or on other activities. The institutional framework for the fifth Kondratiev cycle is only now being shaped.

Most of our institutions and ideologies are still geared to the old technological paradigm of the fourth Kondratiev. Only through social and political debate and conflict shall we determine how we reshape our institutions and our way of life to match the potential of the new technology. The new pattern of employment that will emerge should be of a kind that encourages flexibility in hours of work and continuing education, and ensures to everyone who is seeking paid employment the opportunity to work in socially useful activity. This should mean a renewed commitment to the goal of "full employment," but in a new social context.

The disappearance of these barriers has resulted in the development of existing industries (consumer electronics, computer technology, video games, etc.) and the spawning of new services (electronic commerce and publishing, mobile communication, teleshopping, etc.). These changes have required major investment, underlining the industrial and commercial character of the media and the scale of financing they need. At the same time, the high cost of research and development has led companies to sign alliances setting up multimedia groups on a world scale, their aim being to obtain greater outlets on the international market. Worried by the potential loss of a substantial part of their own media capacity, states have set up authorities to supervise and regulate the market-place at national or regional levels. The present chapter discusses the salient trends of the communication market.

The move towards the information society is characterized by the general dematerialization of the market-place, a feature which has affected every economic sector and has resulted in new modes of economic exchange and corporate organization. It has freed the economy of the conventional constraints of distance and the scarcity of resources. Digital technology and data compression have produced means of creating information that can be multiplied to infinity, making the information economy one of abundance and profusion. Essential wealth no longer resides in the physical substrate on and with which information is conveyed, but in the growing production of paperless goods and in the development of know-how, which has itself become a strategic resource.

On the global information technology market, the value of software and services caught up with that of hardware as early as 1991 and exceeded it in 1992, with sales of almost $200 billion out of a total market worth $380 billion. By the year 2000 it is estimated that services will be worth more than $660 billion out of a total of $1,000 billion. This new development has enabled the program and software industry to overtake manufacturers of hardware.

The real added value is no longer held by computer constructors such as IBM or Compaq, but by the manufacturers of microprocessors and operating systems. Up to the present date, the computer industry has always been dominated by Intel, which supplies 80 per cent of all the microprocessors used around the world, and by Microsoft, which holds an identical market share in terms of operating systems (Windows 95, Windows NT, MS-DOS), hence the nickname of 'Wintel' often given to personal computers (PCs) today.

The operating systems of the one and the microprocessors of the other form the core of more than 80 per cent of the PCs sold around the world, and the two companies lie at the heart of the computer revolution. Microsoft, the creator of the MS-DOS operating system, is worth more on the stock market today than the American giant IBM. It is astonishingly powerful and financially profitable, with sales of approximately $4.6 billion and a net profit margin in the order of 25 per cent. It also has a major advantage: its domination of the program market for microcomputers - tools which are still an essential prerequisite for access to the Web. Since its launch in August 1995, the firm's latest generation of operating systems for general public microcomputers, Windows 95, has sold 25 million copies. Windows NT, the professional version of the system, has just become the world leader. Finally, Microsoft is the fourth-ranking publisher of CD-ROMs worldwide and is now launching projects for broadband operating systems, as well as the development of a programme navigation and guide system for interactive television. Intel, for its part, has become the driving force for growth and profit in the world of information technology. The enterprise, with net sales for 1995 skimming $20 billion, in 1996 announced a leap of 41 per cent in profits. Its turnover has increased every year by more than 30 per cent to reach $20.8 billion in 1996, with a net profit margin of 20 per cent. Financial analysts estimate that Intel will be soon the most profitable company on the planet, ahead of traditional industries, for example Shell or

General Motors. The qualitative level of the human resources in a country and the capacity of its citizens to use new technology and thus make optimum use of their know-how have become vital factors in competitiveness. The correlation between know-how and economic growth is henceforth an established fact. Development strategies around the world now invest in knowledge, education and training, as the new keys to success for modern economies.

At the heart of this movement lies the exponential development of software systems and services. Real added value is no longer contained in technology or production, but in the ways we use them both. This tendency is particularly noticeable when the situation of businesses in the communication sector, whose activities are exclusively paperless, is compared with that of companies producing hardware. Globally, software and services have superseded the manufacturers of computers and other technology in generating revenue, profits and capital gains.

In every country around the world, the demand for information in every form seems to be steadily increasing. The three sectors of the communications industry (telecommunications, information technology and audiovisual products and services) in 1994 totalled sales of $1,430 billion, or 5.9 per cent of the world's gross product. In other terms, for every $ 1,000 that the planet earns and spends, $59 are generated by the sectors of the communications industry. Its high-speed growth-is notably the result of constant demand from the Asia-Pacific region and Latin America.

The communication market can cover a relatively wide range of business activities, including new as well as conventional media: radio broadcasting, information technology, satellites, cable TV, cinema and many other related activities.

In the new audiovisual environment, the most immediate problem perhaps is competition from new forms of image distribution, linked to the development of digital television. The latter has introduced direct pay-per-view systems, thus creating an upheaval in the freedom of television enjoyed up to the present time by commercial advertising. In Europe, the audiovisual market is expanding at a sustained rate, on the order of 10 per cent per year.

Growth of this nature, 1 per cent higher than the world market rate, has every chance of being maintained with the start-up of ninety-eight new television channels in 1995. This increase in supply is the result of the development in European satellite capacity, with the launch in 1995 of the first services making use of digital technology, but also of the continuation of deregulation, notably in Central and Eastern Europe and in the Scandinavian countries. The growth is due to three factors: the expansion in cable TV infrastructures; the growing number of cable subscribers; the upswing in investment in television commercials; and finally the development of pay-per-view channels and the growth in their subscribers (+25 per cent). On the North American continent, pay services are also the driving force behind growth. According to the Institute de l'Audiovisuel et des Télécommunications en Europe (IDATE), 51 per cent of the turnover in the American audiovisual sector comes from pay television, whereas public TV no longer represents more than 40 per cent of the market.

The same trend can be seen in Asia and in Latin America, where the trend in the audiovisual sector is continuing towards direct financing by the consumer, thereby widening the gap with the logic of indirect financing generated by TV commercials or licence fees. One might question whether this new tendency is likely to marginalize general-interest television, but the facts indicate that mass-media broadcasting is far from being a thing of the past. Even if the TV market share has decreased sharply, the size of its audience is still enormous and its power of attraction still strong.

The television market worldwide seems to be based on hybrid forms of coexistence and financing combining the various forms of commercial advertising and direct payment systems. Another feature is the ongoing reconciliation between the cinema and television industries as well as the increasingly international nature of programmes. As a rule, the arrival of private general-interest or pay TV channels is accompanied by an increase in the television commercial market. This current expansion is taking place to the detriment of the advertising revenue for public television channels.

The first concerns the market for electronic components, the key to all technological innovation. Component performance characteristics (miniaturization and computing power) and the ongoing decline in their prices have boosted the market for electronic hardware.

The market for these components is also growing steadily wider with the digitization of every possible electronic product, with outlets in buoyant sectors such as telecommunications, computer technology and multimedia. American and Japanese companies are the leading manufacturers worldwide of electronic components. Since 1984, they have also dominated the professional and general consumer computer markets. The second change concerns the spectacular growth of the multimedia industry.

The health of the market is due to the expansion of the general consumer sector for hardware and products. In 1993, in the United States, the number of CD-ROM readers in homes outstripped the number of CD-ROMs in the workplace. Out of an estimated total installed base at that time of 7 million readers, 4.5

million were in homes and 2.5 million were in companies. From 1993 to 1994, product sales in the publishing sector no less than tripled, generating a growth rate in publishing turnover of 85 per cent, which rocketed to 186 per cent in the first quarter of 1995.

Since then, the computer manufacturers have, started to reposition themselves on the general consumer segment, an upheaval caused by the potential market of hundreds of millions of homes to be equipped in the coming years. The installed base worldwide of personal microcomputers (PCs) has, so to speak, exploded. 'According to the consultancy firm IDC, the European market grew by 7.1 per cent in 1996, thus placing it far behind the Middle East and Africa (20 per cent), the Russian Federation (17 per cent), the United States (21 per cent), China (25 per cent) and Japan (33 per cent). Professional estimates indicate that the world will have 250 million microcomputers at the world of the twenty-first century, with sales of 132 million microcomputers in the year 2000 alone, without counting portables or mainframes.

The market potential represents an annual sales figure of $264 billion in the year 2000 as against $148 billion in 1996 and $125 billion in 1995. This being said, the aforementioned developments in microcomputer technology are taking place in a high-risk market against a backdrop of intense competition.

Microcomputer technology has become a market in which volumes and economy of scale have become essential in order to compensate for decreasing prices and narrowing profit margins. To be profitable today in the microcomputer sector, a company has to sell at least 1 million machines per year. On top of this, ongoing technological changes, never-ending price wars to sell machines that become obsolete increasingly rapidly, and decreasing profit margins have made the microcomputer market vulnerable, and a reshuffle of the players and their cards is likely.

The weakest manufacturers are already winding up their ventures in computer technology. At the same time, other manufacturers are positioning themselves and taking the initiative in innovation, by creating new architectures capable of breathing new life into the multi-purpose microcomputer of the future, combining computer and television technologies.

The issue has more to do with preparing the machine of tomorrow, a user-friendly hybrid resulting from the convergence between television sets, computers and games consoles. All the major' manufacturers have realized the scale of this development and are preparing for a radical change in their end market. in this respect, the Japanese firms are proving to be unusually aggressive. The NEC group, which has a 20 per cent stake in the capital of Packard Bell, claims, with its new partner, second rank worldwide, with 4.2 million machines sold and net sales of $8 billion. The same offensive is being launched by the other Japanese constructors Fujitsu, Hitachi and Sony.

The Internet is a new distribution platform not only for value-added services but also for programs and multimedia works. It is a highly prosperous, new market with some 40 million users to date. In the United States, 11 per cent of American families are already subscribers to on-line services and 19 per cent have regularly used the Web over the course of the last twelve months. In Europe, according to the strategic survey published by the directorate in charge of electronic media for the European Commission (DG 13), service demand seems to make greater use of distribution over an Internet type of network than that via CD-ROM. In fact, these new market opportunities anticipate a major upheaval in the computer industry and foreshadow the impact that the Internet will have on the use of computers. They are all part of a technological, commercial and legal battle for the control of the Web, between computer technology and software majors such as Microsoft, IBM and Compaq and small innovative firms like Netscape for navigation software, or Sun Microsystem for Internet application development tools. The latter's success can be explained more by their aggressive strategy in relation to the dominant position of Microsoft and by their diversification policy, notably with respect to multimedia and Internet applications, than by their technological skills alone.

Faced with these new pretenders, the majors are changing strategy to adapt to the new shape of the computer market. Microsoft is henceforth preoccupied with network navigation-aid software, given the success of firms such as Nets-ape Communications and Sun Microsystem. The first of these two companies has become sector leader with a market share of almost 74 per cent gained with its program Navigator, a software system that has introduced new interfaces such as guidance and navigation instruments for users to find their way through the jungle of addresses on the Internet.

To counter the aims of Microsoft, the firm is striving to maintain its position and title by launching a new version of its Navigator program, that provides users with much wider possibilities for sound and video applications. The firm has also set up a subsidiary whose objective is to develop another version of Navigator to equip televisions as well as cellular telephones or games consoles. In 1997 Netscape also intends to launch a new browser called Communicator, with a small modular knowbot called Constellation. In addition to management of all the standard Net functions (Web, e-mail, newsgroups), the virtual, information-seeking robot will enable internauts to receive personalized information automatically, without having to make regular use of the module themselves.

In the near future this type of knowbot should be able to help people in all sorts of ways, whether to book a plane ticket at the best price, or to sort information in order to have a personalized daily review of the press. Microsoft, which only has a 4 per cent market share in this sector, is trying to make up for lost time by launching three versions of its Explorer software, a program equally capable of navigating through the information found on the hard disk of a computer and that found on the Web. The programs are integrated directly with software systems such as Windows or Microsoft Office and supplied free of charge to endusers. The strategy, aimed at increasing the sales of Windows-based software and operating systems, has not been welcomed by Netscape, and the company has filed a complaint with the American Department of Justice on the grounds of anti-trust practices. Informed sources report that Microsoft held a 28 per cent share of the global 'navigator' market in January 1996 as against only 4 per cent three months later.

The real potential, however, lies in conquering the promising Intranet market, i.e. the application of Internet tools to corporate in-house networks. In this area, Netscape seems to be a few lengths ahead of its competitors. Its software system Navigator 3.0 is apparently compatible with sixteen different types of operating systems, which is a powerful sales argument for companies that generally have a heterogeneous installed base of computers. In comparison, Microsoft's Explorer software can be used only with its own operating systems Windows 95 and Windows NT.

The second of the firms mentioned, Sun Microsystems, has been the first to launch into the supply of computers tailored to operating Centre servers on the Internet. The company is undeniably the current leader on the Internet, with a 56 per cent market share. It is developing new software systems of the Java-OS type, which enable applications to be distributed via the Internet and which work on any type of personal computer or operating system.

Even the players in the computer industry agree about the central role of the Internet and are framing strategies to make the most of this new revolution in the field. As early as June 1996, the IBM group focused its strategy on networking and the development of electronic commerce solutions. Today, all the PCs of the firm are equipped with the latest version of the navigation software system Netscape. The firm also provides on-line aid and direct links with a quantity of Web pages designed to attract a family audience.

The IBM Web site usually offers free software which can easily be downloaded with a simple click of the mouse. Hewlett Packard has similar aims, and has enabled its servers to carry out transactions as well as perform video retransmission. To do so, in May 1996 the firm signed an alliance with Netscape in order to sell the Web server and Netscape navigator in the software package supplied with each HP machine.

Apple, which is currently in economic difficulties, is fighting the same battle: the company is focusing its new strategy on the Internet by proposing an access that aims to be simple, efficient and inexpensive. The constructor is betting heavily on this card by launching the Pippin, a combined CD-ROM reader console and Internet terminal. Apple has also undertaken to integrate Internet functions on all of its machines.

The firm's new strategy breaks with the in-house policy of norms and standards. It is also militating for a policy of all-out reconciliation and partnerships, even with Microsoft, with which the constructor has signed an agreement whereby European users of the PowerMac, the top-of-the-range computer from Apple, will have access to Microsoft Office office-automation applications.

The telecommunications industry entails both the production of hardware and infrastructures (satellites, telephones, wireframe networks, corporate networks and personal radio communications) and the supply of services. It forms the basic infrastructure for any modem economy, as well as being an important link in all international exchange of goods and services. Over the course of the last decade, the telecommunications sector has been shaken by lightning technological changes and competition from powerful networks as a result of the convergence of computer technology, software publishing and the media. These developments have meant that the telecommunications industry has moved away from its conventional role of a public service providing telephone facilities alone, to become a branch of business generating new services and products considered to be key factors in international competitiveness and productivity.

The world telecommunications market boasts a very rapid growth rate projected to continue well beyond the year 2000. Estimated at $800 billion in 1996, it is expected to reach $1,200 billion by the year 2000. The sales figure for telephone lines approached $600 million in 1993 as against $575 million in 1992. On top of this should be added the figure of almost 34 million mobile telephone subscribers in 1994. The region of South-East Asia is seen as one of the strategic zones for telecommunications, a sector considered to be a priority in any development policy. Japan has the largest telecommunications market in Asia.

The penetration rate for telephones has increased by more than 30 per cent since 1984, with 61.7 million subscriber lines and a teledensity (the number of telephone lines per 100 inhabitants) of 49 per cent in 1995. Meanwhile, the digitization of the network is continuing and should be completed by year-end 1997. The Japanese market also serves as a benchmark for other countries in the region. The prospects in China are impressive, with a sector that is genuinely booming. Other development programmes of unprecedented scale have also been set up in Indonesia, the Philippines and Thailand, transforming the region into a battleground between the world's major manufacturers and the main exporters of telecommunications technology. National legislation to protect telecommunications monopolies is gradually being modified in every country. The movement and the philosophy behind it began in the middle of the 1970s in the United States.

The trend then spread to Japan, the United Kingdom and the rest of Europe. In 1997, the movement became global with the agreement signed in Geneva (on 15 February 1997) within the framework of the World Trade Organization (WTO). The agreement marks the gradual end of the monopoly in telecommunication services (telephone, service transmission, etc.). The signatories of the agreement together represent 90 per cent of a world market evaluated at $800 billion in 1996, with an annual growth rate of more than 10 per cent.

According to WTO experts, the complete opening of the market to competition should result in price cuts, benefiting consumers first and foremost, thereby spurring an upswing in growth in every country. In the industrialized countries, the trend has already had a positive effect on the growth of the sector and should make a significant contribution to improving the situation of employment. Africa, on the other hand, shows some sluggishness of growth in the telecommunications sector, no doubt due to the general slowdown of economic activity in the region.

The results recorded by Africa for the period between 1990 and 1995 were lower than those of the other developing regions. The main obstacles to the development of the telecommunications sector are connected with the cost of infrastructures, to their financing, to regulatory problems and to price policies. According to the International Telecommunication Union (ITU), investments of some $7 billion will be needed between now and the end of the century for sub-Saharan Africa to have one telephone line per 100 inhabitants. The information sector, considered to be one of high growth, has a high demand for personnel, although the impact on employment depends on the technology in question and the structure of the market. As a rule, employment is increasingly concentrated in the production of paperless goods and the supply of services. Between 1990 and 1995, the film industry generated 127,000 jobs in the United States - more than the car, pharmaceutical and hotel industries combined.

Hollywood nowadays is a bigger employer than all the manufacturers in the aerospace industry put together. Another noticeable trend is the creation of new jobs in services using new information technology, such as telecommuting and teleshopping. The potential for creating jobs in the information and communication technology sector lies in the use of the technology and not in its production, and in services rather than in industry; this explains the negative trend in employment in the industries that produce new technology, and the relative stagnation in employment among the industries that use new technology and the services that produce it, but the positive employment curve in the services that use the technology.

The environmental sector and non-trading services, particularly education, are also prime areas for creative applications of information and communication technology." The arrival of the networks and the explosion of the Internet, however, have seriously disrupted the organization of work and production. New services such as teleshopping could reduce employment in the conventional industries such as retailing, or result in transfers.

The time and money saved could be devoted to the purchase of products and services which in turn create jobs. When CDs and videos are accessible via on-line servers, all that users will have to do is select the digital file corresponding to the music or film that they wish to hear or watch. The CD or video production line will disappear to the benefit of other surrogaie areas.

The Internet, for instance, could disrupt the conventional software distribution circuits (software shops) by making it possible to distribute software as an on-line service. Remote companies are also being set up, structured as networks and focusing their capital outlay on information systems that form the basic toot of their business activities. Their operations are gradually being enhanced via a maze of collaborators interconnected by interactive networks that are modifying the ways in which people work everywhere.

At the dawn of the twenty-first century, telecommuting is developing in giant leaps. According to the International Labour Organisation (ILO), 7 million people telework full-time or part-time in the United States, with more than 1 million in the United Kingdom, 250,000 in Germany and 200,000 in France. At the heart of this trend lies a series of factors linked to the boom in paperless business, the development of global networking and the decrease in telecommunication costs. Technology no longer poses a problem: it is available, simple to use and relatively inexpensive. In theory there is nothing to stop properly equipped employees from putting their skills to good use hundreds of kilometres away from their company. Like all new technology, however, telecommuting is the subject of heated debate. Its proponents put forward a whole series of items in its favour: savings in travel costs and time, the tailoring of work to personal rhythms, reconciliation between business and the rural environment. Its critics, on the other hand, feel that it does not guarantee employees' social benefits, that it entails a risk of confusion between one's job and one's private life, and that employees have to make themselves more readily available, without any rea' recompense. They also feel that telecommuting eliminates not only manual work, but even certain professional jobs, those that can be replaced by expert systems or intelligent machines.

Others claim that telecommuting does not contribute to the continuing high rate of unemployment, but on the contrary provides an opportunity for new growth of the job market. Others again maintain that a telecommuting economy actually exists, encompassing not only the major corporations which are currently off-shoring, but also the clusters of professional micro-companies that analysts call the 'Soho' (Small Office Home Office) market, one with significant potential, since it comprises a large number of companies, usually with fewer than ten employees.

The various forms of telecommuting

— Telematic work at home or home automation.

— Work in a satellite centre, a delocalized micro-branch of a firm linked to it by telematics.

— Work in telepremises for different companies by independent telecommuters or by employees of the administrative body for the telepremises.

— Nomadic, mobile, itinerant telecommuting, such as sales representatives or technical sales executives in frequent telematic contact with their permanent base. Part-time telecommuting.

— Telecommuting based on teleservices from the home or telepremises (taking appointments for a doctor's surgery, telephone calls for prospecting services, company after-sales services, etc.).

Key figures

— 47 million: the current number of American telecommuters (occasionally working from home), according to the Link consultancy firm. If telecommuting is taken to mean a job in which the home is the main workplace, this figure is much smaller.

— 70 per cent of American companies have already set up some form of telecommuting (Source: Fortune Magazine).

— No more than 55 per cent of the active population in the United Kingdom work full-time inside a company.

— 10 million Europeans will be telecommuting between now and the year 2000 (DG XIII Objectives).

— 35 per cent of the French population say they are ready to try working at home, according to a poll carried out by *Télétravail Magazine* on a sample of 1,000 persons. The outlook is particularly attractive for those under 40 years of age. The main advantage anticipated is better management of working hours (44.5 per cent of sample).

— 7.5 million: the number of working hours lost by people in the Paris area every day in transport.

The globalization of economic activities has resulted in enhanced concentration in the communication sector, strong growth in the world market for new information technology and an acceleration in the development of electronic commerce.

The term refers to the consolidation of corporate positions through takeovers, mergers or alliances, or simply by absorption. It is inseparable from product diversification, of which it is also the financial result. Concentration is increasingly part of the overall process of globalization, involving cross-border investments aimed at acquiring shareholdings in companies in foreign countries. Globalization thus ensures return on initial capital outlay and increases market share.

As early as 1986, the Indian Government launched a development programme to set up a high-quality software industry targeting the world market. Today, the three leading Indian data-processing firms (CIVIC, Tata Consulting Services (TCS) and Tata Unisys Ltd) specialize in the production of software systems. Their rate of development is increasing virtually parallel to that of their installed base, and high-power growth is anticipated in the software market for the coming years. Exports rose from $114 million in 1990 to $351 million in 1994. With a population of more than 900 million inhabitants, India has labour available which is specialized, highly skilled and low-cost. These people are trained in the leading universities and polytechnic schools, from which 250,000 engineers and scientists graduate every year.

To boot, some 5,000 Indian engineers today are members of the research teams of Silicon Valley (California) and serve, on their return home, as intermediaries for setting up Indo-American joint ventures. This means that, given the quality of its computer engineers and the low cost of domestic production, India has become a 'target' for the major foreign groups of computer manufacturers and software publishers. It has also become a key site for service activities.

The scope of action in this sector in India is widening all the time, and the country has become easily the number one supplier of teleservices, with 400 companies and 20,000 programmers and computer engineers. Consortiums such as TCS (4,000 operators) have extremely serious references in computer project management (such as an electronic management system for a British bank, a management system for the administration of the port of Kuwait, etc.). Some of the most important companies in Switzerland, such as the Swissair airline company, financial institutions, and even the Swiss National Bank, have chosen to develop software in partnership with TCS. The company is currently engaged in nearly 500 projects in some forty different countries. Since 1987, its sales figure has more than tripled to more than 1 billion rupees, 80 per cent of which are generated by software exports.

Parallel to teleservices, another system has seen particularly high growth: 'body shopping', or the hire on-site of teams of computer engineers working several weeks abroad as part of a specific contract and at wages significantly lower than those paid to local staff. According to a report by the World Bank, the average monthly salary of a programmer in India is $225, compared with $600 in Singapore and $2,500 in the United States.

The starting salaries paid to Indian computer engineers are approximately 10 to 15 per cent of their American counterparts. In order to develop its software industry and attract customer companies, the Indian Government has set up technopoles such as 'Silicon Platform' in Bangalore, with proper infrastructures and international telecommunication links by satellite.

Companies that have set up in country, including Texas Instruments, Motorola, IBM, etc., benefit from tax breaks and customs duty exemptions on imports.

The Indian Institute of Science, reputed to be the best science university in the whole country, as well as various other institutes, trains specialists on-site in areas ranging from software systems to aeronautics. In all, the Bangalore technopole comprises 70,000 employees, 7,000 of whom are engineers working in high-technology sectors. Like the other sectors of the economy, that of the communication industry also bears the stamp of high corporate concentration, achieved by acquisitions, alliances or the start up of new companies to widen the scope of market penetration and business activities.

In the audiovisual field, as well as the press, publishing and leisure sectors, international conglomerates are emerging with the purpose of controlling not only the transmission system (manufacturing network, cable, satellite, etc.) but also the programmes they convey. The latter have become the key issue in the digital war. The boom in digital programme streams and the advent of information highways has led to the setting up of vast banks of programmes, precisely because these are the raw material which will supply the networks and generate most income on the audiovisual market.

The players in the communication industry have already made their calculations. Ted Turner, owner of CNN, has been buying out production studios, while Microsoft has been buying up the reproduction rights for museum pieces the world over for years. The fact is that film studios and museums are a valuable source of programmes for cultural and leisure applications. Other players are taking part in a frantic race of mergers and acquisitions of firms specializing in the media and in entertainment, Disney with ABC Capital

Cities, Westinghouse with CBS and Viacom with Paramount and Blockbuster). These alliances have resulted in the appearance of conglomerates such as News Corporation, Sony, Time Warner Inc., Finivest, Bertelsmann and Havas, which have reached scales previously unheard of in the media and leisure industries. The features they have in common are globalization, integration and 'critical mass'. The largest group is the giant Time Warner-TBS (Turner Broadcasting System) which, ahead of Disney/ABC-Capital cities and with sales of $20 billion in 1995, combines assets as varied as Time, Fortune and Sports Illustrated magazines, the cable-TV news channel CNN and Warner Bros film studios, not forgetting its music outlets and the Atlanta basketball team. Each of these divisions in itself also comprises a complete range of other companies, publications and professions.

The worldwide, diversified scale of the firm enables it today to generate approximately 25 per cent of its income outside the United States. By the year 2000, that percentage will have risen to 40 per cent. 19 Following its merger with ABC Capital Cities, Disney now tops the world list in the field of leisure. The American giant is active in three branches. The first of these combines cinema and audiovisual. It represents almost half of the turnover. The second branch consists of the theme park industry and represents one-third of all the activities.

Finally, the third branch comprises consumer products and by products (about 20 per cent of the turnover) commercialized in some 600 Disney outlets around the world. The media market is dominated by between five and eight major firms known as the 'World Companies', with other groups of regional or secondary status trailing far behind.

The creation of groups on scales such as these, with such high-power diversification, is an eloquent illustration of the major trends that characterize the media industry at the end of the twentieth century. In this sector, at least four groups in 1994 saw their sales climb over the $ 10 billion mark. Most of the top ten groups in the world today are diversified conglomerates. Of the top ten groups in the sector in 1994, five were American, three were Japanese, one was Dutch and one was German. Many of the major groups also obtain a large part of their earnings outside their country of origin.

In the field of telecommunications. the list of examples of concentration, particularly in the United States, has grown much longer since the law on the deregulation of telecommunications was passed by Congress in February 1996. The first deregulation in 1984 put an end to the monopoly of AT&T (founded by Graham Bell in the nineteenth century) by splitting it up into eight divisions, seven of which were 'Baby Bell' companies, each of which inherited a monopoly in a region of the United States, and an eighth, which kept the name of AT&T and its long-distance communication networks. With the adoption of the most recent law in 1996, legislators brought monopolies to an end in every sector of the telecommunications industry with an eye to greater competition between long-distance operators and regional firms in their respective markets which had hitherto been protected.

However, one year after the adoption of the law, competition is finding it hard to take hold. On the contrary, there is a trend towards concentration that appears to favour the monopoly of regional firms: SBC Communications, the biggest of the local telephone companies, grew out of the purchase of Pacific Telesis by Southwestern Bell.

Two other Baby Bells -Nynex and Bell Atlantic - are preparing a merger. In the view of some analysts these alliances foreshadow a return to the single-operator system as was the case with AT&T before the 'big bang'. Others hold that legislators will oppose any return to such a monopoly. Moreover, the attempted merger in June 1997 between AT&T, leader in national and international communications, and SBC was pronounced anticompetitive and contrary to the spirit of the 1996 telecommunications reform.

An even more important fact, however, is that worldwide deregulation of the telecommunications market has, for the first time, favoured the emergence of cartels with global status. The recent takeover of the American company MCI by BT (British Telecom) has rocked the telecommunication services industry by completely changing its scale. For the first time, a telephone operator will be able to exert strong pressure in the leading business areas around the world. BT, which will have control of the new group, baptized Concert, will be able not only to consolidate its position on a deregulated American market but also to strengthen its penetration of the Asian marketplace, considered to be the most buoyant sector for the future. In the takeover, in addition to its commercial aggressiveness, MCI will contribute its Internet know-how and a customer base of some 3,000 international firms, as well as its shareholding in the News Corporation multimedia group owned by Rupert Murdoch.

The new group now ranks fourth in the telecommunications sector, behind the Japanese company NTT, the American firm AT&T and the German firm Deutsch Telekom. With an annual sales figure of £25 billion and 43 million customers (professional and private) in seventy countries, the group forms a large-scale network more global in scope than any of its competitors.

The information technology market, including software, hardware and other communication products.

currently has the fastest growth rate in the world. In 1996 it represented $650 billion, equivalent to one-tenth of the gross domestic product of the United States. According to the statistics of the World Trade Organization (WTO), the market has expanded each year since 1990 by approximately 15 per cent, when the average growth rate for world trade in the same period was 8 per cent.

The rate of expansion is even more impressive given that prices are rapidly falling, particularly in the program sector and that of all the software tools serving the exponential growth of the Web. The heavyweights in the sector are American, with IBM, Motorola, Intel and Microsoft, or Asian, with NEC, Toshiba, Samsung and Acer, while the Europeans also have several majors, notably Philips, Siemens, Thomson and Alcatel. In terms of exports, Japan and the United States dominate international trade. In 1995, Japan exported some $106 billion-worth of goods, while the United States came close to $ 100 billion. The European Union arrived in third position with $57 billion, but this figure does not include trade inside the European Union.

Many Asian countries figure among the top ten exporters in the whole field of international trade, notably Singapore (fourth position), the Republic of Korea (fifth position), Malaysia and China. The ten leading exporters represent sales of $435 billion out of a total of $595 billion-worth of exports worldwide. A large number of developing countries, however, have trade deficits both in equipment and in services, and are hesitant about encouraging over-rapid deregulation of their foreign trade.

The information technology market saw the signing on 12 December 1996 of a free-trade agreement between the United States and the European Union, to come into effect between now and the year 2000. The purpose of the agreement, drafted as part of the first WTO ministerial conference, is to eliminate trade barriers on imports of computers, semiconductors, telecommunication equipment and integrated circuits.

The emergence of world networks has provided a genuine infrastructure for international trade. This has oriented the development of the industrialized countries towards a global information economy, based on the delocalization of companies and free trade. The very nature of the Web and its capacity for digital data transmission make the Internet a prime channel for trade in any paperless product or service.

The launch, for instance, of virtual telebanks without any branch office could well become the norm in the coming century. As a rule, any product that can be printed in an electronic medium book, newspaper, picture, video, etc.) can be sold and delivered instantaneously via the Internet. In 1995; electronic trading on the Web represented sales worth $0.5 billion, and close to $0.25 billion in the first quarter of 1996 alone. By the year 2000, the experts estimate the world market for electronic trade will be worth more than $7 billion. The difficulties connected with the novelty of the market and with its international character should not be underestimated, however. A number of quandaries still remain, notably with respect to the fiscal and legal status of these transactions.

The global explosion of the Internet has had repercussions in the corporate sector, and fostered the setting up of a new private network, baptized the 'Intranet. It is based on the use of the architecture and protocols of the Internet within a company. The result is a significant reduction in operating and telecommunication costs as well as an improvement in the flow of information.

The network knows no frontiers and enables the telecommunications costs of a company to be reduced by a factor of up to ten. Data transmission costs the price of a local call, no matter what volume of data is transmitted or the distance over which it is sent. When the transmission rates on the network have sufficiently increased, companies will be able to communicate in real time very cheaply by video conference.

Companies connected to the Intranet have a fantastic tool for trade, technology and competitor monitoring. A vast database on be efficiently used to monitor competitors and contact potential partners. Finally, the Intranet is an extremely powerful marketing tool, whereby not only can millions of potential consumers be contacted, but above all personalized dialogue can be set up with each of them, precisely targeting their requirements at extremely competitive cost.

With all these potential advantages, projects are multiplying in every company, no matter what their size, sector of activity or objectives. In 1996, more than 30,000 companies around the world were present on the Internet. Infatuation with the Web has led to a boom in the market for Intranet services and systems.

According to the Californian consultancy firm Zona Research, Intranet programs are currently outstripping the software systems developed for the Internet; in 1996 they represented a market worldwide of $2 billion, which should reach $8 billion by 1998. Finally, the Input company estimates that 75 per cent of the sales realized in 1996, either direct or indirect via the Internet, in fact concern the Intranet. This is no doubt what has motivated companies to find rapid solutions to the data security issues posed by the Internet in order to finalize the adaptation of the network to their in house needs.

7

Internet Revolution

The rapid development of communications on the Internet constitutes an extraordinary collective resource for the international community. However, over the past year several governments have come to consider that the network also represents a serious threat to public order. The dissemination of offensive material - relating to paedophilia, pornography, drug trafficking, the spreading of 'negationist' or pro-Nazi doctrines, and other deviant behaviours - is highlighted by certain politicians and pressure groups who draw attention to the fact that the freedom of the Internet knows no bounds.

For their part, the Internet's users consider that certain abuses and aberrations, relatively rare in proportion to the number of existing services, serve in fact as an alibi for those who wish to police freedom of expression and consequently to censor the Net. This means that politicians have their work cut out for them, all the more so in that the Internet continues to expand and to increase the number of services on offer such as radio broadcasts or, in the near future, television. In an effort to curb misuse of the network without hindering freedom of expression, states are attempting to set up concerted action bodies grouping service of civil society.

In Germany, for example, a federal prosecutor in Munich designated 200 news-groups whose material was deemed to be actionable under German law governing the dissemination of certain forms of pornography (in particular paedophilia). In November 1995, the Munich public prosecutor's office ordered a search to be made of the headquarters of the on-line service CompuServe Germany, in connection with which it launched a preliminary investigation for dissemination of obscene material.

The American company, caught in the act of disseminating pornography, was forced to ban access to its discussion forums by its 4 million clients in nearly 140 countries, on account of the technical impracticability of restricting this measure solely to its German subscribers. Finally, in January 1997, the charges against CompuServe Germany were dismissed.

On the other hand, a draft 'multimedia law' has been published whose objectives are to protect the private sphere, to create a system of certification for electronic transactions and to broaden the scope of the laws against pornography, revisionism, violent and racist literature, and incitement to prostitution in cyberspace. In the United States, the crackdown began, in 1995, with the arrest by the FBI of several individuals charged with trafficking in child pornography on 'the Net.

The same year, the Conservative Senator James Exon, leader of the anti-sex crusade, laid before the American Senate a Bill relating to 'communications decency' aimed at making it an offence to transmit any 'obscene or indecent' words on computer networks. In conjunction, eleven American states passed legislation restricting use of the Internet. Most of these laws were variants of the Exon amendment, and as such they targeted pornography and indecency. At the same time, the State of Georgia adopted a law instituting penal sanctions against not only pornographic material but also other types of material such as works infringing copyright and pirated works. On 8 February 1996, President Bill Clinton signed the new Bill on the deregulation of telecommunications in the United States, and thereby gave his approval, following that of the United States Senate and Congress, to the Communications Decency Act (CDA). This law limiting the dissemination of 'indecent' or 'patently offensive' texts or images on the Internet in order to protect children caused an outcry in the American Cyberspace community.

The American Civil Liberties Union (ACLU) and the American Library Association, assisted by associations representing computer publishing and the industry, took the matter before the Supreme Court which pronounced the Communications Decency Act unconstitutional on 26 June 1997. In its decision the court noted the particular nature of the network, being that of a public forum for the exchange of ideas and knowledge, and refuted any comparison with radio and television where the authorities may intervene if circumstances so warrant. In France, the debate began with the posting on the Internet, in January 1996, of the book Le grand secret by Dr Gubler on the illness of the former President of the French Republic, Francois Mitterrand, the sale of which had been banned.

The same year, the directors of the two main French companies providing access to the' Internet were charged with having disseminated paedophile materials and placed under investigation. On 18 June 1996, the law on the regulation of telecommunications was voted by the French Assembly. Two months later, an interministerial commission published its report on the Internet and proposed 'concrete measures and regulatory developments which, while strictly respecting the freedom of communication, would ensure maintenance of a satisfactory level of public order, notably in regard to young people and consumers'. Generally speaking, states recognize the economic and scientific usefulness of the Internet but continue to grapple with a question that is usually left unanswered: how to ensure that their countries benefit from the wealth of scientific knowledge and materials stored on the Internet while at the same time containing the drift towards pornography or racism.

It is equally true that the discussion forums on the Internet represent a form of opposition for some states. In order to contain such flows, the method proposed by the authorities consists either in monitoring all materials transmitted to subscribers or in banning undesirable sites. For example, in Singapore the authorities have set up programmes designed to block access to a number of Web sites and targeting in particular 'information liable to inflame political, religious or racial susceptibilities'.

Other, no less repressive, methods involve using filtering software to provide personalized access: veritable instruments of censorship serving to cover up certain affairs that are politically embarrassing for the city-state. Several governments are currently interested in systems of this kind. Bahrain, Saudi Arabia and the United Arab Emirates have already ordered software from American companies to enable them to block messages judged to be offensive to moral and traditional values.

The adoption of this series of laws triggered off a vast protest campaign throughout the world, led by numerous organizations concerned with human rights and freedom of expression as well as associations of Internet users. In the United States, the champions of freedom of speech rallied to protest against the Communications Decency Act. Such eminently respectable bodies as the American Civil Liberties Union (ACLU) and the Electronic Frontier Foundation (EFF) attacked the law on constitutional grounds, citing the First Amendment of the Constitution of the United States of 1791. At the same time, thousands of Web servers displayed their home page on a black background or ornamented with a small blue ribbon as a rallying sign of protest against the new law, and urged Internet users to inundate the White House and Congress with electronic messages of protest.

The same mobilization occurred in Japan around the Japanese Internet Association, which considered that the directives of the Bill had been adopted unilaterally, and were likely to lead to self-censorship if not censorship. In France, the various court rulings also sparked off a surge of solidarity among members of the Association Francaise des Professionnels d'Internet (AFPI), who launched a general boycott by deciding to deprive their subscribers of all discussion forums.

Moreover, the entire community of Internet users, from the Association des Utilisateurs d'Intemet (AUI) to the Association Francaise de la Télématique Multimedia (AFTEL), including numerous academics and deputies, condemned the speed with which the law on the regulation of telecommunications was adopted. Finally, in Germany, a similar protest movement led the government to abandon all forms of repression, and to opt instead for minimal regulation by putting the onus first and foremost on the operators and content providers to practise self- censorship.

The government has also stated its intention to curb the enthusiasms of certain Länder which are eager to extend to the Internet and on-line services the legislation in force in the broadcast media sector. Generally speaking, the different protests converge towards the same conviction: that freedom of speech on the Net can admit of no exception.

The measures taken to silence fascists of all persuasions or sexual perverts always backfire eventually, and democracy is the loser. It is better to tolerate their abuses and aberrations, for only at this price can the freedom of all be guaranteed. Moreover, as the Net becomes ever more complex, it will become increasingly difficult to silence anyone having access to a computer.

While it is true that authoritarian regimes have succeeded for several years in jamming international radio broadcasts, banning books, newspapers and satellite dishes, the use of centralized means to censor the Web is, in the view of Nicholas Negroponte, director of the Media Laboratory at MIT, doomed to failure - barring the use of terror tactics to reduce people to silence. Negroponte's conclusion is that 'there is no means of blocking access to all sites, since it is possible to move from "acceptable" pages to pages that are not, or else to use a cellular telephone to break through the barrier'.

Moreover, the efforts to control the Web are pathetically ineffective. This is demonstrated by the ease with which a censored site can spawn subsites. Scarcely had the Web site of Dr Gubler's unpublished (and banned) book been shut down than it became available on an increasing number of other servers, in Israel, the United States and the United Kingdom. Ike Godwin, a lawyer representing the Electronic Frontier Foundation, does not deny the need for some regulation, but criticizes the legislators for having adopted only criteria applied to radio and television. 'On the Internet, material is not sent to passive consumers in their homes . . .; what is legal in a bookshop or a library should be legal on the Internet'.

These different reactions in fact illustrate one of the fundamental misunderstandings that plague the Internet. It stems from the growing divergence between a community of users strongly marked by a culture that is profoundly hostile to all forms of public interference, and the public authorities, increasingly tempted to seek to monitor and even in certain cases to control the network.

National measures for regulating the Internet

Australia

— January 1996: Entry into force of a law on self-censorship by Internet service providers.

Canada

— April 1996: The Minister of Justice calls upon Canadians to express their views on the possible regulation of the portrayal of violence in the media, including on the Internet.

China

— June 1995: The Minister of Telecommunications announces that China intends to exercise control over the content of information circulated on the Internet.

— February 1996: The Bureau of Public Security makes it obligatory for Internet subscribers to register with the authorities within a period of thirty days.

Cuba

— October 1996: Havana is connected to the Internet. Individual access is, however, controlled by a commission of the Academy of Sciences.

European Union

— October 1996: The Commission puts forward

measures to ban the distribution on the Internet of pornographic material and other materials deemed to be illegal.

Germany

— July 1996: The Minister for the Family, Frau Nölte, calls for a commission to be set up in order to define international criteria for monitoring the content of material distributed on the Net.

— November 1995: On the order of the German Government, CompuServe shuts down a number of Internet sites in order to combat child pornography.

— January 1996: Deutsche Telekom blocks access to certain Internet sites containing anti-Semitic material.

— January 1997: Draft 'multimedia law' on the applicability to cyberspace of the laws against pornography, racism and revisionism.

Hong Kong

— March 1996: SuperNet, the country's leading Internet service provider, shuts down several servers containing pornographic material.

Japan

— February 1996: The Ministry of Industry and Foreign Trade publishes a report on the moral principles governing the management of computer networks.

— April 1996: The Police Department sets up a unit with responsibility for computer network security.

— October 1996: The government announces its intention to legislate against offences committed on the Internet.

Malaysia

— March 1996: The government announces its intention to set up a body whose task it will be to monitor the content of material available on the Net.

Philippines

— March 1996: Censorship measures are adopted to control the content of material transmitted on the Internet.

Republic of Korea

— October 1995: The government decides to institute censorship of software and video games available on computer networks.

— June 1996: The government bans access to Democratic People's Republic of Korea pages available on the Internet.

Singapore

— March 1996: The government announces a tightening of legislation on the control of material available on the Internet. (Compulsory use of filtering software, registration by Internet users with the Singapore Broadcasting Authority.)

— June 1996: The Singapore Broadcasting Authority announces that in future all Internet access providers must register with it and must ensure that no sexually explicit material is available on their networks.

— July 1996: The government imposes strict contractual obligations upon Internet access providers. All offenders are liable to lose their licences.

— South-East Asia

— March 1996: The member states of the Association of South-East Asian Nations (ASEAN) announce their intention to set up a regulatory body to deal with the new technologies.

Thailand

— February 1996: The National Electronics and Computer Technology Center (NECTEC), the official agency responsible for new technologies, calls upon Internet access providers to monitor the content of the material circulated on their servers.

Tunisia

— Agence Tunisie Internet (ATI) is assigned responsibility for operating the Internet. Any organization or company wishing to be connected must submit a request to ATI and fill out a special form for 'institutions'.

United Nations

— July 1995: Michael Parker Benton, British Rapporteur of the Committee on the Elimination of Racial Discrimination, proposes a draft resolution calling upon the United Nations General Assembly to canvass the views of an expert body on ways and means of controlling the misuse of global electronic communications networks in matters of incitement to racial hatred and pornography involving children. Not all the experts agree on the advisability of involving the United Nations in this matter, and it is accordingly decided to defer examination of a draft resolution to a forthcoming session.

United States

— February 1996: Entry into force of the Communications Decency Act (CDA). In protest, thousands of sites 'wear black' and launch the 'blue ribbon' campaign on behalf of freedom of expression on the Net.

— March 1996: The FBI secures for the first time a court authorization to put a tap on the Internet in order to track down an Argentinian hacker.

— June 1996: A Federal court in Philadelphia suspends application of the CDA. The Department of Justice appeals to the Supreme Court, which pronounces the CDA unconstitutional (26 June 1997).

— September 1996: The Governor of New York signs an order banning the circulation on the Internet of pornographic material aimed at children.

Viet Nam

— Beginning of 1996: The launching of a public Internet service planned for early 1996 is delayed for want of any form of control or regulation.

By and large, the high courts have ruled in favour of the champions of freedom of expression. In June 1996, a Philadelphia Federal Court declared the Communications Decency Act (CDA) to be unconstitutional, ruling that the Act, promulgated on 8 February 1996, constituted an infringement of the First Amendment to the Constitution, which guarantees freedom of speech, and of the Fifth Amendment relating to the rights of persons involved in criminal proceedings.

The court's ruling included the statement that 'the Internet has served to create the most open area of mass communication that this country - and indeed the world - has ever known.... Any regulation based on the content of communications, whatever its justification. would be in danger of destroying, in addition to its set target, the entire global village. In fact, the federal judges, not content with suspending the law, made a point of reasserting the higher principles incumbent upon the legislature in this matter: on the Internet as elsewhere, 'the strength of our liberty depends upon the chaos and cacophony of unfettered speech'.

The judges also dwelt on the terms indecent' and 'patently offensive' in regard to the cultural practices of contemporary America. In their opinion. the CDA would make it illegal to transmit via the Internet the play Angels in America. which tackles in extremely crude terms the subject of AIDS and homosexuality, despite the fact that it is performed every night on Broadway, and that a number of teachers recommend it to their under-age pupils.

The Department of Justice decided to appeal to the Supreme Court. According to observers, the Supreme Court judges will doubtless uphold the ruling of the Philadelphia Federal Court.

Invoking the need to protect this same freedom, the Paris Tribunal de Grande Instance rejected the petition of the Union des Etudiants Juifs de France (UEJF), which had brought charges against nine Internet access providers for having permitted the dissemination of 'negationist material on the network. Like his American counterparts, the French judge made a point of reiterating that freedom of speech is a fundamental value, of which judicial courts of law are the guardians. and which can be restricted only in specific hypothetical cases in accordance with strictly determined procedures .

Finally, on 23 July 1996, the Conseil Constitutionnel quashed the provisions of the recent law regulating telecommunications, known as the 'Fillon Amendment' whereby the Conseil Superieur de Telematique was to be given powers to issue recommendations in matters of professional ethics, infringement of which would make offenders liable to prosecution. Government measures have henceforth been limited to the obligation imposed on service providers to offer to their clients 'a technical device enabling them to restrict access to certain services or to select those services'.

Court prosecutions, no less than the quashing by the high courts of the lower courts' rulings, highlight the evident difficulties experienced by states in exercising some form of regulatory control over the network. They also raise a number of questions relating to the regulations governing the liability of Internet publishers and to other threats hanging over the Net.

The first issue is bound up with the determination of the legislature to regulate the Internet and other on-line services on the basis of the same regulatory principles as those established for broadcast services. On this level, however, the content of broadcast media productions is the responsibility of editors and directors whose authorizations to broadcast may be withdrawn in the event of any failure to comply with their obligations. This is not true of the Internet, where any individual, association or firm can set up a service hosted by a server without authorization and become, at any time and on their own initiative, a transmitter or receiver of information subject to no precise borders. Nor is it the case of the forums or newsgroups offering 'banned' visual material or information, which may violate national laws with total impunity. It is here, in fact, that the Internet's true challenge lies.

With its millions of interconnected computers, the network has become a gigantic global spiderweb, decentralized, and without frontiers or territorial regulations. Just as the censoring of national sites is a conceivable option, as happened in France with the

Minitel, so any attempt to attack international servers is bound to prove difficult and troublesome.

The list of newsgroups accessible on each computer emanates from other computers that Internauts can contact directly. In point of fact, the access providers operate solely as retailers, and do not influence in any way the content of newsgroups, to which each user can contribute anonymously. They highlight their status as 'carriers', and claim that it is strictly impossible to control or monitor the vast volume of information disseminated daily on their servers. In the case of both the United States and Europe, we are moving towards a situation in which the access providers who have performed a purely technical function will in principle be exonerated from all responsibility.

The draft multimedia law' in Germany illustrates this issue, since the Bill stipulates that access providers will be considered solely as carriers, and may not be held accountable for any actionable materials transiting through their networks unless they have been alerted thereto, and possess the 'technical capacity' to erase such data or to ban access to them. The second problem stems from the other threats, which curiously cause less of a furore but which are just as serious as those highlighted by the champions of regulation.

The rising tide of violence observed in television and other media programmes and in video games poses challenges for the public authorities which are undoubtedly more immediate and crucial than the existence of documents that, though offensive, are relatively few in number and generally not easily accessible to young people on the Internet. Other dangers concern, no less than materials of an offensive nature, the various abuses of which consumers may be victims in their on-line commercial dealings, and the possibilities of 'hijacking, or ,attacking' the servers of an enterprise or a government in order to damage its image.

The increasing intrusion of all types of players, in particular the hackers, those computer pirates who won fame in the United States by gaining access to the most confidential data of the Department of Defense and the American Central Bank and who recount their feats in newsgroups christened the '2600' forums, the threats of spying through interception of sensitive data circulating on the network, the deliberate destruction of software, or the transmission of viruses by the so-called 'crackers', are so many new developments that represent a grave danger alike to states, business and consumers.

How is freedom of speech, the cornerstone of every modem democracy, to be maintained while at the same time preventing the Net from becoming the Trojan horse for all abuses and threats? A wide-ranging debate has been launched throughout the world, and the strategies put forward all point in the direction of solutions of a technical, ethical and professional nature. Many countries take the view that freedom of speech and the protection of minors can be assured only through recourse to technical processes involving the use of filtering (so-called parental control) or encryption software, restrictions on which are currently being lifted.

Parental control software enables parents to select the sites which their children can access on the basis of their content. Parental control is regarded by on-line service providers as a means of escaping the responsibilities that weigh on them by shifting the onus to the users. Some forty companies and organizations, among them Microsoft, America Online, Netscape and CompuServe, have joined forces in order to launch the Platform for Internet Content Selection

(PICS). This scheme will enable each site to be labelled on the basis of a number of criteria (violence, sex, politics), with a rating system for each. It will then be for parents to 'programme' their children's computers so as to deny them access to sites regarded as undesirable.

Encryption techniques

These form part of the technologies for ensuring the security and confidentiality of information. They consist in sheltering information transmitted on the network from the prying eyes of possible industrial spies by encoding such material. In order to satisfy the concerns of enterprises as well as of ordinary citizens wishing to safeguard the confidentiality of their exchanges on the Internet, extremely powerful encryption software has been developed. This is in fact a sensitive and complex issue which is currently giving experts and decision-makers the world over much food for thought.

Governments fear that the dissemination of coding systems that are too powerful may contribute to the illegal activities of criminal or terrorist organizations. Accordingly they regard cryptography as a weapon of war which can be used only under the authorities' express control. Computer industrialists and economic agents are contending on the other hand for the use of encryption to be liberalized. They regard this as a basic tenet for the development of electronic business and company networks constructed on the Internet.

A shield for some, for others a dangerous weapon that threatens the security of states, encryption is being facilitated at present in virtually all the member countries of the Organisation for Economic Co-operation and Development (OECD). The United States is well ahead of other countries in this regard: although the debate on the issue was heated at the time of the Internet's birth, encryption software is at present freely available on the domestic market, but cannot in theory be exported.

However, the first exceptions to the rule are starting to appear thanks to the authorization granted to United States firms to export encryption software for the protection of financial dealings. In France, the law of 26 July 1996 on the regulation of telecommunications has for the first time authorized the encryption of messages, provided that the keys to the codes are deposited with organizations approved by the Office of the Prime Minister. Such a custodianship principle is the subject of discussion in many OECD countries.

While it is being called for by countries such as France, Germany, the United Kingdom and the United States, this principle is meeting with opposition from human rights protection groups fearful, among other things, that the principle may provide totalitarian rulers with the means of monitoring the electronic correspondence of dissidents. Broadly speaking, the OECD is in favour of liberalizing encryption. In March 1997, the organisation published seven recommendations concerning scrambling procedures regarded as essential if users are to place their trust in information and communication systems. In the Russian Federation, the situation appears to be more ambiguous, since there is a presidential decree banning encryption, while the Duma is reported to have voted in favour of total liberalization. Elsewhere, in particular in China and the Republic of Korea, encryption is strictly regulated.

Regulating Internet practices must be the work of the community of its users (access providers, operators, users, on-line services), whose task it is to define ethical rules that guarantee respect for the rights of the individual and the consumer. This method has the advantage of leading to a system based on voluntary participation and consensus, not one that is imposed by law.

The approach ties in with an increasingly used self-regulation process known as 'Netiquette', composed of unwritten rules of conduct that are adopted by all Internet users throughout the world. Indeed it is these users, in the majority researchers, engineers and academics, who over the past fifteen years have forged the Net's code of ethics, a code that engages first and foremost the responsibility of each user. The other players, such as the access providers, are tending increasingly to monitor the exchanges conducted in certain forums, and are reiterating their commitment to stop facilitating access to newsgroups whose names suggest that they harbour illegal documents.

The Internet's international dimension, combined with the challenge represented by the globalization of trade, naturally makes it imperative to develop appropriate international co-operation in order in particular to ensure that the decentralization of servers does not lead to national regulations being rendered null and void. Many states envisage setting up a legal framework specific to the Internet which would be based on the adoption of an international convention to be applied by the competent authorities of each country and enshrining a minimum number of common principles that could serve as the basis for a code of conduct. That framework would include a set of ethical principles applicable to Internet services, under the joint responsibility of the publishers and host services, and, finally, governing legal co-operation between countries.

Concurrently, different lines of inquiry and thinking are -being pursued within international agencies such as UNESCO and the International

Telecommunication Union (ITU). For its part, OECD set up in 1995 a number of workshops to think through issues relating to the information society and the Internet. The topics covered include the pricing of the network's services and the development of competition, as well as issues of professional ethics.

The goal is to finalize a common charter and have it signed by states by the end of 1997. Lastly, some countries consider that international consultation should take place within the Internet's own institutions, such as the Internet Law and Policy Task Force, which can create a common descriptive lexicon for Web services in order to make them easier to use with a view to ensuring respect for the regulations governing trademarks and athe permanence of electronic addres worldwide. In the view of many observers, an international legal framework is likely to present a number of ambiguities, particularly in the matter of agreeing at international level on the criteria for judging the reprehensible nature or otherwise of material distributed in field bound up with different conceptions of civilization. For example, is what is possible in the European context acceptable in certain Asian and Middle Eastern countries? For other observers, the idea of an additional body of universal legal norms specifically designed to protect the Internet would have the sole result of confining yet further an instrument of economic development and a tool for modernizing society in a 'legal gulag.'

The current debate is fuelled more by a desire to see the return of a moral order and perhaps by a fear of the future than by any coherent line of argument. According to the American association Human Rights Watch, 'horrors like negationism and paedophilia are combated not by censorship but by speech'. The same association adds: 'The battle between those who wish to impose norms and those who circumvent them is an age-old one. It is quite possible to comply with international legislation, particularly since it is wholly Utopian to think that one can control everything on the Internet. By definition, that is impossible, particularly since the legislators will find themselves grappling with a two-fold constraint: controlling information and having at their disposal an economic tool of communication'. It is therefore imperative, Philippe Quéau argues, that all freedom-loving citizens of the world should join forces in order to prevent any restriction on the free flow of ideas and images. Even if this obliges us to exercise greater vigilance as regards the education to be given to our children. . . . Freedom of speech is indivisible.

Cyber Crime

Banks often figure in computer crimes because of the increasing use of electronic funds transfer systems, which move huge sums of money among banks with electronic symbols as the only record. Banks are robbed in other ways, too. The American Institute of Certified Public Accountants (AICPA) has conducted one of the few scientific studies of the characteristics of computer crime. Of 85 bank cases studied to date, 13 involved fictitious loans, involved unauthorized lines of credit, and the rest involved various forms of transaction manipulation. Most of these crimes have not been of the spectacular variety, with 70 percent yielding less than $25,000. Computer criminals also favour insurance companies. In fact, one of the largest computer crimes so far discovered-totalling over $27 million, though actual losses may never be known-is the Equity Funding fraud. From 1965 to 1971, the company used its computer to write thousands of phony insurance policies, and then sold those policies to companies called reinsurers.

According to the AICPA study, other kinds of insurance computer crime include fictitious claims, fraudulent loans against customer policies, and the switching of addresses and cancelling of policies to gain premium refunds.

After theft of cash or assets, the next most common computer crime is stealing goods, since inventory items are often easily converted to cash. Falsified computer records can make it seem that goods were damaged and disposed of, shipped to a customer but returned, or simply missing. The Jerry Schneider case is a perfect example. He was an 18-year-old college student when he started stealing from Pacific Telephone, convincing the company's computer that the thefts were actually internal transactions.

Posing as a magazine reporter doing a story about Pacific Bell's parts-distribution system, Schneider learned that requests for parts come in via touch-tone telephones and that parts are delivered to any specified location. Now he was in business, entering daily orders and picking them up at various spots. He then sold the products through his company, Creative Telephone. However, an employee soon caught on, asked for a cut but was refused, and turned his boss in-but not before more than $1 million in phone equipment was stolen. The wealth of information stored in computers, which often has considerable value to business competitors, is another tempting target. For instance, a large computer manufacturer used a computer system to store records of machines ordered but not yet shipped.

Unfortunately, an employee with access to the computer system sold the information to another manufacturer. Thus, the competitor could approach a buyer and offer a similar system at lower cost and with an earlier delivery.

Information theft is destined to grow more troublesome as word processors replace typewriters in many offices. These systems are really small computers and are often connected to a company's central computer. Easy to operate, their potential for misuse is staggering. Typewriters do not store information when a report is finished-but with word processors, data stay in the system for future recall. Another common computer crime involves changing the information stored, often to induce a company to make decisions different from those it would ordinarily make. Such a crime occurred recently at a New York college that was automating its grade-reporting system. Students were hired for the monumental task-which required that earlier grades be key-punched onto computer cards-and some began a land-office business in making a C a B or even an A. Someone should have remembered that foxes shouldn't guard ,chicken coops.

Theft of computer time is also a perplexing problem. Although employees are often urged to use the computer, their use can become improper or excessive. For example, at most colleges computer time is thought of as a free good. Students and faculty often computerize mailing lists for their churches or fraternal organizations, which might be written off as good public relations. But use of the computer for private consulting projects without payment to the university is clearly improper. The picture is similar in business-management often looks the other way when employees play computer games or generate Snoopy calendars. But if this becomes excessive, the employee is "stealing" work time.

And computers can process only so many jobs at once: analysis of biorhythm charts and Uncle Harry's taxes could delay the company's payroll. Although considered less severe than other computer crimes, such activities can represent a major business loss. If a technical employee spends half an hour each day on the computer—which is not unusual—the cost in computer time is over $3000 per year, not including delays in normal processing operations.

Other events sometimes classified as computer crime include theft of programs (software is one of the fastest-growing segments of the industry), theft of computer components or even small terminals, and the destruction of an organization's computer system. For example, a University of Minnesota study indicates that, after only 4.8 days without computers, most companies cannot function properly. Computer destruction is generally due to an accidental event such as a fire or storm, but deliberate destruction has occurred.

It is tempting to liken computer criminals to other criminals; ascribing characteristics somehow different from "normal" individuals, but that is not the case. Donn Parker of SRI believes the computer criminal "often marches to the same drum as the potential victim but follows an unanticipated path." Many otherwise trustworthy employees have committed crimes after accidentally uncovering flaws in the computer system or gaps in the controls monitoring their activities.

If the payoff appears high enough, formerly honest individuals could easily succumb to such temptations. By analysing computer crime reports and interviewing those involved, Parker has compiled an interesting profile of the computer criminal. Such criminals tend to be relatively honest and in a position of trust; few would do anything to harm another human and most do not consider their crime to be truly dishonest. Most are male; women have tended to be accomplices, though of late they are becoming more aggressive.

Between the ages of 18 and 30, they are usually bright, eager, highly motivated, adventuresome, and willing to accept technical challenges. Actually, they sound like the type of person managers would most like to employ. Their positions range from data entry clerk to company president. While direct access to a computer terminal is helpful, they need only a job allowing them to generate data entered into the computer. And, perhaps ironically, most computer criminals who have been caught have-had no formal computer training; only a modest amount of knowledge seems necessary. They commit frauds in the areas they best understand: payroll clerks steal from payrolls, not from accounts receivable.

Asking how many ways a computer can be burgled is much like asking how many angels can dance on the head of a pin—just as you think you have heard them all, a new method appears. But criminals use certain methods repeatedly, though with many variations. Most common is taking advantage of a lack of control on certain types of transactions. For example, dormant bank accounts receive less attention than active accounts, being checked less often by auditors.

A branch manager at New York's Union Dime Savings Bank-who was also a compulsive gambler—knew this and used the computer to "borrow" from such accounts to pay gambling debts. In industry, if a data entry clerk learns that computerized inventory counts are never verified, the clerk could easily enter a lower figure and then take the items from inventor. A similar gambit is to take advantage of an error in a computer program. A "bug" can remain undetected for years, particularly if located in a set of rarely used instructions, and often is found only by chance.

For example, a benefits clerk entering incorrect data on a specific type of medical claim might uncover a program mistake. Although the clerk finds the error, the computer may not-and the clerk faces strong temptation to use the bug to file fraudulent claims. Deliberate changes in a computer program can lead to a variety of misdeeds. Sums that are difficult to monitor or unlikely to be questioned are easiest to manipulate. Checking account fees are in this category.

A bank employee could prepare a program that overcharges randomly selected accounts by a small amount (less than the cost of a postage stamp, for instance, to avoid customer complaints), netting a tidy sum for deposit in the employee's own account. Or, in an actual case, a company employee writing a program to generate annual w-2 statements included instructions to deduct $4 from everyone's federal taxes. He added the total to his own withheld tax' printed his w-2 with the incorrect amount, and received a massive refund from Uncle Sam. However, a janitor complained to the roll department that his w-2 was wrong, and the scheme was unravelled. The programmer's error was in thinking that no one would notice such a small error.

Program can be processed more than once to cover up schemes. Frequently a miscreant will write two programs for a given task, one correct and one fraudulent. After the fraudulent program has generated purchase orders, check of-other financial instruments easily converted to cash, the correct program is processed to cover up evidence of the additional transactions. Many of these frauds can be accomplished by manipulating the computer's "operating system"—basically, a program controlling all the other programs processed by the system.

Programmers who work with operating systems are called "systems programmers" and are assigned a master account number, much like a building superintendent with a key that opens everyone's apartment. If someone can gain control of a computer's operating system by obtaining a master account number, he or she can copy or change data, change programs as they are running and restore them after completion, or restrict access to various users. In the fall of 1980, for example, two teenagers programmed a home computer randomly to generate master account codes for De Paul University's computer. They reached the university computer by telephone, using a device called a "modem" that translates digital signals into analog signals suited for the phone lines. It does the reverse when the signal is returned from the computer. They succeeded after several thousand attempts (taking only a few seconds), and prevented the university from using the system for a week by changing all the master codes.

Computers can also be used as speedy "tools" to facilitate illegal or questionable activities. Several students from the California Institute of Technology wrote a program that churned out 1.2 million entries for a MacDonald's restaurant contest. Having nearly a third of the entries, they won the major prizes and many smaller prizes. What made this possible was the students' free and unlimited access to Caltech's computer and MacDonald's policy of allowing entries to be printed on plain paper. So the students' actual crime was theft of valuable computer time, although MacDonald's officials did not quite see it that way.

Another famous case depending on the speed of computers occurred at a Florida greyhound racetrack. To win a so-called "trifecta," betters must pick the exact order of the top three dogs. There are few winners, and the pay-offs run to several thousand dollars. The number of possible winning combinations is enormous, so the odds are not calculated until after all bets have been placed-and then only the winning payoff is made public.

Nearly every bank has armed guards, video monitors, tellers with alarm buttons, and numerous other security devices. A soft-drink distributor keeps delivery trucks fenced in, with a guard dog on night sentry duty. Why is it more difficult to rob a bank of $2500 than to steal millions from its computers? Why are trucks locked up when almost anyone can enter the soft-drink distributor's computer room?

While many people may not believe that access to computer centres is often easy, my experience proves this true. During a security consulting project at an Atlantic City hotel, I spent the evening with an associate in the casino. At about 11 pm we headed for our rooms, but the elevator stopped at the floor where the computer center was located and we decided to look around. The door marked "Computer Center-No Admittance" was locked but had a bell beside it. A computer operator opened the door when we rang, letting us in without a word. For the next ten minutes we wandered through the center without speaking to the operators on duty. Finally, we said "thank you" and left. They were lucky we were not disgruntled heavy losers!

Industrial security and bank security are fairly well understood, but computer security is not. History provides data from which to estimate the probability of a robbery occurring and the likely take, and this risk analysis shows the costs and benefits of using bank guards and sentry dogs.

However, computer-related crime data are not widely available, making risk analysis harder. How much is a customer mailing list worth to a competitor? How much damage would be done if the inventory file were altered? How likely is a computer crime? All good questions with no good answers. Because computer crime data are not standardized or gathered in a central repository, analysis of the statistics is difficult. Also, the complexity and variety of computer systems means that a risk-analysis method for one system might not work for another, so security programs must be designed specifically for each organization. Managers have contributed to the relative ease of computer crime as well—though certainly some do a good job in maintaining security—and controls over computer systems are generally weaker than in other areas of an organization.

When computers first became important in business, many managers did not understand them and gave free rein to the data-processing people. Computer professionals became enigmas, assumed to be doing a good job because operations proceeded faster. Managers also transferred this attitude to company auditors, who took the approach of auditing "around the computer." Transactions were carefully followed until they went into the computer and were picked up as they exited.

Too often, traditional auditing controls rigorously enforced in manual bookkeeping systems were either eliminated or weakened in favour of the computer's speed. Other standard checks, such as separation of employee duties, have also been forsaken in many firms, partly because the computer's efficiency eliminated the jobs. Fortunately, today more auditors are working "through the computer." These auditors-write programs that can trace transactions or use auditing software packages now available commercially. Such new software packages enable auditors to identify any operator who gains access to certain data during periods when those files are normally closed.

The programs can also detect employees with above-average overtime payments or highlight an abnormal number of correction entries, which often signal computer fraud. Most new auditors learn such skills, but they are playing catch-up since even the largest companies have only a handful of auditors who cannot be outsmarted by computer technicians. Some managers have resisted additional computer security control systems, considering them at odds with performance goals. Added controls might delay a computer's response by several seconds, and if 100,000 transactions are processed every day—such as at a large airline or bank—the extra delay per transaction becomes significant.

A manager must maintain daily production, develop new processing systems, plan future growth, and handle personnel matters. As a result, planning for the rare possibility that a computer crime might occur—and installing the necessary security controls—does not receive much attention. Finger-pointing often occurs, and a well-known "you're-to-blame" loop has developed in the industry. Users of computer services point to computer specialists to solve problems.

Computer people point to auditors, who point to computer management, who point to manufacturers. It's time to recognize that computer security is a management problem, and that only a coordinated effort will make computer crime more difficult.

Finally, computer crime prospers because of an underlying human trait. The perpetrator of a crime can tell a questioning customer, manager, or auditor that the computer must have made a mistake. Then the criminal can correct that transaction and continue with the fraud-since nearly everyone wants to believe that the computer is at fault.

Perhaps the biggest change in business computer systems is the move to distributed data processing. Computers were once so expensive that they were installed at a central site where all processing took place. Now the hardware is much cheaper and smaller, and computer terminals are distributed throughout an organization's various departments, electronically linked together and to a large central computer. Indeed, the number of terminals in the us has more than doubled in the past five years to over 3 million, and operators can gain access to central computer files through most remote terminals. With more processing sites, the problem of controlling computer access is faced many times rather than just once.

Users are physically closer to the equipment, offering greater opportunity for uncontrolled use. And each site needs qualified managers, operators, and programmers-professionals who are in short supply-so companies sometimes settle for less qualified individuals who do not understand or employ normal operating procedures. To control user access, the most common step has been to issue secret passwords. But this is far from foolproof: for example, once individuals have been granted access to the computer, they often have total access.

A rapidly growing market is now developing for access-control software systems that close such loopholes. This software restricts terminal users (identified by passwords) to only those files they are authorized to use, and users can perform only certain functions. What's needed is a system of checks and balances through the entire system: no programmer should test his or her own work; programmers should not operate equipment; and operators should not write programs.

The rapid increase in word processors and other components of the automated office, such as electronic mail and facsimile- transfer devices, also represent a security headache, since many of these devices are linked directly to a company's central computer. As chairperson of the Association of Computing Machinery's Special Interest Group on Security, Auditing, and Control, I have appointed a committee to organize a conference on office automation security issues. The conference is expected to draw participants presenting solutions to word processing security problems.

Another technological development prompting security worries is the anticipated growth of teleworking systems, in which employees work at home or at neighbourhood centers using terminals hooked electronically to a firm's central computer. Then of course there is the rapid growth of home computers, which can be used to tap into commercial data transmission lines. Five years ago just 1500 personal computers had been sold in the us: today that number is 500,000, and by the mid-1980s the total should hit 3 million. Wiretapping was once considered a remote possibility because of equipment costs, but Motorola now gives bankers a demonstration of how data lines can be tapped using simple equipment bought at any computer store.

There is also the worry of accidental data-transmission "cross-talk." Think of a telephone conversation in which you can hear others talking on the line: the same thing sometimes happens in data communication, and in this way one party can gain information belonging to another company without deliberate criminal effort. The communications industry has been working on this problem for years, but no solution is in sight.

To solve some of the security worries raised by distributed data processing and the transmission of electronic information, more emphasis is being placed on encryption or coding techniques. The National Bureau of Standards and IBM have developed the

Data Encryption Standard (DES), a mathematical model that can be implemented (via software or a microcomputer chip) into a coding device. Each DES user has a "key"—a list of 56 zeros and ones—that enables a message or data to be coded, and anyone who knows that key can decipher the information. So in banking, for example, a financial transaction is coded and transmitted to another bank's computer, which uses the key to produce the original message. Perhaps $400 billion is transferred each day around the nation using such systems.

All encryption schemes can be broken, however, and the work required to break a code depends largely on the length of the key. Supporters of DES claim that the effort required to learn the key, using a computer trial-and-error approach, is so great that no one would ever succeed. But some critics claim that the workload is not so great, and the payoff in cracking the encryption schemes for electronic funds transfer systems makes the effort worthwhile. One possible solution, Southern California, is method. Although safer, suggested by Leonard Adelman of the University of to use a newly developed "keyless" encryption the system requires that the message be transmitted three times, greatly increasing the work load associated with data transmission.

It seems likely that DES is adequate for virtually all the information transmitted electronically today. The problem is that few companies actually use such techniques because of what they perceive as high cost and difficult operation. But in reality DES hardware units cost less than $200, and coding a transaction requires no extra work since the unit does it automatically. In fact, all automated bank teller machines use these devices.

A computer criminal seldom goes to court and even less often goes to jail. Companies often do not prosecute, feeling that customers might react unfavourably to perceived security lapses and take their business elsewhere. Also, the current legal definition of certain crimes may not accurately cover computer fraud. For example, in conventional theft the item is physically removed from the victim.

Theft of computer information often involves copying the data but leaving the original tape or disk. Even when a fraud is suspected, gathering evidence is often difficult, and that evidence is not easily understood by a judge or jury. Because current laws are inadequate, much activity has been occurring in both state and federal legislatures. For example, Congress has been considering for several years the proposed Federal Computer Systems Protection Act, which calls for stiff penalties for computer crime.

Just before the Foreign Corrupt Practices Act was passed in 1978 to prevent American companies from bribing foreign officials, the Senate added a brief section requiring adequate controls on company accounting records. The Securities and Exchange Commission (SEC) has interpreted this legislation to mean that all SEC companies must have internal financial controls. If such controls are missing, top corporate officials are subject to prosecution and prison sentences. (Any company with publicly traded stock is subject to SEC review at any time.)

Since most companies use computers to keep their accounting records, this law seems directed primarily toward computer security. Other legislation protects computer data from criminal activities in certain industries or branches of the federal government. For example, the Food and Drug Administration regulates "how computer systems used in manufacturing, packing, and storing drug products should be operated and controlled." This regulation, directed at a single industry, has generally been effective. Computer professionals must take the lead in the drive to improve computer security. As each computerized system replaces a manual system, the potential criminal is provided another opportunity.

Programmers, systems analysts, and others developing new computer systems must be trained in company-sponsored or industry-sponsored programs on security control measures. More auditors with computer training are needed. Just as programmers need to understand controls, auditors need to understand programming, allowing them to participate in the development of new security systems. A healthy working relationship between programmers and auditors will go a long way toward solving the problem.

Computer users, soon to be nearly everyone in many organizations, must be instilled with a healthy respect for computers. They must understand the computer's potential and proper use, and training programs should stress that stealing with computers is no different from robbing the vault in person. Educational institutions should take similar steps, giving more attention to computer ethics, especially since more than 400,000 college students graduate each year with computer experience.

Some teachers now encourage students to break into the school's computer data base, under the misguided belief that this helps them better understand how the system operates. However, teachers can achieve this goal through more positive action. The overriding point is that the tools to stop most computer crimes are available. Encryption devices can be purchased, and security measures can be adapted from other industrial situations.

One hundred years ago, the few records that existed could tell us when a child was born, when a couple were married, when a man or woman died and what the boundaries of the land purchased by a family were. In those days, of course, only a handful of the American people went to college. Social security, income taxes, and life insurance did not exist. Three-quarters of the population was self-employed. Today, fewer than 5 percent of the American people work for themselves. And of the remaining 95 percent, almost half are employed by large corporations that collect detailed information about the education, health, family, and work habits of their employees.

Today, two out of three Americans have life insurance and nine out of ten are covered by health insurance plans. Insurance companies usually collect large amounts of information about their customers—revealing information such as whether they are seeing a psychiatrist, what drugs they use, and whether they have a drinking problem. Today, 60 million students are enrolled in schools and colleges that generally collect detailed personal and financial histories about both the student and his or her parents. The vast scale of information collected by government agencies, private corporations, and institutions such as hospitals and universities would not be possible without large centralized computers or, alternatively, linked series of smaller computers. It is also true, however, that some of these organizations did in fact collect some of this information before the computer. With armies of meticulous clerks, there were a few industries and a few countries like Germany and Chile that did compile massive handwritten records about the lives of an amazing number of people.

The computer, however, has powers well beyond that possessed by human scribes, no matter how numerous, and thus has fundamentally altered the nature of society's records. The first important change is that the computer mass-produces what has come to be called "transactional information," a new category of information that automatically documents the daily lives of almost every person in the US. Exactly when did you leave your home? Exactly when did she turn on the television? Exactly when did he deposit the check? Exactly when were the calls made from their telephone?

How many times have you driven your automobile? In the centuries before the computer, transactional information answering these kinds of questions was almost never collected. And in those very few instances where it was collected, it was not easily available for later inspection. With the computerized filing systems now available, the larger organizations of our society can easily collect and store this new kind of information. Equally important, they can combine it with automated dossiers containing the traditional kinds of information such as a person's age, place of birth, and the material contained in school and work records.

There is one more important development made possible by the computer: the incredible maze of electronic highways that can move the new and old information about the country in a matter of seconds at an astoundingly low cost. The automatic exchange of information between different data bases was not seriously considered in the first years of the computer age. But as the technology has become more subtle and sophisticated, it gradually is reducing the barriers between these giant repositories, increasing their ability to "talk" with each other. The contributions of these linked data bases to our daily lives are enormous.

The swift granting of lines of credit to a substantial number of American people would not be possible without the computerized data bases maintained by credit reporting companies like TRW and Equifax. The hundreds of millions of checks written each year by tens of millions of Americans could not be processed and cleared without the computerized data bases maintained by the separate banks and the Federal Reserve System. Easy movement about the US would be far harder without the computerized reservation systems of the airlines and car rental agencies.

The collection each year of nearly $500 billion in federal taxes from almost 100 million individuals and corporations would be extraordinarily difficult without the computerized data bases of the Internal Revenue Service and the large corporations who each year employ more and more Americans. There are a variety of reasons why understanding the true significance of all of these changes is very hard. First, there is the fundamental difficulty of putting anecdotal flesh on the bones of the abstract truth that information is power and that organizations increase their power by learning how to swiftly collect and comprehend bits and pieces of information.

This difficulty is greatly multiplied by the sheer force of the tools of the new information age: the machines that can locate a single item in a file of millions in the blink of an eye or that can swiftly develop statistical trends by massing these single items, and the communication links that can shuttle the collected information about the world at almost the speed of light. When thinking about the impact of these technical achievements, allow your mind to wander beyond the traditionally narrow boundaries of the computer debate.

Consider how the technology is altering the power of large organizations. Consider how the technology is affecting our social values such as the notion of checks and balances, the role of work, and the importance of spontaneity. Consider the far-reaching changes it is bringing to the nation's economy. What does it mean, for example, that the officials and clerks of the US government, each year armed with more and more computers, have collected 4 billion separate records about the people of the US, 17 items for each man, woman, and child in the country? What does it mean that an internal communications network serving just one multinational corporation now links more than 500 computers in over a 100 cities in 18 countries and has been growing at a rate of about one additional computer a week in recent years? What does it mean that 10,000 merchants all over the country are able to obtain a summary fact sheet about any one of 86 million individual Americans in a matter of three or four seconds from a single data base in southern California? What does it mean that a handful of federal agencies, not counting the Pentagon, have at least 3 separate telecommunication networks stretching all over the US?

Two of the world's largest and most complicated systems of linked data bases are controlled by the American Telephone and Telegraph Company and the Federal Bureau of Investigation. AT&T's gigantic network was deliberately developed by the company's scientists, engineers, and businessmen. The FBI system, which seeks to link the computerized data bases operated by a majority of the 50 states, has developed in a more haphazard fashion. Because the information-collecting and distributing systems of both the telephone company and the FBI began to function long before the birth of the computer, they illustrate the important point that the new tools of information processing usually are extensions of old bureaucracies, not shiny stand-alone machines that can be considered on their independent merit.

A second trait shared by these two very different systems is that neither has been subject to much outside scrutiny during much of their development. AT&T is a private company regulated by 50 state utility bodies of widely varying quality and a federal commission that never had the staff adequately to monitor the company's interstate operations. And very few congressional committees or state legislatures have taken the time or possess the perspective to consider the impact of the gradually growing network linking the FBI to the states.

Computers generate transactional information for many purposes and many organizations. They allow the construction of huge, speedy, and low-cost communication networks to transmit many different kinds of information to thousands of different customers. But the very different information processing systems developed by AT&T and the FBI provide clear examples of how transactional information and mass networks have enhanced the impact of these two pre-computer bureaucracies on all of our lives. First, consider AT&T. Through its millions of miles of cables, microwave highways, and satellite hookups, the American people make 500 million calls a day—four calls, on the average, for each of the nation's 130 million telephones. Thanks to the computerized data bases that are tied into this massive electronic network at a steadily increasing number of junctures, AT&T has become the largest single holder of transactional information in the world. Buried in the computers of the system are records that can be helpful in drawing an amazingly detailed portrait of any single person, group, or corporation that uses the telephone. The astounding power of these records is not appreciated by the public, the courts, or Congress. But for government and industry investigators, they have become an important tool.

A few years ago, for example, the Senate created a special committee to investigate a very sensitive and delicate subject, the relationship between President Carter's brother Billy and the government of Libya. After many months of embarrassed manoeuvring, the Democratic Senate committee issued a report on the antics of the brother of the Democratic president. Almost every other page of the committee's 109-page final report contains a footnote to the precise time and day of calls made by Billy Carter and his associates from at least ten different telephones operating in three different states.

The report said that on November 26, 1979, Billy Carter and an associate began driving to Washington from Georgia. Shortly after beginning the trip, the report said, the two men stopped to telephone the Libyan embassy and request a meeting with a high-ranking official. The assertion was supported by a footnote to telephone company records showing that "a five-minute call at 3:43 was charged to Billy Carter's telephone from [a pay telephone in] Jonesboro, an Atlanta suburb." Another footnote said that calls were made from Carter's office telephone in Georgia to the Libyan embassy in Washington "on March 7, March 10, four times on March 11, twice on March 12, three times on March 13, three times on March 14, March 15 and March 17." The investigations of the special Senate committee were publicly announced and the telephone records that document the report were obtained by a formal legal process. But this sometimes is not the case. One of the top officials in the Nixon White House, for example, claims that, shortly after the automobile accident that claimed the life of Mary Jo Kopechne in Martha's Vineyard, the White House political operatives ordered the FBI to obtain the telephone credit card records of Senator Edward Kennedy.

These records, which almost certainly would have revealed who and when Senator Kennedy called immediately after the accident, obviously would have been considered useful to those Nixon advisers who thought Kennedy was a likely opponent in the coming elections. Though reporters for the *New York Times* determined that the records in question disappeared from the files of New England Bell shortly after the accident, they never found documentary evidence confirming the account of a top Nixon lieutenant that they were obtained by the White House. Both the Billy Carter and Teddy Kennedy cases illustrate why investigators are so interested in transactional information.

First, the information can be extraordinarily revealing. Only considering the data that can be collected from a telephone computer, investigators can learn what numbers an individual has called, what time of day and day of the week the calls were made, the length of each conversation, and the number of times an incorrect number was dialled. Considered as a whole, such information can pinpoint the location of an individual at a particular moment, indicate his daily patterns of work and sleep, and even suggest his state of mind. The information also can indicate the friends, associates, business connections, and political activities of the targeted individual. But there is an even more fundamental consideration at stake. Almost by definition, transactional information is automatically collected and stored in the data bases of the telephone company, the electronic equipment of banks and the computers of two-way interactive television systems. This means that transactional information can be obtained months after the instance when the particular event that is documented by the records actually occurred. This ability greatly enlarges the scope of any investigator. Before the computer age, it was extremely hard to develop concrete evidence about the activities and whereabouts of an individual unless someone had been assigned to follow him.

In most cases, investigators were limited to pursuing the handful of individuals they believed might undertake a forbidden act in the future. Now they can move back in time, easily gathering concrete evidence about any person of interest long after the forbidden act occurred. The broad broom of transactional information, however, can sweep up much more than the highly revealing computer tracks of an individual citizen. In at least two instances, for example, evidence has recently come to light where this same kind of computerized information was used by AT&T to track the activities of several large corporations and even the ethnic and economic groups living in a single state. A significant characteristic of the transactional information collected by AT&T and other major computer systems is that its reach is universal.

Transactional information is collected and stored about the telephone use and banking habits of everyone who lives in America, rich and poor, ethical and unethical, white and black, Republican and Democrat. Though the information ultimately may cast a revealing light on the activities of a single individual, it is collected about the activities of all. The system of data bases that gradually are being linked by the computerized network of the FBI does not share this universal quality. Instead, it collects and distributes information about one segment of the population, the millions of Americans who are arrested each year in the US.

The story of the FBI system begins almost a hundred years ago, long before the birth of either the modem computer or the FBI. The occasion was a meeting of reform-minded policemen who decided the time had come to ask Congress to finance an agency in the federal government to maintain a central record of all American criminals. The policemen, who called themselves the National Chiefs of Police Union, argued that the prompt exchange of information about "criminals and criminal classes" made possible by such an agency would improve the ability of their separate departments to control crime. Nearly nine decades later, in the summer of 1981, a task force appointed by President Reagan's attorney general, William French Smith, acted to bring the original proposal in line with current technology: the panel endorsed a plan to have the FBI make a significant change in its existing communication system to speed up the exchange of the records of millions of people who are arrested each year all over the US. As was suggested by the police chiefs in St Louis, the Reagan administration's task force said the adoption of the proposal would help the government curb serious crime.

There is a good deal of plausibility in the belief of both the police chiefs at the turn of the century and the Reagan administration today that the swift exchange of summary information about an individual's past contacts with the criminal justice system will significantly improve the ability of the police, prosecutors, and judges to catch and punish criminals. Careful examination of the sources of information that lead a policeman to make an arrest or a judge to decide an appropriate sentence, however, suggests that the nearly instantaneous retrieval of criminal history records may be considerably less useful than is generally thought to the business of crime-fighting.

Furthermore, the gradual computerization of criminal history records in most of the states and the development of a single computerized network to link all these state and local data bases raise questions that go to the heart of democratic institutions of the US. So profound are these questions, in fact, that they have provided a handful of critical congressmen, working with communication experts of the Nixon, Ford, and Carter administrations, with the necessary weapons to stall the construction of the federal network for the last decade.

But now, with the blessing of the attorney general's Task Force on Violent Crime, plans to have such a network constructed by the FBI appear to be nearing fruition. Should the FBI get its way, the single most powerful law enforcement agency in the US will control a computerized network linking a system of data bases of almost unimagined size and complexity.

The impact of the information that would be transmitted through the vast maze of telephone lines, data bases, and computer terminals is of even greater concern than the network itself. When FBI officials call for the development of a bureau-controlled network to speed the exchange of criminal history records—rap sheets—most Americans assume the proposal is designed to reduce the chance that they or members of their family will be the victim of a hardened criminal, an experienced mugger, or a drug-crazed rapist.

But the reality of trying to control crime in America is much more ambiguous and complex than is sometimes suggested by advocates of a greatly enlarged computer network for the FBI. For example, only a small portion of the millions of traumatic events logged yearly into the criminal history records involve what are now called career criminals-professional murderers, robbers, and burglars who repeatedly prey on their victims. The sad truth is that many of the murderers and rapists who terrorize the American people are not marauding strangers. Instead they are wives who have been driven to kill their husbands in the dark heat of the night. They are uncles who have been asked to babysit for their young nieces. They are old acquaintances who fell to fighting at the end of an all-night bout of drinking.

An astoundingly large number of Americans have at one time or another been arrested. Because some individuals have records in more than one jurisdiction, and because millions of those with arrest records have subsequently died, it is not easy to estimate how many people have actually been arrested during the course of their lives. A recent authoritative study done for the Labour Department by Neal Miller, however, concludes that about one out of five living Americans has an arrest record somewhere in the US.

In the past few years, local, state, and federal law enforcement officials throughout the country have successfully argued that society should provide them with statewide and national computerized communication systems that can instantly inform a policeman on the street whether the individual he has just stopped is currently wanted on suspicion of committing a crime. These systems make sense from the standpoint of protecting both the patrolman who is making the stop and society at large from the possibility of further hurtful activities by the person who is being temporarily detained. But the acknowledged value of a hot-line system to Inform a patrolman that the person he has stopped *currently is* a suspect for another crime does not necessarily justify a parallel system informing the patrolman that his target was arrested for a crime in a distant city at some possibly *distant period of time.* The computer panders to the natural human instinct to desire more information about everything. But there are some law enforcement officials who question whether more arrest records are actually going to help them do their work. They contend that the value of the arrest record has been greatly diluted, partly because so many Americans have been arrested for so many significant causes that it is hard to separate the wheat from the chaff. They further believe the records are of questionable value because they frequently do not disclose whether the case was immediately dismissed, whether the defendant was found guilty or innocent, and what sentence, if any, was imposed. Beyond the pragmatic judgment about the utility of providing the patrolman instant access to arrest records, they see a larger ethical and constitutional question: do the American people want their police making arrests for *current* activities partly on basis of *past* behaviour?

> The idea that a national rap sheet system would make an important contribution to our work here is just a bunch of baloney. Our problem is not to find out who the guy is. Our biggest problem is, once we catch him coming out of a house with the goods, how do we keep him in jail and how do we make sure he stays in jail? If anything, we have over-information-oriented and over-computerized this department. These critical comments from the police are drawn from a 1981 report to the Office of Technology Assessment as part of a congressional effort to determine the impact—positive and negative—of the FBI's proposed system. This particular report was prepared by Dr Kenneth C. Laudon, a professor at New York's John Jay School of Criminal justice. During its preparation, Dr. Laudon interviewed over 140 experienced criminal justice officials working in four states and six cities. Dr Laudon found that the prosecutors and judges

he talked with were even more doubtful about the utility of the FBI plan than the police.

The complaints of the policemen, prosecutors, and judges interviewed by Dr Laudon went well beyond simply questioning the utility of a summary record that has been lifted out of its original legal and social context. Over and over again, the users complained that the records being moved along the experimental criminal history segment of the FBI's communication network were incomplete and inaccurate.

The subjective judgments of the police officials, prosecutors, and judges about the poor quality of the information was supported by a second investigation undertaken by Congress's Office of Technology Assessment. For this second study, the OTA arranged for Dr Laudon to obtain access to a random sample of the criminal history records that recently had been dispatched to law enforcement and other agencies from five official repositories maintained and operated by three separate states and the FBI.

The information in the records from the repositories was then compared with the information in the original records in files of the county courthouses. Procedures were followed that permitted the comparative analysis without disclosing individual names. The findings are surprising. In North Carolina only 12.2 percent of the summaries were found to be complete, accurate, and unambiguous. In California 18.9 percent were complete, accurate, and unambiguous. In Minnesota the researchers found almost half the sample—49.5 percent—met the same standards. The quality of the FBI files, which of course rests on the information submitted by the 50 states, was not noticeably better. Based on a random sample of 400 records dispatched by the Identification Division during a single week in August of 1978, Dr

Laudon found that 25.7 percent of the FBI rap sheets met the standards suggested by federal law. Assuming the one week sample was valid for the entire year, the OTA study suggests that 1.75 million of the 2.35 million records sent by the FBI to criminal justice and other institutions all over the country had various failings.

The quality of the much smaller number of records disseminated by the Computerized Criminal History segment of the FBI's National Crime Information Center was somewhat better than that of the Identification Division rap sheets. In the computerized system, the comparison of the sample summary and the original records disclosed that 45.9 percent were complete, accurate, and unambiguous. At the request of OTA, Dr Laudon also checked a sample of 400 arrest warrants from the 127,000 contained in the FBI's "hot file" on a single day in August of 1979. Upon comparing the information on the FBI's warrant notices with the information in the local court records, he found that 10.9 percent of the sample already had been cleared or vacated, 4.1 percent showed no record of the warrant at the local agency, and a small additional number of warrants had other problems. Again, assuming the validity of the sample, it appears that on that single day in 1979, 17,340 Americans were subject to false arrest because the FBI computer incorrectly showed they were wanted when the warrants in question had been cleared or vacated.

Official records, of course, were subject to improper use long before the computer became an important part of every major public and private bureaucracy in the US. But an executive in a New York state agency explained how the computer has enlarged the opportunity to abuse. "Technology may not be the only villain, but it is one villain," the official said. "Before high technology, you could actually control information better; at least, it could not spread very far because it was impractical to transmit it. With the computer system, you can't control it any more, largely because of the automatic interfacing of the system, which makes it difficult for even us to know who's getting our information."

The Office of Technology Assessment asked a team at the Bureau of Governmental Research and Service at the University of South Carolina to try to determine exactly who was now receiving criminal history information and to assess the social impacts of computerizing these histories. According to the South Carolina researchers—Lynne Eickholt Cooper, Mark E. Tompkins, and Donald A. Marchand—the use of criminal records outside the traditional confines of the criminal justice system is enormous and growing.

All applicants for federal positions, all military recruits, many of the hundreds of thousands of citizens working for private contractors who are doing jobs for the federal government, and all new employees of federally chartered and insured banks are among the millions of persons who have long been subject to criminal history record checks for many years, the researcher reported.

In addition, with the recent growth in the number of states and cities requiring licenses and permits for almost any kind of job, the population subject to criminal record checks has further exploded. At the last count, more than 7 million Americans must obtain licenses to earn their living. In California, for example, 47 separate licensing boards, 50 state agencies, and 32 out-of-state agencies have access to the criminal history records stored in the state's computerized record system. In New York the use of criminal records by law enforcement agencies has declined in recent years, while its use by private employers has gone up.

Through a variety of federal and state laws, society has made the collective decision that individuals *convicted* of certain crimes may be properly denied certain privileges. Sometimes such individuals lose the right to vote. Sometimes they may not run for public office. Sometimes they are prohibited from bidding on government contracts. The US also pays a good deal of lip service to the principle that an arrest or investigation, *without a conviction*, should not be sufficient grounds to deny an individual an honourable place in the job market. In late 1981, President Reagan provided an eloquent testimonial to this principle when asked why he had not asked three officials in his administration to remove themselves from office after they were accused of illegal activities.

The three men were Labour secretary Raymond Donovan, CIA director William Casey, and National Security Council director Richard Allen.

"I believe in the fairness of the American people, and I believe that in recent years there has been a very dangerous tendency in this country for some to jump to the conclusion that accusation means guilt and conviction," Mr Reagan told reporters. "And I think it is high time we recognize that any individual is innocent until proven guilty of a wrongdoing, and that's what we are going to do."

Mr Reagan's eloquent statement has considerable backing in the laws and regulations of the US. The Civil Service Reform Act of 1978 includes a provision limiting federal suitability checks to conviction records, and only for those crimes that are reasonably related to job performance. Three states have laws explicitly barring employer discrimination against ex-offenders. Many state and local human relations offices have issued rules barring private employers from requesting arrest information and limiting the use of conviction information.

Despite the various restrictions, however, there is considerable evidence that the president's policy for the high officials of his administration frequently does not obtain for the average job hunter. According to one congressional survey, for example, the 50 states handed out a total of 10.1 million criminal history records in 1978. Two million of the records—one out of five—went to private corporations and government agencies that were not part of the criminal history system.

The Labour Department study that concluded that 40 million Americans have an arrest record also estimated that just Under 26 million of them were in the job market. With so many people applying for so many different jobs, it is nearly impossible to generalize about the impact of criminal records on their lives. Certainly, the bank is on solid ground when it decides not to hire a convicted bank robber. Certainly, no one would argue about a hospital personnel director who decides not to hire a convicted narcotics dealer.

But there is good evidence that some employers assume that any kind of record, no matter what the offence, no matter what the outcome, is a powerful mark against the individual. More than a decade ago, two sociologists named Richard Schwartz and Jerome Skolnick attempted to measure this kind of bias in an experiment in which a number of employers were shown the employment folders submitted by 100 men who were looking for a menial job in the Catskill area of New York. The applicants were broken down into four groups. The first group had no criminal records. The second group had been arrested for assault and acquitted of the charge with a letter from the judge explaining the presumption of innocence. The third had been arrested for assault and acquitted, but there was no letter from the judge. The fourth group had been convicted.

The employers were asked whether they would be willing to offer the individuals in each group a job. Thirty-six percent said they would hire the men with no record, 24 percent said they would hire the men who had been acquitted and had a letter from the judge, 12 percent said they would hire the men who had been acquitted but had no letter, and 4 percent said they would hire the men who had been convicted. The findings of this simple study, replicated in a number of subsequent research projects, are a dramatic illustration of the powerful impact of a criminal record, even if the individual under consideration has been acquitted.

The implications of these findings—when considered in terms of the number of Americans with records and the accuracy and completeness of these records—are staggering. Computerized records being rocketed around the country would be a greater help to the police and less damaging to the public if they were accurate and complete. In the pursuit of this worthy goal, after failing to reach a compromise on comprehensive legislation to govern the NCIC, Congress adopted a brief amendment to the Crime Control Act of 1973.

The 139-word amendment, which all parties regarded as an interim measure, contained three very simple principles. First, to the maximum extent feasible, criminal history information disseminated with the help of federal funds should contain disposition, as well as arrest data. Second, procedures would be adopted to require that the information is kept current. Third, the information would be used for law enforcement, criminal justice, and "other lawful purposes." As already noted, the exception for other lawful purpose has become something of a gusher.

The 1973 amendment also offered the citizen an apparent remedy. "An individual who believes that criminal information concerning him in an automated system is inaccurate, incomplete, or maintained in violation of this title, shall upon satisfactory verification of his identity, be entitled to review such information and to obtain a copy of it for the purpose of challenge or correction." Almost three years later, the government followed up on the 1973 amendment by issuing a vaguely worded regulation that nominally required the states to develop policies and procedures to ensure the privacy and security of criminal history records. Individual access and review was one of five specific areas the federal government said the states must cover in their regulations.

Ever since the computer became a major force in the administration of large government and business organizations in the mid-1960s, the individual's right to see and correct his own computerized record has been held up as a miracle cure for many of the potential abuses of the computer age. Alan F. Westin, in his pioneering 1967 book *Privacy and Freedom*, was among the first to find wonderful powers in the cure of public access. The principle was subsequently embraced by both the Privacy Act of 1973 and the 1977 report of the Privacy Protection Study Commission.

But the OTA report indicating that more than half of the millions of criminal history records now circulating in the US are incomplete, inaccurate, or ambiguous is compelling evidence that the remedies prescribed by law and regulation are not every effective. And when the congressional researchers looked at the actual record-keeping practices of four states and six urban areas, they found strong evidence that the promises made in the 1973 Crime Control Act amendment are largely an illusion.

The California criminal justice system, for example, contains more than 3 million records, 1.1 million of which are in computers, the balance in manual files. In a recent year, authorized organizations made 5 million separate inquiries of the system. Despite the huge number of transactions, however, the researchers discovered that only 300-400 individuals each year ask to see their records, 80 find something they regard as incorrect, and 40 are actually successful in forcing California to make a correction.

A second approach to assuring accurate records is to require that the record-keepers periodically check their files and dump those that are inaccurate or incomplete. The government, at least in theory, adopted this alternative approach in 1976 when it required that all the states develop plans for regularly auditing and purging their criminal history files.

In 1980 the Office of Technology Assessment sent a questionnaire to the 50 states about how they managed their criminal history records. One question was whether they checked the accuracy of the records in their files. Four out of five of the 49 states answering this question responded that they had never conducted record quality audits. So much for federal regulations.

The astounding finding that only one out of five states has ever sought to audit and purge the information in its criminal history files may explain why so many of the records are inaccurate or incomplete. It also demonstrates how difficult it is for the federal government to force state and local agencies to meet a standard established by Congress.

Computer scientists and manufacturers purport to believe that their machines are neutral. This is true, of course, as long as the technology remains in the showroom. The neutrality evaporates, however, when powerful officials running powerful bureaucracies harness the computers to achieve their collective goals. Often both the goals and methods of achieving them are in the public interest. History tells us, however, that the organizations of fallible men sometimes lose their way. During the 1960s and 1970s the leadership of the FBI and a number of police departments throughout the country came to believe that their responsibilities went beyond arresting those who had committed criminal acts.

Their job, some policemen thought, extended to trying to channel the political thoughts and lifestyles of the American people along certain narrow paths. Police departments in such cities as Chicago and Los Angeles enormously expanded their surveillance of individuals who did not share conventional police values. The US Army ordered its intelligence agents to attend all sorts of political rallies. The FBI, with the explicit approval of J. Edgar Hoover, undertook a secret program in which it deliberately sought to have critics of the federal government fired from their jobs or otherwise discredited by mailing false and anonymous reports to their neighbours and colleagues.

The FBI's effort to expand its activities beyond the precise boundaries of criminal law did not stop with the anonymous smearing of thousands of Americans who did not happen to share Mr Hoover's view of the universe. From 1971 to 1974 the FBI harnessed the computerized data bases of the

National Crime Information Center to pick up the movements of persons who were not criminal suspects.

Under the public relations establishing the NCIC and how it would operate, the FBI declared that only the names of persons who had been formally charged with a crime would be listed in the NCIC computer. In July of 1975, however, John Tunney, then chairman of the Senate Subcommittee on Constitutional Rights, announced the discovery that the Bureau had violated its own regulations by using the NCIC "to keep track of individuals who might be of interest to the FBI for whatever purpose, including possible political reasons."

Three months later, the justice Department confirmed that from 1971 to 1974 the FBI had instructed its NCIC's computers to sound an alarm any time a local law enforcement agency sent a message to Washington indicating that any one of 4700 individuals was arrested. When it is remembered what a large part of the population have arrest records, and how many persons were being arrested during that particular period for taking part in civil rights and antiwar demonstrations, the automated flagging mechanism can be viewed as a potentially powerful surveillance device.

One indication of how embarrassed the justice Department was about the FBI's secret operation of a surveillance system outside the limits set down in its own regulation was the way the project was abruptly halted on the precise day that the Senate subcommittee staff made its first inquiry. But seven years later, there are indications that the FBI and other law enforcement agencies of the Reagan administration would like to resurrect the use of the NCIC computers to track persons who are not the subject of a formal arrest warrant.

The first hint of this possible shift in NCIC policy came at a meeting of the NCIC advisory board in June of 1980 in a talk by Kier T. Boyd, an FBI inspector and the deputy assistant director of that part of the bureau that controls the FBI's very large computerized telecommunications system. According to the minutes of the advisory board meeting, Mr Boyd openly advocated the startup of the same kind of surveillance that had been so suddenly halted in 1974.

The official began by acknowledging that the tracking of the early 1970s had run into a wave of adverse reaction because "of the political climate of that time" and that the policy under consideration in the spring of 1981 "smacks of the tracking system which in the past has not been very well received by certain quarters of Congress." In an apparent reference to the growing power of conservatives in the Congress, however, Mr Boyd said he now felt "that the climate is very definitely changing and now we have an opportunity to raise the system to a new level."

In the summer of 1982, the justice Department approved the request of the Secret Service to use the FBI computer to keep track of persons it suspects may be a danger to officials. But Representative Edwards, the one-time FBI agent, asked the justice Department not to implement the plan until a thorough public examination of the issues had been completed and possible legislation considered.

Without a law, Mr Edwards said in a letter to Attorney General William French Smith,

> what assurances do we have that this system will not evolve into the sort of system maintained by the Secret Service in the 1970s when "dangerousness" and "threat" were interpreted to include political dissent? In 1972, the Secret Service had nearly 50,000

> individuals on its lists, including such "threats" as Jane Fonda, Tom Hayden, Ralph Abernathy, Cesar Chavez, Benjamin Spock, and Walter Fauntroy. Among the organizations listed were the NAACP, the Southern Christian Leadership Conference, and the John Birch Society.

It is very hard to challenge a Secret Service request for a tool that it declares will provide improved protection for the President. But it is easy to understand that the principle of restricting the FBI's computerized telecommunications network to tracking criminal suspects is an important one. It also is easy to understand that changes in a powerful instrument of federal surveillance should not be made without public discussion, congressional hearings, and legislative authorization.

Logical Security

Logical security refers to the software or hardware-wired controls built into the system to prevent or detect unauthorized entry into the system or unauthorized access to system or business data.

Vendor controls

Vendor controls are primarily to ensure that data are not lost or amended during transmission from the media into main storage.

1. *Parity-bit checking*: Parity-bit checking entails adding one bit to each character processed. Computers are built to accept either even or odd parity. The parity bit is added to ensure that the count of "on" bits is odd or even depending on the type of computer. When the computer accepts odd parity, the count of all "on" bits within a character must be an odd number. Even parity would indicate an error in this case.

2. *File labels*: Vendor-supplied software will generally attach header and trailer labels to data files created. The header labels can be used to determine that the correct file is being used and can also protect the file from being overwritten before a specified date. Trailer labels can contain the number of blocks written into the file. This block count can then be checked after the file has been read to ensure that all the blocks have been read and that additional data have not been inserted. There may, however, be an option to bypass this label processing.

Cryptography

The growing trend toward the data base environment has caused a significant increase in opportunities for the unauthorized access to or disclosure of sensitive information. Additionally, more and more applications are being designed as real-time, on-line systems, with the result that an increasing amount of confidential or sensitive data is being transmitted over telecommunication lines.

Encryption techniques are designed to scramble the data into a form which is unintelligible to the unauthorized observer. Decryption techniques are then used to translate this scrambled text back into its original form. The advantages of encryption are that the encrypted data are secure from unauthorized disclosure or amendment, including the addition of any information. The introduction of the computer has enabled the creation of extremely complex algorithms for encryption, which are almost impossible to decrypt without detailed knowledge of the algorithm or, in some cases, without the actual key used in the encryption.

1. *On-line communications*: Cryptography has been used almost since the introduction of the telegraph and is widely used to scramble

telephone communications as a protection against wiretapping.

Devices now available can be attached between the modem and the compute or terminal. Used in pairs, the sending encryption device translates the text into its encrypted form. The receiving device then translates the encrypted text back into its original form.

2. *Data files:* A great deal has been written about cryptography as it relates to on-line communications. However, the majority of a company's data resides on data files stored on tapes and disks resident either in the data center or at an off-site storage location. There is no reason why sensitive data held on external media should not also be protected by data encryption.

The objective of the following is to present a viable approach which will (1) ensure that sensitive data are made available only in clear text to authorized programs (2) centralize the responsibility for data privacy and security, (3) be transparent to individual programs which access the data, and (4) keep the additional processing overhead to a minimum.

Data held on external media are most often held in clear text forms; i.e., assuming that individuals have access to the file, the data are readily accessible and in a readable form. Obviously, not all data maintained would be considered sensitive. It would be the responsibility of individual companies to determine which information, if disclosed, could cause competitive disadvantage, breach of good faith, or other problems.

The organizational structure of the data processing department would have to be expanded to include a data administrator responsible for maintaining an administration data set describing which files within the installation are considered to contain sensitive data.

The administration data set would contain each production file deemed to contain sensitive data.

Each entry would contain the following information:

— Position and length of the fields to be encrypted/ decrypted

— The key to be used for encrypting the data. Each application would have the facility of specifying a unique key.

— The job names and passwords which are to be considered as authorized; i.e., only certain job names supported by the correct password will be allowed access to the data in clear text format. All other jobs may gain access to the rile but would obtain sensitive data only in an encrypted form.

As each file is opened the administration data set would be accessed using the job name corresponds to an au'horized file name as a key. If an entry is found, job name and the correct password is specified; then an indicator within the data control block (DCB) will be set on to indicate that encryption /decryption is required for this file. The remaining pertinent information from the administration data set entry will be stored in core and an address pointer to this information will be stored in the DCB.

After each record has been read from the file into core storage, the associated DCB will be interrogated to determine whether any data must be decrypted. When a record is to be written to an output file, the associated DCB wi'l be interrogated to determine whether any data must be encrypted before being physically written to the output device. The basis of this proposed system lies within the administration data set.

Security over the information held within this data set is imperative if the proposed system is to attain the desired level of data security. The data administrator also has a key role in ensuring the completeness, accuracy, and authenticity of the entries within the administration data set.

The advantages of this approach to data security are as follows:

1. Actual possession or availability of a production file does not represent an exposure since sensitive information cannot be interpreted.
2. Sensitive data are made available only in clear text to authorized programs.
3. By amending the open, read, and write procedures for all files, the security routines are transparent to individual programs. All programs must go through these routines whenever data are to be accessed or created.
4. The creation of a data administration function with responsibilities as previously described centralizes the responsibility for data privacy and security:
5. The processing overhead will be minimized by, determining at open time which files are to be subject to encryption/decryption and by storing all other pertinent information in high-speed core storage.
6. The data processing department will derive benefit from the standardization of data protection practices. Test files could-be created directly from production riles as any sensitive data would be encrypted and therefore not readily available to other than authorized production programs.

Identification/Authentication of On-Line Users

In a batch environment, control over access to the computer and therefore the data held by the computer is relatively easy to maintain.

Typical examples of these access controls are:

— The remote job entry (RJE) station or card reader is maintained in a restricted access area within the data center with an operator present whose responsibility is to take the jobs and input them into the system.

— Physical recognition of any person submitting a job is possible owing to the fact that jobs have to be handed in at a central location.

— Each job has to have a job submission card which possibly even requires an authorization signature or initial. This card will state the name of the person submitting the job, the purpose of the run, the computer resources required, and the expected output.

An on-line system operated with terminals does not offer the same possibilities for the centralized control over access to the system. An on-line system must devise alternative methods to identify the person operating the terminal. Once an individual has been accurately identified, it is then possible to restrict that person's access to certain transactions or data files.

Identification is usually made by the operator providing some kind of password to the system. The passwords can either be keyed into the system by the operator or can be contained on a badge or card which is inserted into a reader attached to the system. Access to an on-line system would consist of two stages. First is the identification stage, where the operator identifies himself to the system. The operator identification can be considered as non-secure information. It may be the surname of the individual, employee account number, or some other type of ID.

The second stage concerns the authentication that the operator is who he says he is. This authentication password should be unique to each operator and should be kept confidential. It is the authentication of identification which has the direct bearing on the security of the system. Some computer packages can generate passwords randomly. User-selected passwords have been found to be the most easily discovered.

The following points should be considered when designing controls to protect against unlimited access to an on-line system.

- Maintain a password data set identifying authorized personnel who may access the system.
- Establish and document the administrative functions responsible for maintenance of this password data set.
- Clearly define who has access to this data set and ensure that it is protected from unauthorized disclosure or modification.
- Generate passwords randomly by the computer and change as frequently as practicable.
- Suppress the display or printing of any passwords. In this way it is not possible for anyone to gain knowledge of a password by looking over the shoulder of an operator or by reviewing printed output.
- Educate the user to the importance of non-disclosure of passwords and clearly state management policy in the event of unauthorized disclosure.

Various means are being developed for identifying terminal operators by some physical personal characteristic. Although these methods have the greatest potential for unerring identification, they are not yet commercially available.

Data file protection

Passwords

It is possible for the "owner" of a data file to assign a password to the data file at the time of its creation. Access to this file is only available when the password is correctly presented to the system. The advantage of the password system for data file security is that it provides a reasonable level of protection at low cost.

The disadvantages are:

— In a batch environment, the password must be supplied by the computer operator. This may appreciably slow down job throughput depending on the number of riles which require a password and also presents a security exposure in that the password must be shared with someone who is not the owner of the data. In an on-line environment, the terminal operator will be requested to supply the password for any protected files that he tries to access.

— All the data on the file are protected from anyone who does not have knowledge of the password. There may, however, be a legitimate case for allowing someone access to certain portions of the data. If that person is given the password, he has access to all the data but if he is not given the password, he cannot access the portion to which he is entitled.

— The password may not be unique to any individual. Where multiple users have access to a protected data file, additional measures are necessary to identify precisely who has accessed that file.

Date protection

Data files have labels at the beginning and at the end. Part of the information held in the header labels is the date of expiration for the particular file. If an attempt is made to write onto that file prior to the expiration date, a message will appear on the console log.

The operator has the option of cancelling the job or of continuing by overriding the date protection. Where date protection is used as a measure for data security, appropriate administrative controls must be introduced to ensure that only authorized overrides are submitted by the console operator. Reliance on the date protection facility is not a strong control, but it can be strengthened by writing a report to management detailing each system request for date protection override.

— Overriding date protection should be the exception not the rule.

— The report must be reviewed and acted upon.

— There should be a clearly stated management policy regarding any instances of unauthorized override.

Access control software

The growing awareness of the need for comprehensive treatment of data security has led to the introduction of several access control software packages designed to protect data from unauthorized disclosure, modification, or destruction, and to permit access to each user on a strict need-to-know basis. Each package has its own features, strengths, and weaknesses. They are all, however, attempting to provide a level of security based on the following criteria:

— Access authorization is user based.

— Access by the user is limited to information he needs to know to perform his function within the company.

— All attempts at unauthorized access are detected, rejected, and reported.

Before access control software can be introduced, the installation must complete a great deal of preplanning, including setting up the organizational and administrative function necessary to support the software, classifying users according to what they require access to and classifying data according to its relative need for security.

Testing

Before new or amended programs are placed into the production environment, they must be tested using data specially suited to the particular needs of the test. Testing can be carried out by the programming team responsible for creating or amending the programs, the user department that will ultimately use the output from the programs, or the data center in the form of an acceptance test designed to ensure that the programs will run successfully in the production environment.

Using "live" data

The transaction data for the test may be relatively simple to create. In fact, there may not be suitable data on any live transaction files. It may, however, be considered necessary and/or expedient to use a live master file for the test.

The advantages of using a live master file are:

— the majority of possible conditions will already exist on the master file.

— the master file will be up-to-date. The problem with maintaining a test master file is that it is often not kept current.

The disadvantages of using "live" files are obvious. The increase in the potential for unauthorized modification, disclosure, or destruction of these files is tremendous. Where it is considered necessary to use live files in the test environment, consideration should be given to the following points:

— Encrypt all production data and allow the- data to be decrypted only by authorized programs running in the production environment.

— Do not allow access to the actual live file. Insist that a copy of the file is taken and that the copy be used in testing. This procedure will eliminate the risk of modification or destruction of a live file during testing although the risk of disclosure remains.

— Establish and document procedures and standards for copying production files into the test environment. The copying should be under control of the data center as they should have custodial responsibility for all production data.

— Establish procedures for controlling the output from test runs which use live production files.

— Ensure that all copies of production files are scratched after use in the test environment.

— Make use of system reporting facilities to detect unauthorized accesses to production files and clearly state management policy in the event of such an occurrence.

Regression testing facility

A regression testing facility requires setting up a

master file and transaction file containing all known conditions. Each record is documented, stating the content of the record and its purpose during the running of a test. The documentation for the transaction file should also contain a section on the expected results after application of the transaction. Tests of the system are run using these files. Whenever the system is changed, the tests can be rerun and the two sets of output compared.

Output results can be compared either visually, which can be a long, tedious, error-prone task, or by the use of an automated file-compare facility. A regression testing facility requires a high degree of documentation and a commitment to keep both the documentation and the files in line with the current production environment; as an example, when a new condition is encountered in- the production environment, the testing files and documentation should be updated to incorporate this new condition.

Integrated Test Facility (ITF)

An integrated test facility entails the incorporation of certain records into the live master file for use as a testing vehicle. Tests are conducted using these. records, and they can be created and amended according to the needs of the test. The main advantages of an integrated test facility are in problem determination, auditability, and training.

— Where an error condition is suspected, the condition can be recreated in a live situation without affecting the "authentic" records oil the file.

— The auditors have the opportunity of submitting transactions for processing by the production system in its production environment without disrupting the run.

— Employees training on the system can use these "dummy" records until the have sufficient knowledge to work on the authentic records.

To ensure that the ITF records are not confused with live data and are not used in reporting actual company results. An ITF combined with a regression testing facility can provide a powerful tool in ensuring that systems are properly tested prior to their introduction into the production environment.

Library management system

A Library Management System (LMS) consists of the standards and procedures to ensure the security of an installation's program libraries and the integrity of the members that reside on these libraries. Earlier sections discussed some of the available techniques to protect the business data of the company from unauthorized disclosure, modification, or destruction. Now the security of the programs developed to process these data will be considered. It is essential that the application programs executed in the production environment be authorized, meet the criteria for which they were designed, and not perform any additional unauthorized functions.

An effective LMS, therefore, consists of the administra-tive and logical controls to ensure that new or amended library members to be migrated into the production environment are authorized, properly documented signed-off by the appropriate parties, and, once in the production environment, are protected from unauthorized activity.

1. The programmer writes the program using a language similar to English. The programmer's output is referred to as source statements and typically is written to a source statement library.
2. In order to translate these source statements into

a form understandable to the computer, they are input to a compiler which produces machine language statements corresponding to the English language statements coded by the programmer.

3. When all the modules which make up the total program have been compiled, the various object decks are input to a utility program called the linkage editor, which creates an executable program from the various input components.

There should be a distinction between the environment in which this program is created and the environment in which the program will be used to process live data. Where control over production data files limits access to production programs, the LMS need only secure the contents of the production program libraries. Before any program can be migrated into the production environment, it must be thoroughly tested to ensure that it does what it was designed to do and nothing more. After a program has been migrated into the production environment, the LMS must protect this member against unauthorized changes.

That it is the source statement library and the executable library members which are migrated into the production environment after they have been adequately tested. This is a simplistic view of these procedures. In some installations there may be an intermediate set of libraries from which the user testing and data center acceptance testing would be executed. To ensure the integrity of the programs being' tested, the programmers would not have access to these intermediate libraries.

The following is a list of considerations to be made in the development of an effective library management system:

— Determine what libraries require protection. If production data cannot be accessed from test libraries, the level of protection afforded to these libraries may be minimal. Access to protected libraries should then be restricted to authorized, personnel.

— Back-up and recovery procedures should be designed to counter a partial or total loss of the libraries.

— Changes to protected libraries should be authorized by the user department serviced by the programs. This aspect provides for segregation of duties and prevents any programmer from submitting an unauthorized change through established channels.

— An audit trail should be made of changes to source statements in order that such changes can easily be verified to the change that was authorized.

— There should be a way of ascertaining that the most recent version of the executable program corresponds to the most recent version of the related source statements.

— After the programmer has finished testing a program in the testing environment, there should be a method of "freezing" the source and executable code while user and data center testing is carried out.

— Actual changes to the production libraries should be effected by data center personnel, thereby providing an additional level of security through enhanced segregation of duties.

— The documentation supporting any activity to these production libraries should be complete and contain provision for the appropriate sign-offs indicating that the programs may form an authorized part of the production environment. The archival system supported by the LMS should provide for adequate recovery facilities should a new version of a program fail to work in production.

— Management should receive reports from the LMS indicating activity against the protected libraries and also noting any unauthorized accesses, whether they resulted in a change being made or not.

— Management should have a clearly defined policy in the event of any unauthorized activity regarding these libraries.

Provision should be made for controlling the implementation of emergency changes. Emergency changes are usually made because of the discovery of an error in a program running in production.. Time constraints usually do not allow emergency changes to go through the normal channels of authorization, testing, and sign-off. For these reasons, emergency changes must have special provisions for follow-up after the change has been implemented. On no account should emergency changes be accepted as a normal part of the operational environment. A high percentage of emergency changes indicates a lack of proper testing procedures and may even be indicative of an unstable operational environment.

The auditor's function is to assess the adequacy, effectiveness, and efficiency of the system of internal control within an organization. Until the introduction of computer systems on a large scale, the auditor's role in an organization was fairly well defined. In recent years however, an increasing reliance upon computer systems has forced the auditor to adjust to a new environment.

To adequately fulfill his primary function, the auditor must have access to a great deal of information not normally available to one individual. This information will include details of all the data security measures in force within an installation An organization must, therefore, have a degree of protection against any unauthorized activities by its auditors, and the auditors, while still maintaining their independence, must be protected from unwarranted suspicion should an exposure occur.

The auditor's role in a computer environment has been the topic of a great deal of discussion and controversy. The main issue is the question of involvement and the maintenance of the auditor's independence. On the one hand is the argument that if the auditor is actively involved in the design stages of a system, he will not be able to present an unbiased assessment of the controls within the system and may be at a disadvantage if a weakness is subsequently highlighted.

The other side of the argument is that computer systems are substantially different in their approach to security and require the auditor to grow with the system if he is to attest to the adequacy of the controls built into the system.

Although this subject will not be dealt with in detail in this chapter, the following points bear mention:

— Assuming that the auditor finds the system of internal control to be adequate, he should conform to the standards and procedures governing the rest of the installation.

— All attempted violations of the system of internal control by the auditor should be documented, including what was attempted, why it was attempted, and what were the expected result and the actual result.

— More installations have gone through the exercise of identifying the various stages making up the system development life cycle. The output from this exercise is usually a checklist of tasks to be performed which is then used to chart the progress of the developing system. Similarly, it is possible for the auditor to prepare a checklist of the audit tasks which have to be performed in each of the component stages. It is recommended that the auditor prepare this checklist by component stage and issue a sign-off at the end of each stage. In this way there is no confusion between the auditor and the system development team regarding the auditor's requirements. It is also recommended that this checklist be made available to- the system development department in order that they may become familiar with the criteria used by the audit department when reviewing a new system development.

— The auditor.is in the position of acting as a user for any new system. Assuming that the audit department has kept abreast of all projected new system developments, it is possible for the audit department to design its own subsystem and have this programmed into the developing system at the appropriate phase.

8

Opportunities and Prospects

A certain number, the advocates of the 'modernization paradigm', consider that the transfer of new information and communication technology is a major stimulant for the development process that, in the long run, will enable the developing countries to catch up with the industrialized countries. For others, the opponents of 'cultural dependence', any such transfer would merely be a step further not only towards inequality, but even towards the destruction of the cultural identity of societies in the Southern hemisphere. Finally, for others again, both the paradigms of transfer and dependence are outdated. New information and communication technology and its applications provide developing countries with the ability to perform a kind of 'technological leapfrogging' that could enable them to reach the connection capacity required for the information networks far more rapidly. Similar forms of leapfrogging might also enable economies with a high level of skilled labour to switch to 'value-added' economies.

An increasing number of states share the latter point of view and have opted for the most advanced forms of technology to implement or renew their communication infrastructures. To reach their objectives, on the one hand they have adopted policies of adaptation and technological transfer by offering attractive subcontracting capabilities, thereby relocating communication multinationals; on the other hand, they are investing in communication programmes or setting up new communication infrastructures. Other countries, particularly in South-East Asia, have achieved something of a feat in telecommunications and the audiovisual field. Some of these nations even form the driving force for economic expansion that counterbalances the climate of recession elsewhere in the world. South-East Asia currently enjoys the highest rate of economic growth worldwide and operates as an accelerator for the whole continent: 11 per cent per year since 1983 compared with a global growth rate of 6 per cent. Its telecommunication equipment population is now close to that of the industrialized countries and in some areas is even a length ahead of European states.

Thailand, for instance, which started from nothing in 1986, today has the world's highest penetration rate in radio communications. China, India and several countries in South-East Asia have launched their own satellites.

Nevertheless, it would probably be a mistake to think that all developing countries could automatically attain this level of development. The countries in this region of the world find themselves in widely differing economic situations as a result of a series of factors, the most important of which are the ability to attract investment, the educational level of the population, the economic policies adopted by their leaders and, finally, their cooperation with the industrialized countries and the impact of all these factors on new information and communication technology and its applications.

In fact, most of the developing countries are confronted with economic and political alternatives of a strategic nature, but also with constraints and obstacles that they will have to overcome or manage if in the future they wish to set up gateways with the networks and services promised by the information society. These obstacles are financial, technical and political in nature.

Although it began in the industrialized countries, the development of the new information and communication technology is gradually spreading to the whole world, offering tremendous opportunities for every society to access knowledge and know-how. This trend can be seen in the Arab countries, with the installation of communication infrastructures capable of providing new opportunities for distance learning, health and many other development-oriented activities. With 250 million inhabitants, a gross domestic product of $12 billion, an installed telephone base of 450 billion lines (cr more than 5 subscriber lines per 100 inhabitants), the 'Arabsat' regional satellite system, an installed television base ratio higher than 10 per 100 inhabitants, and an installed radio base ratio higher than 25 per 100 inhabitants, the Arab world is well placed to tackle the global information society.

Gulf states, i.e. Bahrain, Kuwait, Qatar and the United Arab Emirates, have practically reached the objective of a universal service. They have almost all fully digitized their networks and offer state-of-the-art services characteristic of developed countries (ISDN, the Internet, GSM standard cellular mobile telephones, digital television, etc.). Less advanced Arab states have inadequate access to the Web. The issue for these countries is how to improve access to telecommunications against a backdrop of low-level economic development. In the third group of Arab states, the level of development in telecommunications is situated between that of the wealthy countries of the Gulf and that of the less advanced countries in the region. This group includes the Maghreb countries and the Levantine countries, together with Oman and Saudi Arabia. Some countries in this group since 1990 have obtained the best results in terms of telecommunications among the Arab states: Morocco, for instance, has almost tripled its network of subscriber lines since 1990; in 1995, Syria increased its telephone line system by 42 per cent, and Tunisia now ranks third in the region for its rate of growth in subscriber lines.

During the coming years, most Arab states will be faced with the task of accelerating progress in their telecommunications sector in order to bring them up to the level that some developing regions have reached (Asia and Latin America) and to expand their service offers, both of which are indispensable prerequisites for active participation in the new global information economy. Arab states have an advantage, compared with other developing regions, in that they can count on diversified sources of potential financing. Private capital in the region also plays a far from negligible role: according to World Bank estimates, Arab holdings overseas total some $350 billion. In addition, telecommunication companies in the Gulf are not only an example of successful development, but can also provide technical and financial support to operators in the other Arab countries.

Full development of the information society in the Arab states will be possible, provided that governments use the new information technology efficiently, notably to reduce the gap in development between nations and within them. With this outlook in mind, satellite operators, and the users and creators of content as well as specialists in information and computer technology, have vast possibilities for initiating innovative approaches in the field of communication, taking into account the potential for development and market opportunities. Within this framework, the ITU and UNESCO are working together to promote the use of telematics for social, economic and cultural development in the region. An important step in this process was the creation in March 1996, endorsed by both organizations, of an association for co-operation in the area entitled the Regional Arab Information Technology Network.

First and foremost, the introduction of new information and communication technology requires extremely heavy-investment, estimated at several hundred billion dollars, a sum that most developing countries can neither raise nor commit. In addition, most of these states are currently confronted with obstacles to development and are subject to structural adjustment plans that force them to limit their expenditure. Second, the hypothetical presence of these countries on the future electronic networks presupposes the installation of terrestrial or satellite telecommunication networks, the management and control of which, seem incompatible with the obsolete and under-equipped level of local telecommunication services. Third, the future information society presupposes fair, universal access to the Web for the whole population of a country. The geographical dissimilarities within these countries, however, are alarming They stem from the political options that have been adopted by governments which are generally centralizing in outlook, resulting in fairly top-heavy media concentration, with telecommunication services located in the capitals and major provincial capitals.

Together, those problems and obstacles clearly illustrate the challenges that the developing countries must face: implementing a new information and communication policy in order to modernize, democratize and diversify the services on offer. The first of these challenges entails favouring a worldwide strategy for the reform of communication services. The need to modernize communication equipment presupposes the transfer of the new technology and intensive use of the services it provides. The funds required, however, are such that modernization inevitably entails monopoly deregulation, a fact which has now become the reference framework for any upgrade or modernization of communication policy.

Most developing countries are fully aware of this need, and have already opted for deregulation or privatization by having their companies join the trend of internationalization and partnerships with the major operators in the industrialized countries. Without subscribing to some form of liberal economic determinism, privatization can probably solve a number of requirements, including that of providing the specific value-added services necessary for any connection with telecommunication's networks. On the other hand, privatization can be seen as a legitimate means of socio-economic change only if every class of society gains some benefit from it. This is precisely the reason why privatization must be accompanied by a statutory framework guaranteeing that all sectors of the population, in particular those people living farthest from the major cities, have access to the basic information and communication services, just as, through partnerships or alliances, it should facilitate access to every form of information and communication flow, whether by telephone, audiovisual programmes, the written press, etc. Finally, the success of privatization presupposes the existence of an open market, strong local enterprise, and fair market rules and regulations to counterbalance the risk, inherent to privatization, of the emergence of new monopolies. The second of the challenges mentioned above is linked to the conditions in which access is gained to technology and to its content. Most developing countries have modest, even outdated telephone services and audiovisual equipment, which cannot easily be adapted to the digital transmission used by electronic networks.

The experts take the view that this deficiency can be made up by satellite technology which will complement the existing terrestrial cellular telephony systems and transport large amounts of data at low cost. The system of transmission by satellite seems to offer several advantages, notably that of covering vast areas and reaching populations in regions with difficult terrain and hostile climates that cannot be covered by Hertzian means. Satellites make it possible to broadcast educational and cultural programmes and distance learning courses throughout a country, and finally to connect up to electronic networks.

This last point seems worthy of note, since the technical capabilities and possibilities of planetary networks, the most well-known of which is the Internet, seem closest to the idea of open, limitless communication. It is also a practical, economical solution for developing countries if they wish to have access to a universal system of communication that can make good a number of deficiencies, notably in terms of point-to-point communication. The third challenge mentioned above concerns the capability of developing countries to adopt an overall strategy that links the transfer of information and communication technology to a training and research policy. Access to know-how and training in every country is a major priority.

The acquisition of know-how and knowledge, which today fill the role played first by land-ownership and later by capital in transforming modem society, has become a priority in national development strategies. New information and communication technology is seen as an important means of completing and consolidating the traditional techniques of teaching and learning. Virtually everywhere around the world, development programmes are making increasing use of satellite television, telematics, and even video-conferences in education, health, family planning and community development. The technology permits transmission throughout the national territory of adult training programmes and distance learning courses tailored to suit all kinds of public (leading to greater flexibility, faster learning and a wider audience).

The technology offers immense possibilities for reaching vast numbers of people, with more efficient and attractive teaching methods than those used in traditional education. In addition to these advantages, if the various costs of training, such as travel in developing countries between badly-serviced rural areas are taken into account, distance learning based on new technology seems particularly cost-effective, and will become even more so as its use develops.

In the medical field, new technology such as picture phoning, video-conferences and medical encyclopedias on CD-ROM are responding increasingly to a demand which already exists at the experimental level. In a few years, doctors, hospitals, laboratories and universities will be networked and capable of telemonitoring diagnoses, analyses and examinations transmitted from one end of the world to the other in record time, via computer and video systems. Examples of experimental applications are already on the increase, notably between hospitals in developed countries.

An international survey entitled 'The Right to Communicate: At What Price? Economic Constraints to the Effective Use of Telecommunications in Education, Science and Culture and in the Circulation of Information', was jointly undertaken in

1992-93 by UNESCO and ITU. The survey details the needs of the education, science, culture, communication and information sectors in terms of telematic services and data transmission. It provides examples of more appropriate pricing systems and other special arrangements successfully used to benefit these sectors, together with an analysis of the factors that affect prices and the international market trends that result from them.

The survey examines some of the options available to the authorities to solve problems of inadequate use of telematic services by sectors of public interest and discusses the balance to be struck between the concept of a public service and the principle of non-discrimination. The survey shows that the Internet - and in more general terms, all forms of co-operative networks oriented towards specific applications - is an important model for improving access to telematics, with advantages for user groups, telecommunications operators and public authorities alike. Overall, the strategies and recommend-ations in the survey point to a promising approach to quality telematic access, at reasonable cost, for users in sectors of public interest linked to development.

The approach implies:

— co-operation among users to identify, consolidate and promote the demand for telematic services;

— the development and expansion of such services on the basis of market principles and possibilities;

— enlightened public policy, the purpose of which should be to promote the setting up of telematic infrastructures and their use by sectors linked to development, including measures for price reforms based on the cost of access.

It is not enough to buy technology to gain access to the information society, however, nor should a straightforward purchase be seen as a miraculous solution. Access entails a considerable degree of effort, information, learning and popularization that developing countries will have to uphold if they wish to benefit from technological change and have the tools necessary for their autonomy, namely new information and communication technology. Nor should the latter be seen as some sort of magic wand far removed from the socio-economic facts of life of the countries into which they are introduced. The technology concerns every, kind of user: researchers, academics, students, company executives, etc., who have to adapt to their new environment and learn to use their navigation system properly in order to optimize its potential. In addition and in parallel to this, technology transfer has to be supported by a research drive. This consists, first of all, in analysing the breakthroughs made in information technology, the conditions permitting its transfer, and its interaction with the local socio-economic environment, and discovering the ways in which all these factors occur and interrelate.

The result will be a clearer understanding not only of the use of technology, its effects, and the economic and technical constraints, but also of its advantages and the room for manoeuvre in its application. Within this global framework, research can provide a genuine form of 'strategic surveillance' used to guide policy-making by developing countries with respect to technological options. Research is also a prerequisite for development which is often put to one side by countries that are consumers of new technology.

Many developing countries since their independence have built highly diversified industrial tools in the field of communication systems, while remaining technologically dependent on supplier countries. They often find themselves confronted with RE&D issues designed, driven and developed in industrialized countries. The latter have taken the high ground in the field of new technology-or are seeking to do so - by developing scientific research, taking the view that the capability to appropriate and assimilate technology depends on the degree of mastery and development attained in the strategic sector of research and development, a branch of activity in which the most advanced countries have dominant positions.

A pilot distance education programme introduced by UNESCO and the International Telecommunication Union (ITU) has been launched in Morocco in collaboration with the Ministry of Education there. The aim is to achieve a link-up between the audiovisual and telecommunication sectors and to explore ways in which it can be applied to the country's education system.

The project will seek to solve the problem of budgetary constraints and meet the most pressing pedagogical needs. These concerns were voiced at the Jomtien World Conference on Education for All (March 1990). A plan of action was subsequently prepared by UNESCO and ITU in May 1995 to estimate the potential of interactive television in regard to schooling and teacher training. The principle of interactivity is vital to learning in that-it fosters constant improvement in the training process, as students and teachers learn to adapt. It also triggers interstudent dialogue, thereby creating interest and curiosity.

The communication of knowledge accordingly is no longer unidirectional, leading as it does to spontaneous reaction and lively comment on the part of students. The purpose of the Moroccan project is to furnish an umbrella blueprint for improved teaching by updating telecommunication infrastructures and upgrading teacher training. The introductory phase of the project will concentrate on elaborating and finalizing the different stages 'of educational studies and teaching methodology with the assistance of a representative sample of teachers. It will then be extended to the country as a whole and in particular to southern Morocco with its largely illiterate rural population. This second phase involves a training programme for some 2,000 teachers, 500 school directors, administrators and technical staff. It also provides for five training centres in each of the main provinces of Morocco. Each centre will be equipped with the latest in technological and information system resources for fifty pupils, and be placed under the supervision of the School of Radio and Television in Rabat, which will circulate and disseminate information.

The teaching documentation centres will be linked to a data transmission network for case of communication with students, principally through e-mail and a CD-ROM system available in a virtual library which teachers may use. The project is to be managed by technicians, engineers and administrators under the supervision of a project chief. This project will be of three years' duration. The first year will be devoted to preparatory work, including staff training and the purchase and installation of interactive equipment. The distance education system will take off in the second year. And finally, by the end of the third year, the teaching methods should be tried and tested and the technological aspects well under control.

The system will be extended to all twenty-two provinces of the country by the year 2008. The overall cost is estimated at $6 million. Half of this sum will be provided by the Moroccan Government, with the other half being paid by international institutions and agencies. Feasibility studies are now under way to assess the possibility of extending the project to other developing countries such as Bangladesh and Cape Verde. The last point in this chapter concerns the issue of international co-operation in the field of communication. The balance sheet, after several decades of international co-operation for development purposes, is disappointing. On the one hand, it shows that very few countries have entered the newly industrialized country category, and that the use of traditional methods of development aid to enhance economic growth must be re-examined. The efforts made by the international community must be upheld and widened to include other underprivileged regions around the world, through a different approach to co-operation. In concerted fashion, this must include international organizations in order to facilitate partnership agreements with the private sector, include professional skills and ensure marketing and management know-how, and enhance understanding and knowledge with respect to the new legislation on the independent written press and the audiovisual field-in short, a different conception of co-operation altogether, leading to an authentic transfer of knowledge, in a spirit of balanced interests, solidarity and sharing.

A major development in the short- to medium-term future will be a substantial growth in multimedia telecommunications in one form or another. In this way, multimedia information networks will correspond more closely to the experience of communication and information interchange in everyday life, with a flexible mix of sound, picture, and words. The exact nature of this experience, and its effect on information networking in general, remains to be determined. A major preoccupation of national governments and regional associations is to build the infrastructure for these developments as quickly as possible (and preferably faster than their competitors).

In the United States, for example, in an attempt to accelerate the extension of fibre optic cabling to the home and workplace on a massive scale, the Federal Communications Commission (FCC) decided in 1992 to allow the regional Bell holding companies to transmit video programmes over their telecommunications lines, in competition with the cable television companies. This attempt to create a communications infrastructure for the next decade is seen by many Americans as crucial to the continued economic dominance of the United States. The FCC, for example, places much weight on multimedia devices such as high definition television (HDTV), a digital two-way interactive television set, as the vehicle for this information expansion, aiming at a 15-year deadline for complete HDTV conversion.

The technological futurism is the subject of much political controversy and manoeuvring at the current time; it seems likely though, that the new presidential administration will lead out more liberalization to support competition-led innovation and technological advances in communications media, and there is a clear emphasis on the use of technology for economic development in the shaping of public policy statements. One more immediate result is likely to be the more rapid development of the National Research and Education Network, sponsored for many years by Vice-President Al Gore.

The building of NREN services will bring into focus many of the issues on information access and price, and of the emerging adjustments in role of all those involved in the information cycle. In Europe, a similar urgency has fuelled a number of projects sponsored by the European Commission to work towards the creation of integrated broadband communications systems by the latter part of this decade. The RACE programme, funding research into advanced communications technology and services, indicates by its name some of its underlying objectives, and the ESPRIT programme has initiated the IDOMENEUS project to co-ordinate and improve European efforts in the development of new information environments in the area of interacting open media. Adopting lessons learned from the French experience in the establishment of the Minitel system, the EC has initiated a number of pilot projects in fields ranging from banking and finance, manufacturing, transport, distribution, and health care; other projects include distributed multimedia publishing, and a broadband network based library for the petroleum and chemical industries, with a 1995 target date for the introduction of commercial services.

The existence of a technology, however, does not always guarantee its success. It is worth remembering that the Picture Phone was launched by AT&T at the World Fair of 1964. This was a first example of the videophone; in 1992, almost 30 years later, British Telecom launched a low-cost consumer videophone, which can be connected directly to the normal telephone socket; this has yet to make any substantial impact in the market-place. A development which is likely to be of more significance, though, is the planned availability of audio-visual workstations based on the standard PC. Such a device will make the full integration of data and voice networks within the workplace a reality, and will open up a wider market for multimedia information services. Many of these exist in prototype form within the existing infrastructure. Multimedia electronic mail, for example, is now possible even in a limited text-based medium such as the Internet.

The multimedia information mail extensions (MIME) to the standard Internet mail protocol permit the inclusion of still images, group III fax images, compressed full motion video, and multipart playback sequences of mixed information types. Desktop videoconferencing, the ability to conduct meetings with a geographically remote person each at their own desk, has been established as a feasible communications technology, although so far finding only a niche rather than global market.

The experience of this videoconferencing raises some key issues since it is clear that, as with most other information technologies, the technical issues are much less important than the social and organisational ones. Technical advances which have made the idea more feasible include the emergence of high bandwidth ISDN networks, video compression techniques, accepted standards, and powerful graphics-based workstations. The degree of success in implementing this technology is determined rather by the extent to which it supports the way people work. The involves an understanding of the communications patterns between individuals and groups, and of their information needs and the uses to which information is put; of the way in which contacts with individuals and formal information sources assists the innovative process, and an appreciation of the interdependent balance between formal and informal communication.

Technology has often been used to support formal communication patterns, rather than the informal, and sometimes is intended to replace rather than support either. Multimedia communications systems cannot replace face-to-face contact any more than the telephone (although a similar argument was made against the telephone at its introduction). Thoughtful design may, however, be used to appropriately support existing human communication patterns. The Cruiser videoconferencing system designed by Bellcore, for example, uses the metaphor of a 'virtual hallway'—floor plan representing the groups of participants—along which a user may navigate. 'cruise' and interact with others in the process. For multimedia multi-user systems such as this, the interface must include some form of social protocol which enables decisions about the nature and style of desired interaction to be taken. Many issues which will effectively delineate the shape of multimedia networking in the future remain as yet poorly understood and little explored. In some areas, however, there is more immediacy on concerns which are being raised by the substantial growth in network traffic and users, and the potential changes which can be perceived in the near future.

The growing importance of digital information and its availability over networks which demand physical and technical access create barriers which are increasingly insurmountable for many groups of potential users.

While there is no space here to discuss the social role of information systems, there are a few examples of attempts to bypass these barriers in recent developments. The Cleveland FreeNet experiment, for example, is an attempt to increase access to Internet information to a wider audience. The vast amounts of information, and the worldwide nature of the Internet, also bring to the fore issues of intellectual property and copyright surrounding electronic information. Much of the information held on this network is freely available, as long as it is used for non-commercial purposes. The subsequent use of information taken from computer networks cannot be controlled, however, once it has been downloaded from the original source. It may appear in many diverse guises, be re-partitioned, amalgamated, and reused, taking on a life of its own. Print-based copyright legislation does not translate easily to the electronic environment. A feature of the legislation to found the advanced NREN network requires the provision of charging mechanisms to be put in place, suggesting a trend towards more control over use and users.

The characteristics which make electronic information difficult to define and 'freeze' at one point in time also raise questions on the nature of bibliographic control and mapping of information resources. Electronic documents and journals which can be updated immediately, replacing the original copy, are difficult to define as a bibliographic entity which has a declared and fixed content, which can be cited for later use.

The identification of various versions of a logical item becomes a complex (or perhaps impossible) task, as does preservation and archiving as a permanent record of publication. These problems also redound upon ethical issues involving the quality and accuracy of the document content. Electronic documents may easily be changed, or 'falsified' with changing intellectual fashions in a way that print fixed at one point in time cannot. The unstructured and fluid process which allows a network user to make information available without recourse to formal publisher or refereeing process has great advantages in stimulating an innovative and creative dialectic, but at the cost of a large proportion of false, misleading, or incorrect information which must also be sorted through and rejected. Whilst the research community, in which much of this type of activity takes place at present, has evolved a fairly sophisticated code of practical ethics for network co-operation and exchange, it is doubtful that this will survive a broadening of access and the introduction of commercial interests.

The increasing ubiquity of the networking environment is raising questions about the relative responsibilities of those involved in the information transfer process. Traditionally, this process could be described in terms of five distinct roles: the information provider, who provides the original source material; the information host, who makes it available and accessible, 'publishing' in a print or electronic sense; the carrier or distributor, providing a channel for the information; the intermediary, traditional role for the information service professional; and the information user, the final consumer. This model has long ago begun to break down when applied to the networking environment. The information provider is often the same as the information host; the common carrier, the telecommunications authority, provides information services in its own right; and the information user more often wishes to find and retrieve the information directly. Many people have begun to question the role of the publisher in the electronic environment: since the author can mount a document in its electronic form on a local computer (quite probably the format it was originally composed in) and the network facilities act as a distribution mechanism, it becomes harder to gauge the function of a traditional publisher. Although this is clearly not appropriate for many types of publishing, in some areas it is possible to see advantages.

For instance, the traditional venue for reporting research has been as a journal article in some summarized form; network publishing would allow a reader to optionally download original datasets and intermediate analysis, as well as authorial commentary, directly and without a time delay. The development of network publishing is likely to involve identifiable changing characteristics compared to the traditional activities:

— a growth in simulcast publishing, with one source file producing a variety of complementary versions in different formats;

— multimedia electronic publishing, integrating database, text, image, sound, and video;

— the use of information tools to skim, navigate, browse, and utilize these new media products;

— selective and customized publishing targeted at particular groups;

— a linking with the concept of a 'virtual library', where access and materials are not constrained by physical barriers.

The information user and the information provider potentially have a much more direct and interactive relationship, possibly to the extent that the information exchange cannot be completely separated from the communication process itself. This raises a question mark against the received role of the intermediary, as a filter between originator, distributor, and recipient.

As the growth in electronic information begins to demand a new philosophy of the nature and function of information so also the activities of the information professional must, in this setting at least, change and adapt. No longer able to adopt a custodial role in managing and organizing the materials and artefacts of information, the librarian or information scientist must adopt a facilitating strategy, aimed at creating the conditions for a user to negotiate the information sphere successfully. The librarian no longer 'owns' the information since it is not contained within any physical institution; and it cannot therefore be 'managed' in the same physical sense. The information user, however, must still negotiate an information space, now across a digital network as much as before within the confines of a library, in order to achieve a successful resolution to the information transfer process.

Index